S0-CCF-292

HINDU
PREDICTIVE
ASTROLOGY

Books on Astrology by Dr. B. V. Raman

Astrology for Beginners
A Manual of Hindu Astrology
A Catechism of Astrology
Hindu Predictive Astrology
How to Judge a Horoscope Vol. I
How to Judge a Horoscope Vol. II
Three Hundred Important Combinations
Prasna Marga Vol. I
Prasna Marga Vol. II
Prasna Tantra
Notable Horoscopes
My Experiences in Astrology
Nirayana Tables of Houses
Bhavartha Ratnakara
Ashtakavarga System of Prediction
Graha and Bhava Balas
Hindu Astrology and the West
Planetary Influences on Human Affairs
Muhurta or Electional Astrology
Studies in Jaimini Astrology
Klachakra Dasa
Raman's One Hundred Ten Years Ephemeris (1891-2000)

HINDU
PREDICTIVE
ASTROLOGY

BANGALORE VENKATA RAMAN

Editor: THE ASTROLOGICAL MAGAZINE

📖 UBSPD®
UBS Publishers' Distributors Pvt. Ltd.
New Delhi • Bangalore • Kolkata • Chennai • Patna • Bhopal
Ernakulam • Mumbai • Lucknow • Pune • Hyderabad

UBS PUBLISHERS' DISTRIBUTORS PVT. LTD.

5 Ansari Road, **New Delhi**-110 002
Phones: 011-23273601-4, 23266646-47, 23274846, 23282281, 23273552

10 First Main Road, Gandhi Nagar, **Bangalore**-560 009
Phones: 080-22253903, 22263901, 22263902, 22255153

8/1-B Chowringhee Lane, **Kolkata**-700 016
Phones: 033-22529473, 22521821, 22522910

60 Nelson Manickam Road, Aminjikarai, **Chennai**-600 029
Phones: 044-23746222, 23746351-2

Ground Floor, Annapurna Complex, Naya Tola, **Patna**-800 004
Phones: 0612-2672856, 2673973, 2686170

Z-18, M.P. Nagar, Zone-I, **Bhopal**-462 011
Phones: 0755-4203183, 4203193, 2555228

No. 40/7940-41, Kollemparambil Chambers, Convent Road,
Ernakulam-682 035 • Phones: 0484-2353901, 2363905

2nd Floor, Apeejay Chambers, 5 Wallace Street, Fort, **Mumbai**-400 001
Phones: 022-66376922, 66376923, 66102067, 66102069

9, Ashok Nagar, Near Pratibha Press, Gautam Buddha Marg, Latouche Road,
Lucknow-226 018 • Phones: 4025124, 4025134, 4025144, 6531753

680 Budhwar Peth, 2nd floor, Near Appa Balwant Chowk, **Pune**-411 002
Phone: 020-24461653 • Fax: 020-24433976

3rd & 4th Floors, Alekhya Jagadish Chambers, H.No.4-1-1058,
Boggulkunta, Tilak Road, **Hyderabad**-500 001
Phones: 040-24754473, 24754474 • Telefax: 040-24754472

Visit us at www.ubspd.com & www.gobookshopping.com

© Mrs. Rajeswari Raman

Twentieth Edition	1992	Nineteenth Reprint	2004
First Reprint	1993	Twentieth Reprint	2005
Twelfth Reprint	1998	Twenty-first Reprint	2006
Thirteenth Reprint	1999	Twenty-second Reprint	2006
Fourteenth Reprint	2000	Twenty-third Reprint	2007
Fifteenth Reprint	2001	Twenty-fourth Reprint	2007
Sixteenth Reprint	2002	Twenty-fifth Reprint	2008
Seventeenth Reprint	2002	Twenty-sixth Reprint	2009
Eighteenth Reprint	2003		

ISBN 978-81-85273-54-9

All rights reserved. No part of this publication may be reproduced or transmitted in any form or by any means, electronic or mechanical, including photocopying, recording, or any information storage or retrieval system, without prior permission in writing from the publisher.

Printed at: Ram Printograph, Delhi

DEDICATION

This work is respectfully
dedicated to the
memory of my revered grandfather

Prof. B. SURYANARAIN RAO

PREFACE TO THE TWENTIETH EDITION

The fact that the twentieth edition of HINDU PREDICTIVE AS-TROLOGY has been called for within a few months of the publication of the nineteenth edition is sufficient proof of the value attached to my writings on Astrology and the wide popularity my works enjoy. What may be regarded as still more satisfactory is that the demand for it has been considerable.

The twentieth edition herewith presented has been revised. The table of Ayanamsa has been revised upto 2000 A.D. The book is made quite useful and complete. The public are the best critics and I am thankful to them for their continuous patronage and support.

I am obliged to UBS Publishers' Distributors Ltd., New Delhi for having brought out this edition attractively.

B.V. RAMAN

"Sri Rajeswari"
Bangalore-560 020
1st February, 1992

Preface to the First Edition

The appearance of a new book on Hindu Astrology in these days of superfluous journalism and book publication might be deemed an uncalled-for luxury. A little reflection will show that such a view is rather unfounded and such a conclusion too, premature. For quite a long time, there has been a great demand for an up-to-date, concise and comprehensive text-book on Hindu Astrology that is in itself complete and self-contained so that the necessity of purchasing additional volumes may be done away with. In order to meet this need and to enable the reader to extend his talents to spheres of research and investigation, the present volume has been designed.

All the necessary and useful information has been treated with great care and scrutiny. Many of the planetary combinations given in this book are of such rare value that I did not like to omit them. They are the outcome of much practical study and have not been merely chosen at random from some Sanskrit Astrological work or other. This book is intended both for the beginner and the advanced student as all the details needed for scientifically deciphering the future have been fully described without obscuring at the same time those very elementary portions so essential for the beginner. Wherever necessary, explanations are given to facilitate comprehension of the difficult portions.

One who reads the book carefully and dispassionately and understands the principles incorporated, will not only be able to make fairly correct predictions but will be induced to take to the study of more advanced works and thus help the cause of the science.

The Western reader might omit Chapter IX as it deals with the method of casting horoscopes on the basis of Indian Almanacs, and devote himself to Chapter X. Chapter III deals with general information regarding the Cycle of Years, Ayanas, etc., and the reader, if he so desires, may omit this chapter also. However a perusal of it is sure to benefit the reader. It is needless to remark that both in the matter and method, I have touched fresher grounds and I feel confident that I have supplied a real and long-felt want by ushering in this publication for the acceptance of the educated public.

I take this opportunity of expressing my thanks to my many friends for their suggestions and in particular to the late Prof. B. Suryanarain Rao (whose recent demise the whole world deplores), without whose guidance the work would never have been produced. I must also acknowledge my thanks to Miss Laurie Pratt of Los Angeles, U.S.A., who read the manuscript and offered helpful suggestions; to Mr. N. R. Thiruvenkatachar, B.A., of Madras, who has kindly assisted me in preparing the Oblique Ascension tables; to my well-wisher Mr. C. G. Row of Gulbarga, for his valuable suggestions and lastly to my friend, Mir Abdul Huq, for expediting publication and for his personal attention to the details of printing, and to the staff of the Modi Press for the special zeal they displayed in the publication of the work.

If the reader should be enabled, by a study of this volume, to acquire a working knowledge of the science, my labours will have been amply rewarded.

BANGALORE   B. V. RAMAN
1st February 1938

Introduction

Astrology is the most ancient of all sciences. It is not a science like Mathematics, Botany, Zoology, Chemistry or Physics, the study of which requires strict adherence to the world's conventionalities of commonsense reasoning and ordinary logic. Astrology comprehends something higher, mysterious and subtle. It is not a mere appeal to the reasoning faculty of man but it is an appeal to his hidden powers and capacities. Astrological predictions cannot be simply based upon strict hypothetical principles or vague guesses but a certain amount of intuitive capacity must be brought to bear upon such attempts. The various rules given for future predictions are merely intended for our guidance and we must substantiate them by recourse to the study and examination of a large number of practical horoscopes. Collect the horoscopes of a number of people of all grades, ranks, temperaments and peculiarities and study them in the light of the principles enumerated in the following pages and then you will really get some precious intellectual food for your mental refreshment and you will be doubtless convinced that astrology is a practical and useful science.

Astrology relies more upon the skill and intuitive capacities of the interpreter than upon complicated rules. It gives a sketch of life. It is a mirror in which one's own figure is clearly reflected. Astrology comprehends the manifestation of a sort of relationship among all objects in nature, animal, vegetable and mineral. It records the interaction of influences of all things, visible and invisible. While Ayurveda ranks as an *Upaveda*, *Jyotisha* or Astrology is one of the Vedangas. It was not a mere accident that distinguished practitioners of one of these arts were generally proficient in the other also. Cosmos is a unity and knowledge cannot be cut up and confined in rigid water-tight compartments.

Astrology when properly understood will be most useful in the daily transactions of life. A repetition of this idea would be superfluous as the very first chapter of the book deals with the "Necessity for the Study of Astrology".

This science had been cultivated to a high degree of perfection by the Hindus long before the so-called period of authentic history. Their researches may be brought under the following three important divisions : (1) Parasari, (2) Jaimini and (3) Tajaka. Almost all astrological books in India are after Parasara who is said to have lived before the dawn of Kali Yuga (more than 5,000 years ago). Even eminent authors and commentators like Varahamihira, Bhattotpala, Venkatesa and others, who have enriched the astrological field by the effusions of their fertile brains, have held Parasara in high esteem and have based all their writings on the principles propounded by him. Thus there is absolutely no ground to doubt the accuracy of the Parasari system. The Jaimini School of Astrology* considerably differs from that of Parasari inasmuch as the method followed by the former in the treatment of even the fundamental principles, is at considerable variance from that of the latter. In spite of Jaimini being held in very high esteem as the author of the great Poorva Meemamsa Sastra or the subtle and recondite system of philosophy, his astrological methods are not in

---

* The beautiful Astrological Aphorisms of Jaimini have been rendered into English by Prof. B. Suryanarain Rao. My own publication *Studies in Jaimini Astrology* may also be studied with advantage.

vogue in India excepting that they are consulted as an alternative to Parasari. The Tajaka* is entirely devoted to the deciphering of Varshaphal or the annual results and its importance is revealed only in recent times. Thus the Parasari is the most common method having won the general acceptance of all eminent people in all ages.

I have mainly followed Parasara in the collection of material for this book and have devoted myself to a clear exposition of the various principles of astrology by following which the future of man can be revealed with sufficient accuracy.

In chapters dealing with Casting the Horoscope, Ashtaka-varga, Death, Horary Astrology, Medical Astrology, Lost Horoscopes or Unknown Birth Times, etc., every effort has been made to illustrate the theoretical principles with practical examples.

The chapters on Death and Unknown Birth Times open fresh fields for research and investigation. It is with a view to drawing the attention of the reader to the necessity of instituting inquiries into the problem of Unknown Birth Times that these chapters have been included.

The chapters are systematically arranged. As a matter of fact *the book is so graduated as to make even the beginner well acquainted with all the principles easily, while the advarced student will find much useful information with which he will not have come into contact hitherto.*

The theory of Astrology has been fully dealt with by my grandfather Prof. B. Suryanarain Rao in his *Introduction to the Study of Astrology* and by me in my book *Astrology and Modern Thought*. Both these books may be studied with great benefit.

---

* See my book *Varshaphal* or *The Hindu Progressed Horoscope* a nique treatise based on Tajaka.

I trust that my honest and humble endeavours to further the cause of Astrology will not go in vain and that this humble venture will be appreciated by all well-wishers of knowledge.

BANGALORE
1st February 1938

B. V. RAMAN
Author

CONTENTS

CHAPTER I

Necessity for the Study of Astrology

Various theories have been set up to discover the influences of planets upon the terrestrial phenomena. While some people admit the intimate relationship that exists betwixt the movements of those "mysterious intelligences" in the heavens and the fortunes and misfortunes of men, rise and fall of Empires, ebb and flow of human passions and the regeneration and degeneration of Arts, Sciences, Literature and Philosophy, there are others who always deny the existence of any sort of connection between the stars and the inhabitants of this earth. This attitude is due to the fact that they do not approach the subject with an unbiassed and unprejudiced mind. Dispassionate enquiry alone can enable one to appreciate the truth behind any branch of knowledge. In any field of enquiry, the student will find it useful to remember, it is a major error of the intellect to attempt to oppose prejudices based on *a priori* arguments to the evidence afforded by facts. The final test of a theory is that it should work satisfactorily in practice. This is the test by which astrological theory should be judged.

No science or art is more interesting, instructive and useful to mankind in contributing to his moral and material advancement than the sublime science of astrology. This is the most ancient of all sciences and had reached considerable perfection in India thousands of years ago.

While the modern scientists acknowledge astronomy, some of them sneer at astrology and reject it with contempt charging it with the dogmatism of charlatanry and superstition. They preach frankness and research as fair and reasonable; but show the greatest bigotry, when the subject of astrology is taken up or introduced.

Astrology is the science which comprises the foretelling of the regular movements of the planets, the fortunes and misfortunes of men, fates of nations, inundations, earthquakes, plagues, volcanic eruptions, pestilences, and other incidents relating to terrestrial phenomena. In Sanskrit it is called *Hora Sastra* meaning the science that treats of Time. It is also called *Jyotisha* or the *Knowledge* of *Light* from Jyoti or Light which is the root-cause for all known creation. According to the Western interpretations, Astrology is derived from *Aster*—a star, and *Logos*—reason or logic.

No sane brain could ever deny the influence of planets upon man and how they affect, deter and facilitate his future career on the three planes of human existence, *viz.*, physical characteristics, mental peculiarities and spiritual aspirations.

That a certain subtle power, derived from nature, pervades the entire universe, and the earth we inhabit is also subject to this mysterious and subtle power is evident to all. The various elements, encompassing all matter, are altered by the motions of this ethereal power. The acts of creation (*srishti*), protection (*sthiti*) and destruction (*laya*) are embedded in the womb of the All-Powerful Time and these variations are brought about as a consequence of this subtle power. The Sun by his daily movements and the change of seasons brings to perfection the embryo in plants and animals and brings about various changes on the earth. The Moon being nearest to the earth exercises much influence on it and as she wanes and waxes rivers swell, the tides of the sea are ruled and the plants and animals affected.

The Sun as the central figure predominates over the entire arrangement of the celestial system and the other planets and stars are directed by his rays.

Thus, it invariably follows, that all bodies in nature, whether animate or inanimate, are subject to the motions of the celestial bodies.* Not only those that are already in existence are influenced by the movements and configurations of planets, but also the impregnations and growth and developments of the seeds from which all bodies emanate are moulded by the quantity and quality of these influences at the time of impregnation.

Astrology must not be confused with fatalism, witchcraft, palmistry and card-shuffling. It interprets what it conceives to be the future of man as moulded by his previous Karma and indicated by the planetary positions at the time of birth.

The greatest men of the world believed in and practised astrology. Dante declared it to be "the highest, the noblest and without defect". Kepler, Bacon, Pythogoras and Democrates were masters in astrology. The ancient Hebrews called the astrologer *Asphe* meaning "the mouthpiece of the star". It is recorded that Newton was attracted to the study of mathematics and astronomy by the contemplation of an astrological figure of the heavens

---

* *Vide* my book *Astrology and Modern Thought* for an exposition of the rationale of Astrology, in the light of modern concepts.

When one has acquired a thorough knowledge of the ever-lasting and ever-changing influences of the stars, he will be able to prognosticate correctly the mental and physical qualities of any man and the fortunes and misfortunes that await him and his progress in the world whose actual moment of birth is accurately known.

By thus knowing the future correctly, man can so create an environment that, he can cope with the adverse periods of his life and alleviate the evils, indicated by the planets to a great extent. The human will is free to a certain extent and advance knowledge of the future can enable one to mitigate many evils. There is a proverb : "Fools obey planets while wise men control them."

CHAPTER II

The Zodiac and the Solar System

The zodiac is a broad band or belt in the heavens extending 9 degrees on each side of the ecliptic. The ecliptic or the path of the Sun passes exactly through the centre of the zodiac longitudinally. It is an imaginary circle of 360 degrees and the ancients divided this zodiac into 12 equal parts of 30 degrees each, each being named after the constellation. Though each of these signs differs considerably from the other, yet there is a sort of continuity through all the twelve. The quality of each sign is not equally spread, but every degree in a sign has its own peculiar qualities. The zodiac, known as the *Bhachakra* in Sanskrit, revolves on its axis once in a day from east to west.

The planetary orbs, which the ancients recognised as having the most powerful influences on our earth are seven, leaving aside the shadowy planets, Rahu and Ketu, and the so called newly discovered planets Uranus, Neptune and Pluto which Hindu astrology does not recognise.

As inhabitants of the earth, we are concerned with the influences of these celestial bodies on our planet. All the planets perform the double function of not only revolving on their own axes once in a day (from west to east) but also round the Sun. According to *Suryasiddhanta*, Saturn is the most distant planet from the earth. Jupiter, Mars, the Sun, Venus, Mercury and the Moon come next in the order of their distance from the terrestrial globe. Thus we see that the nearest planet to our own orb is the Moon. The velocity of each planet diminishes as its distance from the earth increases.

The Sun moves at the rate of roughly 1 degree of this Circle of Light (zodiac) in one day composed of 24 hours or horas, and takes 365 days and 6 hours to complete a circuit round the zodiac. The Moon takes the average rate of 4½ ghatis or 1 hour and 48 minutes to traverse through a degree of this space. Mars moves at the average rate of 45 days for 30 degrees or takes 1½ days per degree. Mercury moves at the average rate of 1½ degrees a day; but on account of his closeness to the Sun and due to the solar influence, he is very unsteady. He completes his average run in 27 days. He gets into forward and backward motions from the Sun and attains what is called *astam* or combustion. He hardly takes a day to move in each degree, but moves on more rapidly for some time, gets in front of the Sun and then begins to move slowly and goes backwards from the Sun. These two states of combustion, *viz.*, moving forwards and backwards from the position of the Sun, are designated in the astronomical works as *pragasthambha* and *paschadasthambha*—*prag* indicating towards the East of the Sun, and *paschad* indicating towards the West of the Sun. In these double motions of backwards and forwards, Mercury never gets away more than 28 degrees in either direction from the Sun. Though the time allotted to Jupiter is one year in each sign of 30 degrees, there is also some variation and the Jovian year or *Barhaspathyamana* will be a little less than 12 years in the 12 signs. Venus moves at the rate of 1 degree per day. Saturn is the

slowest moving planet of the lot.   He takes about 2½ years or
30 months to move in a sign of 30 degrees and thus he takes
1 month to move in a degree. Rahu and Ketu which revolve
in the *Apasavya* order, *i.e.*, from east to west, take 18 months
to travel through each sign of the zodiac.

All the planets, excepting the Sun, the Moon and the
shadowy planets Rahu and Ketu, undergo retrogression or
vakra and this will be fully explained in a future chapter.
This much of the explanation of the solar system seems to be
necessary to facilitate comprehension of the astrological terms
described in the subsequent chapters. For further details
about the astronomical peculiarities. I must refer the readers
to my *A Manual of Hindu Astrology*.

CHAPTER III

Hindu Time Measure

Among the Hindus, 60 lunar years constitute one cycle; they are :—

1.	Prabhava	26.	Nandana
2.	Vibhava	27.	Vijaya
3.	Sukla	28.	Jaya
4.	Pramoduta	29.	Manmatha
5.	Prajotpatti	30.	Durmukhi
6.	Angirasa	31.	Hevilambi
7.	Srimukha	32.	Vilambi
8.	Bhava	33.	Vikari
9.	Yuva	34.	Sarwari
10.	Dhatu	35.	Plava
11.	Eswara	36.	Shubhakritu
12.	Bahudhanya	37.	Shobhakritu
13.	Pramadi	38.	Krodhi
14.	Vikrama	39.	Viswavasu
15.	Vishu	40.	Parabhava
16.	Chitrabhanu	41.	Plavanga
17.	Swabhanu	42.	Kilaka
18.	Tarana	43.	Soumya
19.	Parthiva	44.	Sadharana
20.	Vyaya	45.	Virodhikritu
21.	Sarwajitu	46.	Paridhavi
22.	Sarwadhari	47.	Pramadicha
23.	Virodhi	48.	Ananda
24.	Vikriti	49.	Rakshasa
25.	Khara	50.	Nala

51. Pingala	56. Dunhubbi
52. Kalayukti	57. Rudhirodgari
53. Siddharthi	58. Rakthakshi
54. Roudri	59. Krodhana
55. Durmathi	60. Akshaya

The first year of the cycle denotes the evolution of a new creative force which apparently is supposed to end in the last or 60th year after getting fully matured, when the new year gives rise to a new force. In Vibhava this force is expanded ; Shukla denotes its vitality ; Pramoduta causes development ; Prajotpatti increases activities ; Angirasa connotes the different forms the newly evolved force takes and similarly the names are given for all the 60 years indicative of the function that the force is supposed to do, till the year Akshaya or destruction sets in which means that the force generated in Prabhava has been destroyed.

Ayanas

There are two *Ayanas*—periods—in a year, the *Uttarayana* commencing from the winter solstice, when the Sun enters Capricorn or *Makara* and moves in a northerly direction, and *Dakshinayana* beginning with the summer solstice or the ingress of the Sun into Cancer or *Kataka* when the Sun takes a southerly course.

Ruthus or Seasons

The principal seasons among the Hindus are *six*, whereas the Europeans consider only four, *viz.*, Autumn, Spring, Winter and the Summer.

The six seasons are :—

Vasantha Ruthu: Chaitra and Vaisakha (Spring), Greeshma Ruthu : Jyeshta and Ashadha (Summer), Varsha Ruthu :

Sravana and Bhadrapada (Rainy season), Sarad Ruthu :
Aswija and Kartika (Autumn), Hemantha Ruthu : Margasira
and Pushya (Winter), Sisira Ruthu : Magha and Phalguna
(Winter).

The twelve lunar months are :—

Chaitra	March–April
Vaisakha	April–May
Jyeshta	May–June
Ashadha	June–July
Sravana	July–August
Bhadrapada	August–September
Aswija	September–October
Kartika	October–November
Margasira	November–December
Pushya	December–January
Magha	January–February
Phalguna	February–March

The name of each lunar month is given as a result of the
constellation falling on the Full Moon day of the particular
month.

Solar months with their Tamil and English equivalents

Solar Months	*English*
Mesha—Chittirai	Aries
Vrishabha—Vaigasi	Taurus
Mithuna—Ani	Gemini
Kataka—Adi	Cancer
Simha—Avani	Leo
Kanya—Purattasi	Virgo
Thula—Alpisi	Libra
Vrischika—Kartigai	Scorpio
Dhanus—Margali	Sagittarius
Makara—Tbai	Capricorn
Kumbha—Masi	Aquarius
Meena – Panguni	Pisces

Shukla and Krishna Pakshas

Shukla Paksha consists of the bright half of the lunar month when the Moon waxes. The fifteen days from the next day of the New Moon to including the Full Moon constitute the Shukla Paksha. The dark half of the lunar month or the other 15 days from the next day of the Full Moon to the New Moon day make up the Krishna Paksha.

CHAPTER IV

Planets, Signs and Constellations

Nine important planets are considered in Hindu astrology as affecting the terrestrial phenomena. Their Sanskrit equiva-lents and the symbols used by Western astrologers are also given here for ready reference :—

Sun	Surya or Ravi	☉
Moon	Soma or Chandra	☽
Mars	Kuja or Angaraka	♂
Mercury	Budha or Soumya	☿
Jupiter	Guru or Brihaspati	♃
Venus	Sukra or Bhargava	♀
Saturn	Sani ot Manda	♄
Dragon's Head	Rahu or Thama	☊
Dragon's Tail	Ketu or Sikhi	☋

The twelve signs of the zodiac are :—

1. Mesha	Aries	the Ram	♈
2. Vrishabha	Taurus	the Bull	♉
3. Mithuna	Gemini	the Twins	♊
4. Kataka	Cancer	the Crab	♋
5. Simha	Leo	the Lion	♌
6. Kanya	Virgo	the Virgin	♍
7. Thula	Libra	the Balance	♎
8. Vrischika	Scorpio	the Scorpion	♏
9. Dhanus	Sagittarius	the Centaur	♐
10. Makara	Capricorn	the Crocodile	♑
11. Kumbha	Aquarius	the Water-bearer	♒
12. Meena	Pisces	the Fishes	♓

The zodiac is a circle of light and consequently it knows no beginning or end. In order to measure the distance an astronomical point (end of the constellation of Revati) is established which is called the first point of Aries. The zodiac is marked by 27 constellations or nakshatras. The first point of the Aswini, the first constellation, synchronises with the first point of Aries, which is the starting point of the fixed zodiac. Each nakshatra measures $13° 20'$ of arc and consists of four quarters or padas of $3° 20'$ each. Thus $2\frac{1}{4}$ constellations or nine quarters comprise a zodiacal sign. The Rasis (signs) and Nakshatras (constellations) are both reckoned from the same point, *viz.*, the zero degree of the zodiac or the first point of Mesha (Aries).

The constellations are :—

1. Aswini—*β Arietis*, 3 stars resembling a horse's face.
2. Bharani—41 *Arietis*, 3 stars resembling a female sexual organ.
3. Krittika —*η Tauri Alcyone*-2, 6 stars resembling a razor.
4. Rohini—*Aldebaran*, 5 stars resembling a chariot.
5. Mrigasira —*λ Orionis*, 3 stars resembling a head of a deer.
6. Aridra—*α Betelgeuse*, one star resembling a head.
7. Punarvasu—*β Geminorium Pollux*, 5 stars resembling a bow.
8. Pushyami—*δ Cancri*, 3 stars resembling a flower.
9. Aslesha—*ε Hydare*, 6 stars resembling a serpent.
10. Makha—*ρ Leonis or Regulus*, 5 stars resembling a palanquin.
11 and 12. Pubba and Uttara—*δ Leonis*, and *Denebola* 4 stars resembling the legs of a cot.

13. Hasta—*δ Corvi*, 5 stars resembling a palm.
14. Chitta—*Virginis Spica*, one star resembling a pearl.
15. Swati—*α Bootis or Arcturus*, one star resembling a sapphire.
16. Visakha—*α Librae*, 3 stars resembling a potter's wheel.
17. Anuradha—*δ Scorpii*, 3 stars resembling an umbrella.
18. Jyeshta—*Antares*, 3 stars resembling an umbrella.
19. Moola—*λ Scorpii*, 6 stars resembling a crouching line.

20 and 21. Poorvashadha, Uttarashadha—*δ* and *σ Sagittarii*, 4 stars resembling a square.

22. Sravana—*α Aquila*, 3 stars resembling an arrow.
23. Dhanishta—*β Delphini*, 4 stars resembling a drum.
24. Satabhisha—*λ Aquarii*, 100 stars resembling a flower.
25. Poorvabhadra—*β Pegasi* ⎫ 4 stars resembling the legs
26. Uttarabhadra—*γ Pegasi* ⎭ of a cot.
27. Revati—*ζ Piscium*, 3 stars resembling a fish.

The following quarters (padas) of the constellations comprise the twelve zodiacal signs :—

No.	Rasi (Sign)	Nakshatra (Constellation)		Padas (Quarters)	Space on the ecliptic from 0° Aries	
1.	Aries	1.	Aswini	4	13°	20
		2.	Bharani	4	26	40
		3.	Krittika	1	30	0
2.	Taurus		Krittika	3	40	0
		4.	Rohini	4	53	20
		5.	Mrigasira	2	60	0
3.	Gemini		Mrigasira	2	66	40
		6	Aridra	4	80	0
		7.	Punarvasu	3	90	0
4.	Cancer		Punarvasu	1	93	20
		8.	Pushyami	4	106	40
		9.	Aslesha	4	120	0

No.	Rasi (Sign)	Nakshatra (Constellation)	Padas (Quarters)	Space on the ecliptic from 0° Aries	
5.	Leo	10. Makha	4	133	20
		11. Pubba	4	146	40
		12. Uttara	1	150	0
6.	Virgo	Uttara	3	160	0
		13. Hasta	4	173	20
		14. Chitta	2	180	0
7.	Libra	Chitta	2	186	40
		15. Swati	4	200	0
		16. Visakha	3	210	0
8.	Scorpio	Visakha	1	213	20
		17. Anuradha	4	226	40
		18. Jyeshta	4	240	0
9.	Sagittarius	19. Moola	4	253	20
		20. Poorvashadha	4	296	40
		21. Uttarashadha	1	270	0
10.	Capricorn	Uttarashadha	3	280	0
		22. Sravana	4	293	20
		23. Dhanishta	2	300	0
11.	Aquarius	Dhanishta	2	306	40
		24. Satabhisha	4	320	0
		25. Poorvabhadra	3	330	0
12.	Pisces	Poorvabhadra	1	333	20
		26. Uttarabhadra	4	346	40
		27. Revati	4	360	0

The above table interpreted means that four quarters of Aswini, four quarters of Bharani and the first quarter of Krittika make up Aries or Mesha. The remaining three quarters of Krittika, four quarters of Rohini and the first two quarters of Mrigasira compose Taurus or Vrishabha and so on. This will enable one to fix the positions of planets in a horoscope, as in most Hindu almanacs, the planetary positions are generally given in constellations and quarters.

CHAPTER V

Peculiarities of the Zodical Signs

Each zodiacal sign has certain peculiarities attributed to it by ancient Maharishis. For instance, each sign represents some element in nature, such as fire, air, earth and water.

Moveable signs *(Chara Rasis)* are Aries, Cancer, Libra and Capricorn. Taurus, Leo, Scorpio and Aquarius are fixed signs *(Sthira Rasis)*. Gemini, Virgo, Sagittarius and Pisces are said to be common signs *(Dwiswabhava Rasis)*. Aries, Gemini, Leo, Libra, Sagittarius and Aquarius are odd signs. Taurus, Cancer, Virgo, Scorpio, Capricorn and Pisces are classified as even signs. All odd signs are cruel and masculine and all even signs are mild and feminine. Again, we have an account of fiery signs *(Agnitatwa Rasis)*, viz., Aries, Leo and Sagittarius. Taurus, Virgo and Capricorn are earthy signs *(Bhutatwa Rasis)*. Gemini, Libra and Aquarius are airy signs *(Vayutatwa Rasis)*. And finally Cancer, Scorpio and Pisces are classified as watery signs *(Jalatatwa Rasis)*. Cancer, Leo, Virgo, Libra, Scorpio and Sagittarius are signs of long ascension and those of short ascension are Capricorn, Aquarius, Pisces, Aries, Taurus and Gemini.* Cancer, Scorpio and Pisces are fruitful and Gemini, Leo and Virgo are barren. Gemini, Leo, Virgo, Libra, Scorpio and Aquarius

* Of course, this order has to be reversed for places situated in South of Equator.

rise by their heads and are consequently called *Sirodaya Rasis* which, excepting Gemini, are said to be powerful during the day. The *Prushtodaya signs* (rising by hinder part) are Aries, Taurus, Cancer, Sagittarius and Capricorn. These signs along with Gemini are said to be powerful during the night. Pisces forms a combination of the two and is called *Ubhayodaya Rasi* with power both during day and night. Gemini, Virgo, Aquarius and the first half of Sagittarius are the signs of voice.

These details would be highly useful in the delineation of character and mental disposition.

Quadrants (*Kendras*) are 1, 4, 7 and 10. Trines (*Trikonas*) are 5 and 9. Cadent houses (*Panaparas*) are 2, 5, 8 and 11. Succeedent houses (*Apoklimas*) are 3, 6, 9 and 12 (9th being a trikona must be omitted). *Upachayas* are 3, 6, 10 and 11.

CHAPTER VI

Astrological Terminology

The allocation of sign rulership does not appear to be arbitrary. For instance, the Sun rules Leo. If we replace the Sun by the earth, then we find that the nearest planet to the Earth, *viz.*, the Moon, rules the nearest sign to Leo, *viz.*, Cancer.

Guru (Jupiter) ♃	Kuja (Mars) ♂	Sukra (Venus) ♀	Budha (Merc.) ☿
Sani (Saturn) ♄			Chandra (Moon) ☽
Sani (Saturn) ♄			Ravi (Sun) ☉
Guru (Jupiter) ♃	Kuja (Mars) ♂	Sukra (Venus) ♀	Budha (Merc.) ☿

According to *Suryasiddhanta*, Saturn is the most distant planet from the Earth ; Jupiter, Mars, Venus, Mercury and the Moon come next in the order of their distance. Based on such an arrangement, the rulerships are allotted. The planets and signs are related by what is known as sign rulership.

Aries and Scorpio are ruled by Mars. Venus rules Taurus
and Libra. Mercury governs Gemini and Virgo. The Moon
owns Cancer. The Sun is the lord of Leo. Jupiter governs
Pisces and Sagittarius. Capricorn and Aquarius are ruled by
Saturn. Leo and Ketu rule Scorpio. Rahu owns Leo and
Ketu rules Scorpio.

Exaltations.—The Sun is exalted in the 10th degree of
Aries; the Moon in the 3rd degree of Taurus; Mars in the
28th degree of Capricorn; Mercury in the 15th degree of
Virgo; Jupiter in the 5th degree of Cancer; Venus in the 27th
degree of Pisces; and Saturn in the 20th degree of Libra,
Rahu in 20° of Taurus and Ketu in 20° of Scorpio.

Debilitations.—The 7th house or the 180th degree from
the place of exaltation is the place of debilitation or fall. The
Sun is debilitated in the 10th degree of Libra, the Moon in the
3rd degree of Scorpio and so on.

Benefics and Malefics.—Planets are benefic or malefic
according to their inherent nature. They tend to do good or
evil. Jupiter, Venus, Full Moon and well-associated Mercury
are held to be good planets. New Moon, badly associated
Mercury, the Sun, Saturn, Mars, Rahu and Ketu are evil
or malefic ones: From the eighth day of the bright half of
the lunar month the Moon is full and strong. She is weak
from the eighth day of the dark half.

Sexes.—Jupiter, Mars and the Sun are males; Venus,
Rahu and the Moon are females; and Saturn, Mercury and
Ketu are eunuchs or hermaphrodites. This enables us to
determine the sex of the child in the birth horoscope and the
sex of the person involved if it is a horary chart.

Colours.—Each planet represents a certain colour which
is as follows: —Sun—copper, Mars—blood red, Moon—

white, Saturn—black, Mercury—green, Jupiter—bright
yellow and Venus—mixture of all colours.

Moolatrikonas.—There are certain positions called Moola-
trikonas which are similar to those of exaltation. The Sun's
Moolatrikona is Leo (0°–20°); the Moon has Taurus (4°–20°);
Mercury—Virgo (16°–20°); Jupiter—Sagittarius (0°–10°);
Mars—Aries (0°–12°); Venus—Libra (0°–15°); and Saturn—
Aquarius (0°–20°).

Planetary Natures.—The Sun, the Moon and Jupiter are
divine in nature and indicate *Satvikaguna* or philosophical and
philanthropic dispositions. Venus and Mercury represent
Rajasa or imperious disposition. Mars and Saturn denote
Thamasa or dull nature.

The Sun and Mars are fiery planets; Mercury is earthy;
Saturn is airy; Jupiter is ethereal; and Venus and the Moon
are watery.

The Sun represents ego or *atma*; the Moon *manas* or
mind; Mars—martial power; Mercury—good and eloquent
speech; Jupiter indicates wisdom; Venus shows voluptuous-
ness and gross sensual pleasures; and Saturn indicates sorrows
and miseries.

The Sun and the Moon are kings; Mars—commander-in-
chief; Mercury—Yuvaraja or heir-apparent; Jupiter and
Venus—Prime Ministers; and Saturn a servant.

Planetary Relations.—By the term friendship and enmity
among planets we have to understand that the rays of one
planet will be intensified or counteracted by those of the other
declared to be its friend or enemy respectively. Friendship
will be both permanent and temporary.

Permanent Relationship

Planet	Friends	Neutrals	Enemies
Sun	Moon, Mars, Jupiter	Mercury	Saturn, Venus
Moon	Sun, Mercury	Mars, Jupiter, Venus, Saturn	None
Mars	Sun, Moon, Jupiter	Venus, Saturn	Mercury
Mercury	Sun, Venus	Mars, Jupiter, Saturn	Moon
Jupiter	Sun, Moon, Mars	Saturn	Mercury Venus
Venus	Mercury, Saturn	Mars, Jupiter	Sun, Moon
Saturn	Mercury, Venus	Jupiter	Sun, Moon, Mars

Temporary Relationship

Besides Naisargika or natural friendship, planets become temporary friends also by virtue of their sign positions. Planets found in the 2nd, 3rd, 4th, 10th, 11th and 12th signs from any other planet, become its temporary friends. Those in the remaining signs become temporary enemies. In judging a horoscope, both types of relationships should be carefully considered thus:

Permanent Friend	+	Temporary Friend	=	Best Friend
(Naisargika Mitra)	+	(Tatkalika Mitra)	=	(Adhi Mitra)
Permanent Friend	+	Temporary Enemy	=	Neutral
(Naisargika Mitra)	+	(Tatkalika Satru)	=	(Sama)
Permanent Enemy	+	Temporary Enemy	=	Bitter Enemy
(Naisargika Satru)	+	(Tatkalika Satru)	=	(Adhi Satru)
Permanent Enemy	+	Temporary Friend	=	Neutral
(Naisargika Satru)	+	(Tatkalika Mitra)	=	(Sama)
Permanent Neutral	+	Temporary Friend	=	Friend
(Nasargika Sama)	+	(Tatkalika Mitra)	=	(Mitra)
Permanent Neutral	+	Temporary Enemy	=	Enemy
(Naisargika Sama)	+	(Tatkalika Satru)	=	(Satru)

In the illustration given below, let us find out the temporary and permanent friendships and enmities between the
planets. Take for instance, Jupiter. The Moon is in the
seventh, therefore he becomes temporary enemy of Jupiter.
But from the table of permanent relationship given above, it

✶ Rahu	♈	♉ Moon Saturn	♊
♒ Ascdt	Horoscope of a male born on 8-8-1912 at 7-43 p. m. (I.S.T.) Lat. 13 North ; Long. 77° 34′ East.		♋ Sun
♑			♌ Mars Merc. Venus
♂	♏ Jupiter	♎	♍ Ketu

will be seen that the Moon is the friend of Jupiter. Now
adding the two :—Temporary enemy *plus* permanent friend,
we get the compounded relation as neutral. Thus the Moon
is a neutral of Jupiter. Similarly, ascertain the relations with
reference to other planets

Planetary Castes.—Venus and Jupiter are *Brahmins* or
holy people; the Sun and Mars are *Kshatriyas* or belong to
the warrior caste; the Moon is *Vaisya* or trader; Mercury is
Sudra or farmer and Saturn is *Antyaja* or untouchable. One
should not confuse this with the so-called caste system.
According to Lord Krishna, *varna* is based on *guna* and
karma.

Planetary Directions.—The Sun, Venus, Mars, Rahu, Saturn, Moon, Mercury and Jupiter indicate East, S.-E., South, S.-W., West, N.-W., North and N.-E., respectively.

Conjunctional Peculiarities (Vakra or retrogression).—According to Hindu astronomy, planets in the course of their journey in the zodiac are said to be obstructed by certain invisible forces called *mondochcha, seeghrochcha* and *patha* as a result of which they become stationary for a while, get backward movements and again after some time, they regain their natural course. This phenomenon of going backwards is called retrogression. The astronomical aspect of the retrograde movements of planets is somewhat cumbersome and for details readers may refer to any standard texts on astronomy.

Athichara or Acceleration.—If a planet moves from one sign to the other faster than its usual speed it gets what is called *Athichara* or Acceleration.

Stambhana or Stagnation.—Residence in the same sign for more than the usual period makes a planet get this stage.

Astangata or Combustion.—Planets in intimate conjunction with the Sun get combustion and become utterly powerless.

Samagama.—Planets with the Moon acquire Samagama.

Arohana.—The ascending direction from the debilitation to the exaltation.

Avarohana.—The descending direction from exaltation to debilitation.

CHAPTER VII

Planetary Strengths and Avasthas

Planetary conjunctions play an important part in the determination of the various sources of strength and weakness of the planets in a horoscope. Conjunction of good planets always produces beneficial results while the reverse holds good when malefic planets join together.

Planets on account of their incessant movements get into certain states of existence called *avasthas* which are ten in number. Each *avastha* produces its own results. In the judgment of a horoscope all these details have to be fully considered.

Deeptha or Exaltation.—Gains from conveyances, respect from elders, fame, wealth and good progeny.

Swastha or Own House.—Fame, wealth, position, lands, happiness and good children.

Muditha or in the House of a Friend.—Happiness.

Santha or an Auspicious Sub-division.—Strength and courage, helping relations, comfort and happiness.

Sakta or Retrogression.—Courage, reputation, wealth and progeny.

Peedya or Residence in the last quarter of a sign.—Prosecution, incarceration, pilfering habits and expulsion from country.

Deena or in Inimical House.—Jealousy, mental worry, brain trouble, sickness and degradation.

Vikala or Combustion.—Diseases, orphanage, loss of wife and children and disgrace.

Khala or Debilitation.—Losses, mean birth, troubles from various sources, quarrels with parents and relations, imprisonment and hating God and sacred literature.

Bhita or Acceleration.—Losses from various sources, torture, foes, mean habits and danger in foreign countries.

The Shadbalas or Six Sources of Strength and Weakness of Planets.— Each planet is supposed to get a particular share of strength when it occupies a particular position. The source of strength can be numerically measured by a certain unit called Rupa. (For full details, see my book *Graha and Bhava Balas.*) There are six kinds of strength considered in Indian astrology.

1. *Sthanabala.*—This is the positional strength which a planet gets as a result of its occupying a particular house in the horoscope. A planet gets Sthanabala in its exaltation, own house, moolatrikona, and friendly house and Swa (own) Shadvargas (for Shadvargas *vide* Chapter XI).

2. *Digbala.*—This is the directional strength. Jupiter and Mercury are powerful in the East (ascendant). The Sun and Mars get their directional strength in the North (10th house). Saturn in the West (7th house) gains Digbala. Venus and the Moon acquire directional strength in the South (4th house).

3. *Chestabala* (Motional strength).— The Sun and the Moon in the signs of Capricorn, Aquarius, Pisces, Aries, Taurus and Gemini which constitute the Uttarayana (Sun's northerly course) and Mars, Mercury, Jupiter, Venus and Saturn in retrogression or in conjunction with the Full Moon get

Chestabala. If Jupiter, Venus, Mercury and Saturn are with Mars, they are said to be defeated in the planetary fight or Grahayuddha and get Chestabala.

4. *Kalabala*.—Kalabala means temporal strength. The Moon, Mars and Saturn are powerful during the night. The Sun, Jupiter and Venus are powerful during the day. Mercury is always powerful. Malefics and benefics are powerful during the dark half and bright half of the lunar month respectively. Mercury, the Sun, Saturn, the Moon, Venus and Mars are powerful at sunrise, noon, evening, first part of the night, midnight and the last part of the night respectively. Jupiter is always strong. Planets in their weekdays, months and years are said to be powerful.

5. *Drugbala*.—Drugbala is reckoned as a result of the aspect to which each planet is subjected to by the other. The houses of aspect are given in the next chapter. Aspects of benefics give full Drugbala or strength, and aspects of malefics take away the Drugbala

6. *Naisargikabala*.—This means permanent or natural strength. Each planet is supposed to produce a particular measure of strength permanently irrespective of its position. The Sun, the Moon, Venus, Jupiter, Mercury, Mars and Saturn are strong in order. The Sun is the most powerful and Saturn is the least powerful.

The strengths of planets can be numerically calculated as per my book *Graha* and *Bhava Balas*.

CHAPTER VIII

Hindu Method of Casting the Horoscope

The horoscope is simply a scheme or a plan representing an accurate picture of the heavens, of the positions of the planets and the stars for the time at which a child is born or at any particular moment. The map of the heavens containing the 12 divisions is drawn in either a square or circular form. I give below the most common kinds of diagrams now in vogue in India and abroad.

For the benefit of my Western readers, and such Indian readers who have no access to almanacs, I have also explained the method of casting the horoscope according to the Western system and its reduction to the Hindu, in the next chapter. The following are some of the maps used by different countries :—

S. INDIA   N. INDIA

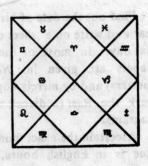

For all practical purposes almanacs published by competent
Hindu astronomers, giving the planetary positions, can be
used by beginners, and after acquiring a thorough familiarity
with the various rules for the computation of horoscopes on
the basis of such almanacs, the student may refer to modern
ephemerides for greater accuracy.

Western Countries

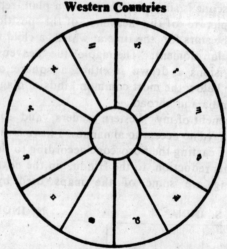

Find out the date of birth in the almanac in the particular
year and write on a sheet of paper all the details given for
that day. In most of the almanacs, the positions of the
planets are given in *Nakshatra Padas* (Constellational
quarters) and by merely copying them, one would be able to
mark the *Rasi* (zodiacal) and *Navamsa* (one-ninth division)
diagrams.

Ascertain the exact moment of birth and sunrise. If the
time is in English hours, convert it into *ghatis* (2½ *ghatis*
make one hour, 24 minutes make one *ghati* and 24 seconds
make one *vighati*). If the birth has occurred after midnight,

it must be taken as belonging to the previous day as among the Hindus a day is reckoned from sunrise to sunrise. Ascertain how many hours after sunrise the birth has occurred and convert this into ghatis.

In the almanac, if there are any planets marked on the day of birth and if the ghatis given against each or any of them are below the time of birth, reproduce them as they are; otherwise trace back and find out the positions of planets nearest to the date of birth. For the Moon some calculations are necessary. Find out the constellation on the day of birth which can be readily seen in the almanac and note down its duration. If it be the one that ends on the same day, then add to this duration, the number of ghatis and vighatis obtained by subtracting from 60, the extent of the preceding asterism on the previous day. The sum represents the entire duration of the constellation in question. One-fourth of this gives the duration of a quarter or pada. Add birth time to the duration of the constellation on the previous day. This gives how much of time has elapsed in the constellation at the time of birth. Dividing this by the duration of each quarter, we get the particular quarter of the constellation in which the Moon is.

In case the constellation be the one that ends on the next day, the duration of the asterism on the day of birth and that on the next day must be obtained thus :

Let us assume that the sunrise on the day of birth of the following illustrative horoscope is at 5–35 a.m. The birth has taken place at 5–35 p.m. Deducting sunrise from birth time (5–35 p.m. = 17 hours, 35 minutes) we get 12 hours. This converted into ghatis at 2½ ghatis per one hour gives 30 ghatis as the time of birth after sunrise. From the almanac, we find that on the day of birth the constellation Rohini ruled for 21–59 ghatis. Subtract from 60 ghatis, the number of ghatis and vighatis at which the Moon left the previous constellation. Add to this, the number of ghatis and vighatis when this constellation terminates the next day. The total duration of the constellation is obtained. Subtract from the time of birth (in ghatis) the time when the Moon left the previous asterism. The time elapsed from the beginning of the constellation to the moment of the birth is obtained. Now it will be easy to find in what quarter the Moon is placed.

The following illustration enables the student to grasp the principles enumerated above easily.

Illustration.—Born 8th August 1912 A.D. at 5–35 p.m. or 30 ghatis after sunrise, Long. 78° E., Lat. 13° N. :

On 8-8-1912.		On 9–9–1912	
Duration of day = Gh. 60–0		Extent of Mrigasira	
Extent of Rohini	21–59	= Gh. 19–15	
Extent of Mrigasira	38–1		

on 8–8–1912

∴ Total duration of Mrigasira

$$= \text{Gh. } 38\text{–}1 + \text{Gh. } 19.15 = \text{Gh. } 57\text{–}16.$$

Dividing this by 4, we find that each quarter lasts for

$$\underline{\qquad} = \text{Gh. } 14\text{–}19$$

Again, Birth time	...	Gh. 30–0
Duration of Rohini	....	21–59
Time elapsed is Mrigasira	...	8–1

Since the balance is less than ghatis 14–19, the first quarter of Mrigasira rules at birth, *i.e.*, the Moon occupies the first quarter of Mrigasira. Tracing back, the positions of other planets are obtained thus:

Sun in the	**II quarter of**	**Aslesha**
Moon	**I do.**	**Mrigasira**
Mars	**III do.**	**Pubba**
Mercury	**II do.**	**Makha (Retrogression)**
Jupiter	**II do.**	**Jyeshta**
Venus	**I do.**	**Makha**
Saturn	**I do.**	**Rohini**
Rahu	**III do.**	**Revati**
Ketu	**I do.**	**Chitta**

♓ Rahu	♈	♉ Moon Saturn	♊
♒ Ascdt.			♋ Sun
♑	**RASI**		♌ Mars Merc. Venus
♐ Jupiter	♏	♎ Ketu	♍

Take the Sun. He is in the second quarter of Aslesha.
Count from the constellation Aswini upto the constellation
of the planet. It is 8. Convert this into padas or quarters
(one quarter is equal to 31/3 degrees of ecliptic arc); 8 × 4 = 32.
Add the two quarters already passed by the planet in Aslesha.
32 *plus* 2 = 34. Since 9 padas make one Rasi, divide this by
9 ; 34/9 = 3 7/9. The remainder is 7. That is, the Sun passed
three signs from Aries and is in the fourth sign, namely
Cancer. All this trouble can be saved by referring to the

Table of constellations given on page 14. The Sun, as we know, is in the 2nd pada of Aslesha. From the table, it will be seen that the last quarter of Punarvasu, the four quarters of Pushyami and the four quarters of Aslesha constitute the sign Cancer. As the Sun is still in the 2nd pada of Aslesha, we can readily place him in Cancer. Similarly, fix all the other planets in their respective signs.

Ascendant or the Lagna

The next step after fixing the planets is the correct determination of Lagna or the Ascendant. The earth is egg-shaped and rotates once a day on its axis and thus all the zodiacal signs are invariably "exposed" to the solar influence. As the earth is egg-shaped, certain signs are exposed to a greater extent of time than others. The 12 solar months are named after the 12 signs of the zodiac. On the first day of Aries the first degree of that particular sign rises in the eastern horizon at sunrise and the remaining signs gradually ascend till the next day at sunrise when the sunrise takes place in the second degree of Aries. The sunrise takes place in the last degree of the zodiac on the 30th day of Pisces, when the solar year ends. Thus the Lagna or the Ascendant is that particular point of the ecliptic considered with reference to the particular horizon. Therefore, certain periods of time are allotted to each of the zodiacal signs to rise, the duration of such periods depending upon the latitude of the place. The duration of the signs varies in accordance with the degree of the latitude of the place and the student is referred to Appendix B at the end of the book by means of which the rising periods of the various signs for the different degrees of latitude can easily be ascertained.

*The degree and the sign in which the Sun rises will be the ascendant at the particular time. The solar date of birth is readily found out in the almanac. In the illustration given, the solar date is the 24th of Cancer. The rising sign in that month will be Cancer itself. But the Sun rises in it on the first day in the first degree of Cancer. The person was born on the 24th evening and therefore the Sun has passed 23 degrees of Cancer and rose on that morning in the 24th degree.

Therefore the Sun on the day of birth was in Cancer 24 degrees. Time of birth is 30 ghatis. Cancer extends for about 5-31 ghatis (see Appendix B) at Lat. 13° N. Therefore each degree requires $5\text{-}31 \times 60/30 = 1\frac{1}{30}$ vighatis to rise. Therefore the Sun has $23 \times 11\frac{1}{30} = 253\frac{23}{30}$ vighatis or 4 ghatis and $13\frac{23}{30}$ or 14 vighatis.

		Gh.
Duration of Cancer	...	5-31
Ghatis gained by the Sun	...	4-14
Ghatis remaining to be covered by the Sun	...	1-17
Leo	...	$5\text{-}20\frac{5}{6}$
Virgo	...	5-6
Libra	...	5-6
Scorpio	...	$2\text{-}20\frac{5}{6}$
Sagittarius	...	5-31
	Total	$27\text{-}41\frac{2}{3}$

* The method of finding the Lagna given here is of a general character intended to serve the purpose of a beginner. The exact situation of the Sun must be ascertained and then the rising sign and degree found out. Full particulars with examples will be found in Chapter VIII of my book *A Manual of Hindu Astrology* to which the reader is referred.

Birth has taken place at 30 ghatis and since Sagittarius ends at 27–41 2/3 ghatis after sunrise the ascendant is Capricorn, *i.e.*, 2 ghatis and 18 1/3 vighatis have elapsed in Capricorn.

The positions of the planets and the Lagna in their exact degrees are thus calculated with the aid of the almanacs.

Each sign is composed of 30 degrees. In the illustration, Capricorn is the ascendant. Its duration is 312 2/3 vighatis at 13 degrees north latitude. *Therefore as 312 2/3 vighatis are to 30 degrees, so are 138 1/3 vighatis to the degrees required* = $30/312\frac{2}{3} \times 138 \ 1/3 = 13$ degrees 17 minutes. Thus the ascendant is 13 degrees 17 minutes Capricorn. This is the Bhavamadhya or the mid-point of the first house, and the first house or the first Bhava extends roughly 15 degrees on either side of this point. For determining the cusps of houses (Bhavamadhya, etc.) reference may be made to my *A Manual of Hindu Astrology*. For ordinary purposes*, it may be supposed that each Bhava extends 15 degrees on either side of the mid-point. In the illustration, 13 degrees Capricorn is the Bhavamadhya of the first house and it roughly extends from 29 degrees of Sagittarius to 28 degrees of Capricorn. The second house extends from 28 degrees Capricorn and so on.

In "Table of Houses" the cusps of the houses are readily available and the student will not find it difficult to enter them in the chart. At the outset, the beginner will do well to confine his attention to these primary rules without worrying himself with the technique of mathematical astrology.

The exact Nirayana longitude, say of the Sun, is to be determined at the birth of a person on 8th August 1912 A.D., at 5–35 p.m. (I.S.T.). That year's almanac will give the following information :—

---

* Even this supposition holds good only with reference to places that lie near the equator.

5th August 1912—Sun enters 3rd quarter of Aslesha at 46–30 ghatis.

9th August 1912—Sun enters 3rd quarter of Aslesha at 17–44 ghatis.

Therefore the period taken by the Sun to pass through one pada or 3 1/3 degrees of the ecliptic are is :—

5th August Gh.   13—30 subtracting the time of entry from 60 gh. being duration of the day.

6th	do.	60— 0
7th	do.	60— 0
8th	do.	60— 0
9th	do.	17 44

Total   ...   211—14 or 12,674 vighatis.

Time elapsed from the entry of the Sun into the 2nd pada of Aslesha (which is nearest to the time of birth) upto the moment of birth.

5th August Gh.	13—30
6th do.	60— 0
7th do.	60— 0
8th do.	30— 0 (moment of birth)

Total ....   163—30 or 9,810 vighatis.

In 12, 674 vighatis the Sun covers $\frac{10}{3}$ degrees.

In 9,810 vighatis the Sun covers $\frac{10}{3} \times \frac{9810}{12674}$ i.e., equal to 2 degrees, 34 minutes and 48 seconds of arc.

In the 2nd pada or quarter of Aslesha, the Sun has passed 2 degrees, 34 minutes and 48 seconds. We know that the last quarter of Punarvasu, the four padas of Pushyami and four padas of Aslesha compose Cancer. Upto the 2nd pada of Aslesha, the number of padas passed in Cancer is :—Punarvasu 1 plus Pushyami 4 plus Aslesha 1, total 6 padas or $6 \times 10/3 = 20$ degrees. This added to the number of degrees passed in the 2nd pada of Aslesha gives the exact Nirayana longitude of the Sun at the time of birth, *viz.*, 20 degrees *plus* 2 degrees, 34 minutes and 48 seconds will be equal to 22 degrees, 34 minutes and 48 seconds. Thus in the illustrative horoscope, the Nirayana Sun is in 22 degrees, 34 minutes and 48 seconds Cancer. For other planets the longitudes must be computed similarly.

CHAPTER IX

Western Method of Horoscope Casting and Its Reduction to the Hindu

A short account of the difference existing between the Hindu and Western zodiacs seems necessary before explaining the method involved in the erection of the heavenly map according to the Western system and its reduction to the Hindu zodiac. The Hindu astronomers of the Nirayana school trace their observations of planets to the fixed zodiac while the Western astronomers, belonging to the Sayana system, consider the moving zodiac commencing from the ever-shifting vernal equinox. The exact period when both the zodiacs were in the first point is doubted by a number of astronomers and accordingly the Ayanamsa—precessional distance—or the increment between the beginning of the fixed and moveable zodiacs, varies from 19 to 23 degrees. This Ayanamsa is reckoned roughly at 50 1/3 seconds of arc per year (see Appendix A).

Erect the horoscope as per rules given below. Subtract the Ayanamsa for the year of birth from such positions and the Hindu horoscope is obtained. In one year the Ayanamsa gains by 50 1/3 seconds of arc so that precession for odd days may conveniently be omitted.

In an *ephemeris (Raphael's or Die Deutsche's or any standard one) the longitudes of planets are calculated daily

* "Raman's Ninety-year Ephemeris" (1891-1980) can be used with great advantage by Indian as well as Western students of astrology.

for Greenwich Mean Noon. Therefore Local Mean Time of the place of birth must be turned into its equivalent Greenwich Time. Add to the Local Mean Time of birth, if the birthplace is west of Greenwich, four minutes for every degree of longitude. Subtract four minutes from the Local Mean Time of birth for every degree of longitude, if the birthplace is east of Greenwich. Having converted this Local Mean Time of birth into Greenwich Mean Time the planetary longitudes can be calculated from the ephemeris easily. To find out the exact longitude of the planet for a given time the difference of longitude between the previous noon (if birth is a.m.) and the noon of the birthday or the difference between the noon of the day (if birth is p.m.) and the next noon must be noted. (In some publications the daily movements of planets will be given in a separate section). This difference is the motion of the planet in 24 hours. Then the following rule must be applied: *As 24 hours are to the daily motion so is the difference between the given time and noon to the motion required.*

Illustration—Born 8th August 1912, Thursday 7 hours 23 minutes p.m., L.M.T., longitude 77 degrees 35 minutss east and latitude 13 degrees north.

Long. 77 degrees 35 minutes = 5h. 10m. 20s. in time.

Local Mean Time of birth	7	23	6 p.m.
Long. of birthplace (in time)	−5	10	20 p.m.
∴ G.M.T. of birth	2	12	46 p.m.

Since the place of birth is east of Greenwich subtracting the difference of longitude in time from Local Mean Time, we get the corresponding Greenwich Mean Time, which is equal to 2 hours, 12 minutes and 46 seconds p.m. Referring to Ephemeris for 1912, for 8th August 1912, the Sun's longitude on that noon is given as Leo 15 degrees, 32 minutes and 4 seconds. On page 35 the daily motion of the Sun on the day is given as 57 minutes and 34 seconds.

Sun's motion in 24 hours   57′ 34″

do. ,,   2h. 12m. 46s. $\dfrac{57′ 34″}{24}$ × 2h. 12m. 46s.

                = 5′ 17″

Long. of Sun at noon   15° 32′ 4″

Add Sun's motion in 2h. 12m. 46s.   5′ 17″

∴ Long. of Sun at birth moment   15° 37′ 21″

This is according to the Western method. Subtract from this the Ayanamsa for 1912 to get the Hindu longitude.

Sayana Longitude   ···15° 37′ 21″ in Leo.

Less Ayanamsa for 1912   ...21   11   29

Hindu Nirayana Longitude   24   25   52 in Cancer.

If a planet is in retrogression, it will be mentioned so in the ephemeris. Similarly, the planetary positions for other celestial bodies must be computed. Calculation of the Moon's longitude, or for that matter the longitude of any planet, may be conveniently done by means of logarithms. Her position for 12 noon on 8th August 1912 is found to be Gemini 15° 0′ 56°. Her motion for that day is 14° 24′ 57″ or 14° and 25′. Turning to Tables of logarithms at the end of the ephemeris, we find that :

Motion Log for 14° and 25′   ... 0.2213

Time Log for 2 hours and 13 minutes   ... 1.0345

                                     1.2558

In the Table of logarithms we find that for the nearest number (this exact number is not found there) to 1.2558 at the top of the column degrees and on the left of the table, minutes showing the number of degrees and minutes the Moon has progressed in 2 hours and 13 minutes, *viz.*, 1° 20′

Moon's Sayana Long. at noon ...   15°   0′   56″ Gemini

Plus Moon's Motion for 2h. 13m. +   1   20   0

              Total   ...   16   20   56 Gemini

Less Ayanamsa for 1912   ...   21   11   29

Hindu Longitude of Moon   ...   25°   9′   27″ **Taurus**

Thus we find that the Moon is in Taurus 25 degrees, 9 minutes and 27 seconds according to the Hindu method. Taurus is composed of three quarters of Krittika, four of Rohini and the first two of Mrigasira. Table of constellations on page 15 will tell us that 25° Taurus corresponds to the first quarter of Mrigasira, *i.e.*, the Moon is in the first pada or quarter of Mrigasira.

Lagna or the Ascendant.—Find out the Sidereal Time at G.M.T. which will be found in the first column of the ephemeris. This is calculated for 12 noon Greenwich Time. Add to this the Local Mean Time of birth (number of hours passed after the local noon), and also add 10 seconds per hour since noon as this represents the difference between the Sidereal Time (S.T.) and the Mean Time. If the place of birth is east of Greenwich, deduct at the rate of 10 seconds per hour of every 15 degrees of longitude (or 1 hour in time) and if the place of birth is west of Greenwich, add a similar quantity. This quantity represents the Sidereal Time at the moment of birth and when this is converted into degrees it represents what is called the R.A.M.C. of birth. Then refer to the table of houses for the place of birth or for the latitude nearest to the place of birth. The ascendant and the cusps of the six houses will be found marked. Considering the same illustration, we proceed thus :—

	h.	m.	s.
Sidereal Time for noon preceding birth ...	9	6	30
Number of hours passed since noon upto birth ...	7	23	6
Corrections between S.T. and Mean Time at 10s. per hour }	+ 0	1	14
	16	30	50
Less correction for the difference of time between the place of birth (east of Greenwich) and Greenwich ...	− 0	0	52
Local Sidereal Time of birth ...	16	29	58

16 hours	...	240°	0′	0″
29 minutes	...	7°	15′	0″
58 seconds	...	0°	14′	30″
R.A.M.C. of birth	...	247°	29′	30″

The *Table of Houses for Madras must be referred to as the latitude of Madras (13° N.) is nearest to the latitude of birthplace and as no tables of houses are available for the birthplace itself.

Having found the nearest Sidereal Time corresponding to 16 hours, 29 minutes and 58 seconds (under the column Sidereal Time) we see in the next column (10) the sign Scorpio and the number 17° 35′, opposite the Sidereal Time showing that 17° 35′ of Scorpio is on the cusp of the 10th house. In the next column (11), we find 15° 35′ Sagittarius, Capricorn 13° 35′ on the 12th and 11° 34′ Aquarius on the ascendant or first house. The cusps of the six houses are thus obtained and adding 180 degrees to each of these, the cusps of the other opposite six are ascertained. Now for example, by adding 180 degrees to the cusp of the 10th house, that of the fourth can be found and so on. If you consult a Sayana table of houses, deduct the Ayanamsa from the figures obtained and you will get the Nirayana longitudes of houses. From the Sayana ascendant so obtained and the cusps of the houses, deduct the *Ayanamsa*, viz., 21 degrees, 11 minutes and 29 seconds and the houses (*Bhavas*) and the ascendant (*Lagna*) of the Hindu zodiac are obtained. $Cusp of the Western

---

* *Vide* Page 111 of *The Nirayana Tables of Houses* 0° to 60° by Dr. B. V. Raman and Prof. R. V. Vaidya.

$ There is a slight difference in the mode of reckoning cusps of non-angular houses between the Western and the Hindu systems. This may be ignored for the present as it will not materially affect further procedure of interpreting horoscopes as explained in the pages of this book. *The Nirayana Tables of Houses* by Dr. B. V. Raman and Prof. R. V. Vaidya calculated according to Hindu methods may be used in preference to Raphael's or any other Western publication.

houses less *Ayanamsa* will give the *Bhavamadhya* (mid-point of
the house) of the Hindus.

Cusps of the first house or ascendant   2°   45′ Pisces
Less Ayanamsa for 1912   ...   28° 11′

Bhavamadhya of the first house
     or Lagna   ...   ...   11° 34′ Aquarius

The illustrated horoscope is to be represented as follows
diagrammatically :

Rahu 24° 16′	Sat. 11° 37′ Moon 25° 11′	
Ascdt. 11° 34′		Sun 24° 26′
	RASI	Mars 22° 50′ Merc. 15° 50′ Venus 3° 43′
Jupiter 14° 26′		Ketu 24° 16′

Similarly, deduct the Ayanamsa from the cusps of the
other houses obtained above and you will get the corresponding Hindu Bhavamadhyas (mid-points of houses).

CHAPTER X

The Shadvargas

The Shadvargas are the six-fold divisions of a zodiacal sign. A consideration of the *Shadvargas* will enable us to estimate the strength of planets. They are Rasi, Hora, Drekkana, Navamsa, Dwadasamsa and Trimsamsa. Generally most of the astrologers mark the Rasi and the Navamsa diagrams and base their predictions on these two. The Navamsa system is the most important division. The readers will do well at the beginning to cast the Rasi and Navamsa diagrams and see how accurate some of the predictions based on these two charts turn out. For determining the strength of planets Sapthavargas (seven-fold divisions) are taken into account. This has been fully explained in my *Graha and Bhava Balas*.

Rasi.—The arc of 30 degrees forming a zodiacal sign is called Rasi. The twelve zodiacal signs are the twelve Rasis. The limits and lordships of the various Rasis have been already named.

Hora.—When a sign is divided into two equal parts, each is called a hora. In odd signs like Aries, Gemini, etc., the first hora is governed by the Sun and the second by the Moon. In even signs like Taurus, Cancer, etc., the first hora is governed by the Moon and the second by the Sun.

Example.—*Ascendant 11° 34′ Aquarius. It falls in the first hora as it is within 15 degrees. Aquarius is an odd sign and the first hora is governed by the Sun; therefore, the ascendant falls in the Sun's hora.*

Drekkana.—When a sign is divided into three equal parts, each is called a drekkana getting 10 degrees. The first drekkana is governed by the lord of the Rasi; the second by the lord of the 5th from it; and the third by the lord of the 9th from it. Take Aries: the first drekkana is governed by Mars, its lord; the second is ruled by the Sun, the lord of the 5th from Aries; and the third Jupiter rules over, as he is the lord of the 9th from Aries.

Example.—*Ascendant 11° 34' Aquarius. Since it falls between 10° and 20°, the birth has occurred in the second drekkana whose lord is the lord of the 5th, viz., Mercury.*

Navamsa.—The most important sub-division of a zodiacal sign is the navamsa. When a sign is divided into nine equal parts, each part becomes a navamsa measuring $3\frac{1}{3}$ degrees. In Aries, Leo and Sagittarius, the navamsas are governed by the lords of the nine signs respectively from Aries. Take Aries, and divide it into nine equal parts. The first navamsa is governed by the lord of Aries, *viz.*, Mars; the 2nd by the lord of the 2nd, *viz.*, Venus; the 3rd by Mercury, lord of the 3rd; and so on, till the last or the ninth navamsa which is governed by Jupiter, lord of the ninth from Aries. Now divide Taurus into nine equal divisions. We have left the counting of the navamsa at the 9th from Aries, *viz.*, Sagittarius. Therefore, the first navamsa of Taurus is governed by the lord of the 10th from Aries—Capricorn, *viz.*, Saturn; the 2nd by the lord of the 11th, *viz.*, Saturn; the 3rd by the lord of the 12th, *viz.*, Jupiter; the 4th, 5th, 6th, 7th, 8th and 9th by Mars, Venus, Mercury, the Moon, the Sun and Mercury respectively. Then the first navamsa of Gemini is governed by the lord of the first Libra, *viz.*, Venus, the last of Gemini by the lord of the 9th from Libra, Mercury. Again the first of

Cancer is governed by the lord of the first, *viz.*, the Moon. Again the cycle begins from Aries. It invariably follows that for Aries, Leo and Sagittarius the navamsas must be counted from Aries to Sagittarius; for Taurus, Virgo and Capricorn from Capricorn; for Gemini, Libra and Aquarius from Libra; and for Cancer, Scorpio and Pisces from Cancer.

Example.—*Taking the Sun in 24 degrees, 25 minutes, 52 seconds Cancer (vide page 41); each navamsa is* equal to

$3\frac{1}{3}$ degrees $\dfrac{24° \; 25' \; 52'' \times 3}{10°} = 7$ navamsas.

The Sun has passed 7 navamsas and 1 degree, 5 minutes and 52 seconds in the 8th navamsa. The 8th navamsa in Cancer is Aquarius and the Sun must be placed there.

In the horoscope illustrated on page 42 the navamsa positions are as follows :—

	Saturn	Venus	
Rahu Sun	NAVAMSA		
Ascdt.			Moon Merc. Ketu
	Jupiter	Mars	

In Chapter VIII, the positions of planets of the horoscope illustrated are marked in constellations and quarters. Take the Sun. He is in the 2nd pada of Aslesha. Counting from Aswini upto Aslesha we get 8 constellations. This converted into padas or quarters gives 32. Adding the two quarters passed in Aslesha, it is 34. Divide this by 9, the number of padas for each sign $\frac{34}{9} = 3\frac{7}{9}$. The remainder is 7. Each pada is equal to a navamsa. The Sun has passed 3 signs from Aries and 7 padas or navamsas in the 4th sign Cancer. According to the above rule, for Cancer, Scorpio and Pisces, navamsas must be counted from Cancer itself. The 7th from Cancer is Capricorn. Its lord is Saturn. Therefore, the Sun is in the navamsa of Saturn. In the navamsa diagram, mark the Sun in Capricorn.

Dwadasamsa.—When a sign is divided into twelve equal parts each portion is called a Dwadasamsa getting 2½ degrees. The lords of the 12 Dwadasamsas are the lords of the 12 signs from the sign in question.

Example.—*Sun is in 24 degrees, 26 minutes Cancer.* He has passed 24 degrees 26 minutes

$$\frac{24° \ 26'}{2\frac{1}{2}} = 9 \text{ Dwadasamsas.}$$

9 Dwadasamsas having been passed and the Sun is in the 10th. The 10th from Cancer is Aries, therefore in the Dwadasamsa diagram, place the Sun in Aries.

Trimsamsa.—When a sign is divided into thirty equal parts, each becomes a Trimsamsa.

In odd signs—

Mars	Saturn	Jupiter	Mercury	Venus	
5	5	8	7	5	= 30

In even signs—

Venus	Mercury	Jupiter	Saturn	Mars	
5	7	8	5	5	= 30

In odd signs, the first five degrees are governed by Mars, the second five by saturn and so on. In even signs, the first five are governed by Venus and so on according to the above rules.

Sapthamsa.— I may also casually refer to Sapthamsa. When a sign is divided into 7 equal parts, each is called a Sapthamsa getting $\frac{30}{7}$ $4\frac{2}{7}$ degrees. In odd signs, they are governed by the lords of the seven Rasis from it and in even signs, by the lords of the seventh and following signs.

In fact, according to Parasara, there are sixteen divisions (*Shodasavargas*) to be considered. Each division is made use of for studying certain aspects of the horoscope—*e.g.*, Navamsa for wife, Dwadasamsa for parents, Sapthamsa for children, Dasamsa for profession, etc. It is not necessary for a beginner to bother himself with these technicalities at this stage.

CHAPTER XI

On Birth Verification and Rectification

The importance of the exact moment of birth need not be stressed. And one of the toughest jobs of an astrologer is to find the exact moment of birth before venturing to make any predictions. In most cases, the precise time of birth will not have been recorded for it is natural that considerable time will have elapsed from the moment of birth to that of recording it. While the importance of the correct instant is so much, we cannot lay any hard and fast rules which will enable us to find out this exact instant. It is accepted by eminent astrologers that the time of birth means the time of the first cry of the child which generally accompanies the first breath.

According to Varahamihira, there is an intimate connection existing between the planetary positions at conception and those at birth. Based on this, the Westerners have developed their so-called "Prenatal Epoch Theory". The Moon is the source of impregnation. Therefore it is possible to rectify the time of birth by adjusting the Moon and ascendant *at birth* and *at conception.* Varahamihira observes thus in Stanza 26 of Chapter IV of *Brihat Jataka* (Eng. Trans. by B. Suryanarain Rao) :

"Find the number of Dwadasamsas occupied by the Moon at the time of conception. Note the zodiacal sign whose name the Dwadasamsa bears. Count from the next sign as many signs as the number of Dwadasamsas by which the Moon may have advanced in any particular sign. When the Moon comes to such last sign, the birth of the child will occur."*

The author has been investigating into this theory and proposes to place before the learned readers, the fruits of his labours in due course. This branch of astrology does not come within the scope of a beginner or an amateur. And birth times can be rectified only by men of experience by a consideration of pronounced life events.

The following are some of the rules which are generally employed by astrologers:—

1. Multiply the time of birth in vighatis by 4 and divide the product by 9. The remainder must give the ruling constellation when counted from Aswini, Makha or Moola.

Example :

Time of Birth 7^h 42^m 44^s p.m. (I.S.T.)
Time of Sunrise : 6^h 25^m 32^s a.m. (I.S.T.)
Janma Nakshatra—Mrigasira.

∴ No. of hours passed from sunrise to birth 13^h 17^m 12^s. Converting this into ghatis and vighatis we get 33–53 ghatis or 2033 vighatis.

∴ $\dfrac{2033 \times 4}{9} = 903\frac{5}{9}$

Rejecting the quotient and counting 5 from Aswini, we get Mrigasira as Janma Nakshatra (birth constellation) which is correct.

If suppose the remainder in the above is say 8, which means Pushyami. In such a case adjust the remainder in such a way as to give the Janma Nakshatra and rectify the time of birth accordingly.

* Based on this, a series of articles has appeared in THE ASTROLOGICAL MAGAZINE, Volumes 28, 29, 38 and 39.

2. Multiply the number of ghatis from birth by 6 and add the longitude of the Sun (the number of degrees passed in the sign). Divide the sum by 30. The quotient *plus* 1 counted from the Sun's sign will give the rising sign.

Example :

The Sun's position 3ˢ 24°

Number of ghatis passed from birth— 33-53.

Multiply the number of ghatis from birth by 6 and adding the Sun's longitude (devoid of the sign) we get :

Gh. $33 - 53$

$= 33.88 \times 6 + 24°$

$= 203.28 + 24$

$= 227.28$

$\therefore \quad \dfrac{227.28}{30} = 7\dfrac{17.28}{30}$

Quotient *plus* one $(7+1)$ added to the Sun's sign, *viz.*, Cancer, we get Aquarius as the ascendant.

The above can also be stated thus :-

The number of hours passed from sunrise to time of birth should be multiplied by 15, the Sun's longitude (devoid of signs) added, the sum divided by 30, remainder rejected and the quotient *plus* one counted from the Sun's sign gives the ascendant.

Example :

The Sun's position   3ˢ 24°

No. of hours passed from sunrise to birth

$$13^h \ 17^m \ 12^s$$

$$= 13^{h}.287$$

$$= \dfrac{(13.287 \times 15) + 24}{30}$$

$$= \dfrac{199.305 + 24}{30}$$

$$= 7.4435.$$

The quotient, *viz.*, 7 + 1 counted from Cancer gives Aquarius as the ascendant which is correct.

3. The 5th or the 9th sign from the house occupied by the lord of the sign in which the Moon is placed becomes the Janma Lagna or the ascendant. The 7th from the sign occupied by the lord of the Moon's sign or the 5th or the 9th from the similar sign and in some cases the sign where the Moon is at radix itself becomes the ascendant.

CHAPTER XII

Dasas and Bhuktis

(Periods and Sub-periods)

The vexed question of timing events is solved to a great extent by the Dasa system in vogue among the Hindus. From a scientific point of view, we cannot say with any sort of definiteness, upon what basis each planet is allotted a certain number of years as its term of Dasa. But in actual practice, the Dasa system yields very satisfactory results.

There are any number of Dasas in vogue among the Hindus, but we propose to deal with Vimshottari. In the choice of any particular type of Dasa, the criterion must be that of experience and Vimshottari has answered this test.

The position of the Moon at birth is important in the calculation of the Dasas. Every constellation covers $13\frac{1}{3}$ degrees of the zodiacal space. Each nakshatra has a planet assigned as its lord and the Dasa at birth is determined rather indicated by the constellation occupied by the Moon at the moment of birth.

Table of Dasas

		Years
Krittika, Uttara and Uttarashadha	Sun	6
Rohini, Hasta and Sravana	Moon ...	10
Mrigasira, Chitta and Dhanishta	Mars ...	7
Aridra, Swati and Satabhisha	Rahu ...	18

Punarvasu, Visakha and Poorvabhadra	Jupiter ...	16
Pushyami, Anuradha and Uttarabhadra	Saturn ...	19
Aslesha, Jyeshta and Revati	Mercury ...	17
Makha, Moola and Aswini	Ketu ...	7
Pubba, Poorvashadha and Bharani	Venus ...	20

The total of the different periods, *viz.*, 120 years is considered as the natural life period of a human being. But there
are examples of persons having lived longer. The combinations
for such horoscopes have been mentioned in the future
chapters. The position of the Moon at birth determines the
ruling period. And the next Dasas succeed in the order given
above. If, at the birth time, the Moon is in the first degree
of the nakshatra (constellation), the full period assigned to
the planet will run. If the Moon occupies some intermediate
degrees, accordingly the period must be reduced.

We shall give below two methods of finding the ruling
Dasa and its balance at birth. The first method is intended
solely for readers who still follow the Panchangas taking into
consideration the balance (in ghatis) of the ruling constellation.

Take an example.—The Moon is in the first quarter of
Mrigasira in the example horoscope given in Chapter IX.
Therefore, Mars' Dasa rules the native at birth. If the Moon
were in the very beginning of Mrigasira, Mars would control
the native for the full period of 7 years assigned to him. But
8 ghatis and 1 vighati have already passed in Mrigasira out of
the total duration of 57/16 ghatis which means the corresponding period must be deducted out of the Dasa of Mars.

By ascertaining the duration of the nakshatra or constellation in question, we say in this case—if 57/16 ghatis give 7
years, what will 8 1/60 ghatis give :

$57\frac{16}{60} : 7 :: 8\frac{1}{60} :$ required number of years.

$$57\frac{6}{0} \quad \frac{7 \times 8\frac{1}{60}}{1} = 11 \text{ months, 23 days.}$$

		Years	Months	Days
Total of the Dasa of Mars	....	7	0	0
Expired period	...	0	11	23
Balance of the Dasa of Mars at birth	...	6	0	7

Similar results can also be obtained by knowing the exact degree in which the Moon is situated.

To give an example.—Take a birth when the Moon is in Taurus 25 degrees, 10 minutes. Reference to the table on page 14 shows that the sign Taurus is composed of the last three parts of Krittika, four of Rohini and the first two of Mrigasira. Each quarter is equal to $3\frac{1}{3}$ degrees in extent. Therefore, 3 of Krittika and 4 of Rohini = 23 degrees, 20 minutes; and 25 degrees, 10 minutes *minus* 23 degrees, 20 minutes = 1 degree, 50 minutes should be accounted for as Moon having passed in Mrigasira at the time of birth. We know that Mrigasira is ruled by Mars whose period is seven years. Each asterism being 13 degrees and 20 minutes we must find out what will be the period for 1 degree and 50 minutes.

13 degrees and 20 minutes : 1 degree and 150 minutes : 11 months 16 days.—This period has expired before birth and from the time of birth only the balance of (7 years—11 months and 16 days) = 6-0-14 days of Mars Dasa will go to the benefit of the native.

After finding out the Dasa, the sub-periods in each of the particular period must be determined :

Table of Bhuktis
(Sub-periods)

Sun's Dasa—6 Years				**Moon's Dasa—10 Years**			
Bhuktis :			*Y.M.D.*	*Bhuktis :*			*Y.M.D.*
Sun	...		0 3 18	Moon	...		0 10 0
Moon	...		0 6 0	Mars	...		0 7 0
Mars	...		0 4 6	Rahu	...		1 6 0
Rahu	...		0 10 24	Jupiter	...		1 4 0
Jupiter	...		0 9 18	Saturn	...		1 7 0
Saturn	...		0 11 12	Mercury	...		1 5 0
Mercury	...		0 10 6	Ketu	...		0 7 0
Ketu	...		0 4 6	Venus	...		1 8 0
Venus	...		1 0 0	Sun	...		0 6 0
Total Years	...		6 0 0	Total Years	...		10 0 0

Mars' Dasa—7 Years				**Rahu Dasa—18 Years**			
Bhuktis :			*Y.M.D.*	*Bhuktis :*			*Y.M.D.*
Mars	...		0 4 27	Rahu	...		2 8 12
Rahu	...		1 0 18	Jupiter	...		2 4 24
Jupiter	...		0 11 6	Saturn	...		2 10 6
Saturn	...		1 1 9	Mercury	...		2 6 18
Mercury	...		0 11 27	Ketu	...		1 0 18
Ketu	...		0 4 27	Venus	...		3 0 0
Venus	...		1 2 0	Sun	...		0 10 24
Sun	...		0 4 6	Moon	...		1 6 0
Moon	...		0 7 0	Mars	...		1 0 18
Total Years	...		7 0 0	Total Years	...		18 0 0

Jupiter's Dasa—16 Years

Bhuktis :		Y.	M.	D.
Jupiter	...	2	1	18
Saturn	...	2	6	12
Mercury	...	2	3	6
Ketu	...	0	11	6
Venus	...	2	8	0
Sun	...	0	9	18
Moon	...	1	4	0
Mars	...	0	11	6
Rahu	...	2	4	24
Total Years	...	16	0	0

Saturn's Dasa—19 Years

Bhuktis :		Y.	M.	D.
Saturn	...	3	0	3
Mercury	...	2	8	9
Ketu	...	1	1	9
Venus	...	3	2	0
Sun	...	0	11	12
Moon	...	1	7	0
Mars	...	1	1	9
Rahu	...	2	10	6
Jupiter	...	2	6	12
Total Years	...	19	0	0

Mercury's Dasa—17 Years

Bhuktis :		Y.	M.	D.
Mercury	...	2	4	27
Ketu	...	0	11	27
Venus	...	2	10	0
Sun	...	0	10	6
Moon	...	1	5	0
Mars	...	0	11	27
Rahu	...	2	6	18
Jupiter	...	2	3	6
Saturn	...	2	8	9
Total Years	...	17	0	0

Ketu's Dasa—7 Years

Bhuktis :		Y.	M.	D.
Ketu	...	0	4	27
Venus	...	1	2	0
Sun	...	0	4	6
Moon	...	0	7	0
Mars	...	0	4	27
Rahu	...	1	0	18
Jupiter	...	0	11	6
Saturn	...	1	1	9
Mercury	...	0	11	27
Total Years	...	7	0	0

Venus Dasa—20 Years

Bhuktis :		Y.	M.	D.
Venus	...	3	4	0
Sun	...	1	0	0
Moon	...	1	8	0
Mars	...	1	2	0
Rahu	...	3	0	0
Jupiter	...	2	8	0
Saturn	...	3	2	0
Mercury	...	2	10	0
Ketu	...	1	2	0
Total Years	...	20	0	0

I shall also give an easy method by means of which the sub-periods (Bhuktis) can be independently calculated.

Multiply the number of years of the Dasa period of the planet by the number of the years of the Dasa period of the planet whose sub-period is desired. Then cutting off the last digit of the product, multiply it by 3 and keep that figure as days, the other figures in the product will be months. Suppose we want to find the sub-period of the Sun in the major period of Venus. Multiply the Dasa term of Venus 20 years by that of the Sun 6 years, *i.e.*, $20 \times 6 = 120 = 12$ months. There is a zero for the last digit of the product and therefore the sub-period is 12 months.

Find the sub-period of Rahu in Jupiter's major period --

Rahu's period being 18 years and that of Jupiter 16 years, $18 \times 16 = 288 = 28$ months and 24 days.

The Bhuktis are further sub-divided into still more minute divisions called the antarams or inter-periods; these into antarantarams and so on, till swara or the period necessary for the inhaling and the exhaling of breath is reached. Nevertheless, for all practical purposes the antaram (inter-period) will be found to be quite sufficient. The antarams (inter-periods) have to be determined for each Bhukti (sub-period).

Example.—*Required the antaram (inter-period) of Jupiter in the sub-period of Saturn in the major period of Ketu:*

Ketu's period 7 years.

Saturn's sub-period in Ketu is 13 months and 9 days.

In 120 years—Jupiter's 16 years.

In 13 months and 9 days.........$\frac{16}{120} \times 13$ months 9 days $= 1$ month, 23 days and 4.8 hours.

We know how to find the unexpired (balance of) Dasa at birth. With the expired portion of Dasa at birth there are certain sub-periods (Bhuktis) ruling under the period which have also expired. After determining them, we can say under what sub-period one's birth has occurred. To do this, find

all the sub-periods (Bhuktis) in a period (Ďasa). Add together
the Buktis from the beginning of Janma Dasa (ruling period)
one by one till the total is a little in excess over the expired
portion of Dasa at birth. Diminish the aggregate by the
expired part of birth Dasa and the remainder gives the
balance of unexpired Bhukti (of the planet in question) at
birth.

Illustration.—Required the balance of Bhukti at birth in
the case of a person born with a balance of years 5-11-28 in
Mars' Dasa.

The ruling period = Mars 7 years
Expired period = 11 months, 16 days

			Y.	M.	D.
Mars' Bhukti	...	....	0	4	27
Rahu	...	...	1	0	18
	Total	...	1	5	15

Therefore, 1y. 5m. and 15d—11m. and 16d., *viz.*, 5 months
and 29 days ; is the balance of Rahu Bhukti in Kuja Dasa at
birth.

The balance of Dasa at birth can be easily ascertained
without any calculations by referring to Appendix 'C'. Take
for instance the same example. The Moon being in Taurus
25° 10 :

	Y.	M	D.
Table I : For 25° balance of Mars' Dasa is	6	1	15
Table II : For 10' (deduct)	0	1	1
Balance of Mars' Dasa at birth	6	0	14

The results likely to happen during such periods, sub-
periods and inter-periods as a result of planetary positions
have been sketched in a separate chapter.

CHAPTER XIII

On Aspects

The power of a planet to produce good or inflict evil, on an individual, is modified to a great extent by the natural sympathies or antipathies of the aspecting and the aspected planets.

According to Hindu astrology, all aspects are impersonal and the aspects are counted from sign to sign. An aspect is good or bad according to the relation between the aspecting and the aspected planet. All the planets aspect the *3rd and 10th houses from their location with a quarter sight ; the 5th and 9th houses with half a sight : the 4th and 8th houses with three-quarter of a sight and the 7th house with a full sight. Saturn, Jupiter and Mars have special aspects. Saturn powerfully aspects 3rd and 10th houses ; Jupiter, 5th and 9th houses ; and Mars, 4th and 8th houses.

It will be seen that Jaimini and Tajak writers consider an altogether different method of reading aspects. Beginners should never mix the one system with the other. According to Jaimini all moveable signs aspect all fixed signs, except the adjacent ones. Similarly, all fixed signs aspect all moveable signs except the adjacent ones. Common signs aspect each other. In this book we are devoting ourselves exclusively to Parasara.

---

* 3rd house 60° to 90° ; 10th house 270° to 300° ; 5th house 120° to 150° ; 9th house 240° to 270° ; 4th house 90° to 120°; 8th house 210° to 340° ; and 7th house 180°.

The aspect is signified by referring to the number of signs from the significator which the aspecting planet may hold. Thus if the Sun is in Cancer and Saturn is in Taurus, we say that the Sun is in the third from Saturn and consequently receives the aspect (3rd house aspect) of Saturn.

The opposition aspect becomes extremely good when it is produced by Jupiter and the Moon. It is held to be good when benefics aspect each other (7th house aspect). A planet, aspecting its own house, whether by the 7th house aspect or special aspect, will naturally increase the signification of that house.

We have said that Mars aspects the 4th and 8th houses in addition to the usual 7th house aspect. The 8th house aspect is a square aspect and sometimes this is evil and sometimes beneficial. For instance, if Mars, as lord of the 4th and the 9th houses (see Chapter on Key Planets) in which circumstance he gets special qualification as a *Yogakaraka* to produce good, aspects by the 4th house aspect a friendly planet, the significations of the aspected planet and the house are greatly enhanced. The same principle applies even in case of the 8th house aspect.

Jupiter aspects the 5th and 9th houses which, in Western astrology, are trine aspects. The results vary according to the natural and temporal dignities of the aspecting and the aspected bodies. Jupiter's aspect over any planet as a natural benefic is of weighty importance apart from the fact that he may be temporarily ill-disposed.

Saturn aspects the 3rd and the 10th houses. As a natural malefic, his aspects are bad. But the aspects produce good in case Saturn acquires beneficence by temporal situation.

Here some observations on aspects have to be made. The exact quantum of an aspect cast by an aspecting body on an aspected body can be mathematically measured by following the method given in *Graha and Bhava Balas*. But for the general purposes of predication, until the reader is quite familiar with astrological mathematics, it will be in order if full aspects (7th house or 180) for all planets and special aspects of Saturn, Jupiter and Mars are taken into account.

In the chart illustrated on page 42 the following aspects are present : Saturn aspects the Sun (3rd house), Jupiter (7th house) and the ascendant (10th house). The Moon aspects Jupiter (7th house). Mars, Mercury and Venus aspect the ascendant. Mars also aspects Jupiter (4th house), and Rahu (8th house). Jupiter aspects Rahu (5th house), Saturn and the Moon (7th house) and the Sun (9th house).

According to Western astrology, aspects are reckoned from mutual longitudinal distances of planets. When one planet is at a certain number of degrees away from another body, they are said to be in aspect.

The following are the major aspects : –

Conjunction :—Two heavenly bodies in the same longitude.
Opposition :

The distance between the two bodies is		180°
Trine :	do.	120°
Square :	do.	90°
Sextile :	do.	60°

Parallel*'declination : When two bodies have the same declination (Kranti).

The effect of an aspect is felt even if the planets are not exactly in the mutual distances mentioned above. Therefore a so-called orb of aspect—and this varies in each aspect—is allowed. The orbs of aspects are :

Conjunction σ	...	8°
Square ▢	...	8°
Sextile *	...	7°

---

* For an explanation of Kranti vide *Graha and Bhava Balas*.

Trine △   ...   8°
Parallel *P*   ...   1°

The influence of an aspect (*e.g.*, sextile) starts when the
planets are 53° away from each other, gradually increase
(applying) and it will be maximum at 60; it then decreases
(separating) when the effect is almost nil at 67.

Take for instance Saturn and the Sun in the example
chart. The angular distance between the two planets is 72°
49. The sextile aspect ceases at 67. Therefore there is no
aspect between them. Take again Saturn and Mercury. The
mutual distance is 94° 13'. It is a square aspect (separating)
between Saturn and Mercury. There are also other variations
of aspects brought about by two planets remaining in the
same sign and not in conjunction but another planet occupying a trine in respect of the two. Readers will do well to
refer to any text-book on Western astrology for more details.

The good or bad nature of aspects depends upon the angle
of aspects. For instance, opposition (180°) and square (90°)
are always held to be evil irrespective of the nature of the
planets forming the aspects. The trine and sextile are generally held to be good.

Such a classification of aspects is erroneous. If for
instance Jupiter is in Cancer and Mars in Aries, Western
astrologers hold this bad. Commonsense suggests this is an
excellent aspect and Hindu astrology says so. Why should a
square aspect be always bad unless planets involved are
malefics ? I am not convinced of the soundness of this view.
The reader need not worry with these controversial points.
But he may take it that aspects as considered by the Hindu
system have a sound and scientific basis.

CHAPTER XIV

Ayurdaya or Longevity

Many advantages can be derived by ascertaining before-hand, the presence or otherwise, of combinations, indicating early death of the child. We know very well that despite the utmost care on the part of the parents, diseases of a dangerous nature and violent accidents do happen to children and place their lives in jeopardy. Astrology can forewarn the parents of such times of danger to their children. Astrologers, not the rank and file, those really well-versed in the science, do hold that they can afford the physician a certain prognosis. An astrologer's work in this respect is priceless in value when compared to that of the doctor.*

After the horoscope is cast, the primary question is necessarily the probable duration of life. For, when a child has a poor longevity to its credit, it would be unnecessary to examine the other favourable combinations. However promising the horoscope may be, it will be futile to study the future, unless long life is assured.

The span of human life can be brought under four important divisions. They are :

1. *Balarishta* (infant mortality).—The combinations of planets rendering the child die before it is 8 years.

2. *Alpayu* (short life).—Death between 8 and 32 years.

---

* In my work *How to Judge a Horoscope* I have dealt with the question of longevity more extensively with suitable examples.

3.   *Madhvayu* (middle life).—Takes the life as far as 75 from the 33rd year.

4.   *Purnayu* (full life).—From 75 to 120.

Some authors hold that Madhyayu extends from 32 to 70 and Purnayu extends to 100 years. But this classification does not seem to have won general acceptance as the natural span of life is 120 years according to Vimshottari Dasa and consequently, Purnayu must extend to this limit.

I shall take the reader through all these various divisions in separate paragraphs. First, the nature of the horoscope, *viz.*, whether it is a Balarishta, Alpayu, Madhyayu or Purnayu must be ascertained ; then the marakas (death-inflicting planets) determined.

Balarishta (Infant mortality) :

The following combinations produce Balarishta :

1.   Malefics in the last navamsa of Rasis (signs).

2.   The Moon in a kendra (quadrant) with malefics.

3.   The Moon in the 7th, the 8th and the 12th houses from the ascendant with malefics and without being aspected by benefics.

4.   Birth 48 minutes before sunrise and 48 minutes after sunset when the Moon's hora is rising and when malefics are posited in the navamsas of signs ruled by malefics.

5.   Malefics in the 2nd, 6th, 8th and 12th houses.

6.   Weak Moon in the ascendant or in the 8th and malefics in quadrants or kendras.

7.   The Moon in the ascendant, Mars in the 8th, Sun in the 9th and Saturn in the 12th.

8.   Week Moon in the ascendant. and the 5th, the 8th and the 12th being aspected by evil planets.

9.   The Moon in the 8th, Mars in the 7th, Rahu in the 9th and Jupiter in the 3rd.

10. The lord of the Dasa (major period) at birth in conjunction with many evil planets.

11. Birth when the Sun is rising with malefics in kendras (quadrants) or trines, and Venus in the 6th or the 12 house.

12. Lord of the ascendant or the lord of the 5th and the 9th in enemy's houses and in the 8th and the 9th.

13. Ketu in the 4th with or aspected by malefics.

14. Rahu in the 7th aspected by the Sun and the Moon.

15. Ascendant lord's Dasa (major period) at birth or the Dasa of the lord of the 8th or the inter-period (antara) of the lord of the 8th in the Dasa of the lord of the ascendant or *vice versa.*

16. Lords of the ascendant, and the navamsa lagna and the lord of the sign occupied by the Moon in conjunction with the Sun.

17. The ascendant and the 8th from the Moon's sign being aspected by malefics.

18. The Moon in the 8th, Mars in the 7th and Saturn in the ascendant.

19. The Moon being aspected by Saturn in his 3rd Drishti (90° aspect).

20. The Moon in the 6th or 8th without having any aspects.

21. The Moon in the ascendant with malefics and without beneficial aspects bring the death of the child with the mother.

22. The Moon in the ascendant with Rahu and Mars in the 8th produce death of the child and the mother.

23. The Sun in the ascendant with Saturn, and Rahu and Mars in the 8th produce the death of the child and the mother after surgical treatment.

24. Evil planets in the 5th, the 8th and the 9th houses and the Sun or the Moon in the ascendant without the conjunction or aspect of benefics.

5

25. Saturn in the 12th, Sun in the 9th, Moon in the ascendant and Mars in the 8th without Jupiter aspecting any one of these. If Jupiter is in the 5th this misfortune is cancelled.

26. Saturn and Mars in the Lagna (ascendant) or in the 8th or in the 7th without being aspected by any good planets.

27. When the Moon attains *Mrithyubhagas* (fateful degrees) *viz.*, Aries 26, Taurus 12, Gemini 13, Cancer 25, Leo 24, Virgo 11, Libra 26, Scorpio 14, Sagittarius 13, Capricorn 25, Aquarius 5 and Pisces 12, and is at the same time posited in a *kendra* or 8th house, death of the child will occur soon.

28. When the lord of the ascendant or of the sign occupied by the Moon at birth is weak and badly posited, the child is said to die within as many years as are represented by the said sign when counted from Aries.

29. The child may live upto 4 years if the Moon occupies the 6th or 8th house from the ascendant and receives the aspects of both malefics and benefics.

30. The Moon in a similar situation, as mentioned above but being aspected by benefics alone, confers longevity which may last upto the age of 8.

In certain charts evil afflictions will be present indicating early death to the infant, but certain other configurations try to act as antidotes. Children born under such combinations suffer a lot in their early years from all kinds of diseases, but survive the attacks.

The following are a few of the many combinations indicating counteraction of Balarishta :—

1. Jupiter powerfully posited in the ascendant removes Balarishta.

2. Balarishta is averted if the lord of the Lagna is powerfully situated and has beneficial aspects.

3. Even if the Moon is in the 8th sign no danger of Bala-rishta is indicated provided she occupies the *Drekkanas* of Mercury, Jupiter or Venus.

4. Full Moon in a beneficial sign with good aspects causes destruction of Balarishta.

5. The strong position of Mercury, Venus or Jupiter is an antidote for Balarishta.

6. Even when the Moon is placed in the 6th house, Balarishta is overcome if she occupies *Drekkanas* of Jupiter, Venus or Mercury.

7. If the Full Moon is between two benefics, there will be no danger to the child.

8. If the Full Moon is in the 8th or the 6th, she will protect the child born during the night of Full Moon days.

9. If the Full Moon aspects the Lagna with Jupiter in quadrants, there is no fear.

10. Malefics in beneficial *Shadvargas* aspected by benefics posited in auspicious *navamsas* overcome Balarishta.

We shall give below a few examples as illustrating the above combinations :—

Illustrations :—

♓ Jupiter	♈	♉ Rahu	♊
♒ Ascdt.	RASI Chart No 1 (Sign Position)		♋
♑			♌ Moon
♐ Sun Mars Merc.	♍ Venus Ketu Saturn	♎	♏

Horoscope No. 1—Female child born on 11th January 1928 at 7 ghatis after sunrise. Longitude 74° E., Latitude 12° N. The sub-period of Venus in the major period of Venus rules for 16 months at birth. Mark the following combinations:—

1. Moon in a kendra (7th) powerfully aspected by Saturn without beneficial aspects.

2. The lord of the Dasa at birth, *viz.*, Venus, in conjunction with the planets Saturn and Ketu and aspected by Rahu. The child died within 16 months.

♓ Rahu	♈ Ascdt.	♉ Moon Saturn	♊
≈			♋ Sun
♑	RASI Chart No. 2		♌ Venus Merc. Mars
♐	♏ Jupiter	♎	♍ Ketu

Horoscope No. 2.—Male born on 6th August 1912 at 42-30 ghatis after sunrise (at Bangalore). Balance of Sun's period at birth: years 4–3–9. (1) Ascendant between two malefics, Rahu and Saturn, (2) Moon is afflicted by a malefic Saturn, and (3) lord of Dasa is also powerfully aspected by Saturn. Died in his 13th month on 14th August 1913.

Horoscope No. 3.—Male born on 12th February 1856 at 12 noon at Chicacole, Orissa State. (1) Mark the malefics on either side of ascendant, (2) Moon is in the grip of Rahu, and (3) Rahu is powerfully aspected by Mars and Ketu; suffered very much till 8 years. The redemption from Bala-

	♈ Rahu Moon	♉ Ascdt.	♊ Saturn
♓			
♒ Jupiter Sun Merc.	RASI Chart No. 3		♋
♑			♌
♐ Venus	♏	♎ Mars Ketu	♍

rishta is seen by the strong position of Jupiter in a quadrant. Died in his 82nd year.

We next come to what is called Alpayu or short life, which extends from 8 to 32 years of age. The following combinations indicate Alpayu :—

Alpayu—Life between 8 and 32 years

1. Saturn in the 8th house, Mars in the 5th and Ketu in the ascendant.

2. Malefics iu 6–8–12 cause Alpayu.

3. Saturn in the Lagna (ascendant) and the Sun, the Moon and Mars in the 7th.

4. Alpayu is caused if the lord of the 8th is in the ascendant with Ketu.

5. If malefics are in the ascendant and the Moon is in conjunction with evil planets, Alpayu occurs.

6. If the lord of the 8th is in the ascendant and *Lagnadhipati* (ascendant lord) is powerless, death takes place at a similar period.

7. If Scorpio is Lagna with the Sun and Jupiter there and if the lord of the 8th occupies any quadrants, the person dies at 22.

8. If Rahu and the Moon are in the 7th and 8th respectively with Jupiter in the ascendant the person lives upto 22.

9. Saturn in the ascendant owned by malefics with benefics in 3, 6, 9 and 12 makes the person die between the age of 26 and 27.

10. Death takes place in the 27th year if the lords of the 1st (ascendant) and the 8th join together in the 8th with malefics and without beneficial aspect.

11. Evil planets in the 1st, 2nd and 8th houses with benefics in houses other than *kendras* make the person die in the 28th year.

12. If the lord of the birth is weak and the lord of the 8th is in a kendra, death comes in the 30th year.

13. Death comes in the 32nd year if the lord of the ascendant and that of the 8th are in quadrants with a planet in the 8th and no planets in kendras.

14. The person dies before the 32nd year if strong malefics occupy kendras and with no beneficial aspects.

15. If Lagna is a common sign and if the Moon occupies a common sign, death takes place before the 32nd year.

Combinations for Madhyayu or Middle Age : 32 to 75 years

1. If lord of the 3rd or of the 6th is in a kendra, the person gets Madhyayu.

2. A person gets Madhyayu if out of the lords of the 8th, the 11th, ascendant and the 10th, at least two are powerful.

3. Mercury, Jupiter and Venus in the 2nd, 3rd and 11th houses from the ascendant confer Madhyayu.

4. Madhyayu is conferred if all the planets occupy the middle 4 houses from the Lagna.

5. Sun in the Lagna which must be his enemy's house between two evil planets, thoroughly powerless, with no beneficial aspects, kills the person in the 36th year.

6. A person lives upto 46 if the birth lord is in 6 or 8 with malefics unaspected by benefics.

7. Death occurs in the 51st year if Saturn is in birth, the Moon in 8 or 12 and other planets in the 11th.

8. The person dies in his 57th year if Scorpio is Lagna with Jupiter in it and Mars and Rahu in the 8th.

9. Lord of the 8th in the 7th and the Moon afflicted, takes the life in the 58th year.

10. 60 years of life is assured provided evil planets are in the quadrants with Jupiter in the 8th and the Lagna is Aries.

11. 60 years of life is assured if Saturn is in birth, Moon in the 4th, Mars in the 7th and Rahu in the 10th with Jupiter, Venus and Mercury in unfavourable houses.

12. If Mars and Mercury are in quadrants, Venus in the ascendant and exalted planets occupy 3 and 11, 60 years of life is guaranteed.

13. A person lives upto 70 years if good planets occupy quadrants, do not aspect the birth and the lord of the birth has the aspect of evil planets.

14. Mars in the 5th, the Sun in the 7th and Saturn debilitated make the person live upto 70.

15. Benefics in kendras (quadrants) and Trikonas (trines) with Saturn powerful, confer 75 years of life.

Combinations for Purnayu or Full Life : 75 to 120 Years

1. If Lagna is aspected by its own lord, the 8th house by its lord and Jupiter is in a kendra, the person gets *Purnayu*.

2. If the first 6 houses are occupied by all the benefics and the last six by all the malefics, 80 years of life will be granted.

3. A person lives for 100 years if Jupiter is in a quadrant from the lord of the birth with no malefics in the quadrants.

4. Long life will be given if Cancer is birth with Jupiter there and when one or more planets are exalted.

5. If the birth lord and the Sun are in the 10th, Saturn in the birth and Jupiter in the 4th house, a person lives long.

6. Jupiter in the Lagna, Venus in the 4th and Saturn and the Moon in the 10th make a person live for a long time.

After ascertaining to which class a particular horoscope belongs, the marakas or the death-inflicting planets must be determined and the death predicted under the Dasas of such planets.

CHAPTER XV

Marakas or Death inflicting Planets

Marakas are planets possessed of the power of inflicting death. Death generally occurs during the periods and sub-periods of such planets. Suppose a horoscope indicates middle life or *Madhyayu* whereas the Dasa of a most powerful maraka comes into operation after 80 years. In such a circumstance the period of a planet, no matter even if it is less malicious in causing death which comes within the maximum number of years allotted for Madhyayu, must be considered as bringing about death, in preference to the most malicious one. Ascertain beforehand, whether a horoscope indicates short, middle or long life; determine the maraka planets and the times when their influences will come to fruition.

The 8th house from **Lagna** (ascendant) and the 8th from that, *i.e.*, the 3rd from **Lagna** are termed houses of life. The 7th house and the 2nd house are called houses of death. The 2nd house is always stronger in inflicting death than the 7th. Planets who occupy the 2nd are stronger than the planets who own it, in tending to cause death and the planets who are in association with the lord of the 2nd are the most powerful in causing death.

Thus the lords of the 2nd and the 7th, their occupants and the planets who are in conjunction with them are the *maraka* planets. If marakas cannot be found out of these three, then the planet in conjunction with the lord of the 12th, even if it is a benefic, causes death in his *Dasa* (period), in the *Bhukti* (sub-period) of a *papa* (malefic) if he is the lord of the 3rd or 8th house. If the Dasa of *Vyayadhipathi* (lord of the 12th) does not come, then one most powerful among the lords of the 3rd, 6th and 8th becomes maraka. If the Sun and Sukra (Venus) or lords of the 2nd and 7th get *Kendradhipatya* (lordship of quadrant)—they are sure to become marakas.

Summarising the above, death will be caused by :

1. Planets who occupy the 2nd and 7th houses.

2. Planets who are lords of the 2nd and 7th houses.

3. Planets who are not owners of the 2nd and the 7th houses, and who are not occupying those houses but who join with the lords of those houses, *i.e.*, the 2nd and the 7th.

4. If the periods of the planets occupying or owning death houses do not come in time, then death may occur in the Dasa of planets who are not *Yogakarakas* but who become evil and conjoin lords of the houses of death.

5. Lords of the 3rd and the 8th are also probable causers of death if death does not occur in the Dasas, etc., mentioned in item 4.

6. If the Dasa of a death-inflicting planet does not at all come into operation, then the most malicious planets in the horoscope will cause death.

Saturn, inclined to produce evil by his conjunction with the lords of death houses, will cause death in preference to any of those planets.

There are many rules to ascertain the probable time of death knowing beforehand *Maraka Dasas*. Any detailed information in regard to this would increase the bulk of the book beyond reasonable proportion.

Add together the longitudes of Saturn, Jupiter, the Sun and the Moon. This gives us a point in the zodiac after expunging multiples of 12. In the case of short, middle and long life, death occurs when Saturn transits over this point, in his first, second and third cycles respectively.

CHAPTER XVI

Judgment of a Horoscope

The notable triumphs in Hindu astrology so far as the predictive portion is concerned are entirely due to the great scrutiny the planetary influences are subjected to in the analysis of a horoscope and the relative values of the good and evil sources of strength of different planets and bhavas.

The following points are noteworthy in the consideration of a horoscope : —

The lords of trines are always auspicious and produce good. When benefics own kendras (quadrants), they become evil. When malefics become lords of quadrants, they invariably become good. The lords of the 2nd and the 12th houses give good results if they are in conjunction with favourable planets. The lord of the 8th, if he happens to be the lord of the 1st, or is in conjunction with a benefic, becomes good. Mars in addition to the 10th house, if he also becomes the lord of the 5th, produces good, Rahu and Ketu produce good results when they are posited in the signs of benefic planets.

Good and evil planets become more and more powerful as they are lords of the 1st, 4th, 7th or 10th houses; 5th and 9th houses ; or 3rd, 6th and 11th houses respectively.

Lords of the 3rd, 6th, 8th and 11th do evil and cause miseries in life. The lords of the 2nd and the 12th remain neutral. Jupiter and Venus owning quadrants become very inauspicious. In addition to this, when they occupy the 2nd and the 7th houses they become very powerful and conse-quently inflict death upon such natives. Mercury as the lord of a quadrant is less malicious than Jupiter and Venus and the Moon, less than Mercury. Mars does not become good when he owns the 10th house. Rahu and Ketu in evil signs produce evil.

The lords of quadrants and trines in conjunction, without any other bad aspects, become extremely powerful in producing good results.*

If the lords of the 9th and 10th houses exchange places, they produce much good.

The greatest assets of a man in this life, apart from the shadowy wealth and fame, are self-respect, courage and prowess. In a horoscope these can be determined by consider-ing Mars and the characteristics attributed to him which are discussed in the future chapters. But here I shall confine myself to the discussion of the most salient points involved in the judgment of a horoscope. The lord of the 3rd also must be considered ; both of them must occupy a friendly house and must be found not in a *Bhavasandhi* (junction of two houses) but in a *Bhavamadhya* (mid-point of a house). Mars must occupy the 10th for good courage and the lord of the 3rd and the 11th occupy favourable and friendly navamsas. The position of Jupiter also considerably improves the situa-tion by making the person not depend upon another but to earn the name of a self-made man. Jupiter adds to the dignity of the person in a sure but silent way.

Marriage is a landmark in the history of the human race. With regard to the number of wives, the character and tem-perament of one's wife, her disposition towards the husband and her own health and happiness, much information is incorporated in Chapter XIX under the caption 7th house or

_____

* See *How to Judge a Horoscope.*

Saptamabhava, and the student must pay special attention to the chapter for fuller details. Venus gets the Commander-in-Chief post over matrimonial alliances and all things concerned about them and the 7th house controls marriage in general. In hundreds of horoscopes, it has been observed that Venus, when afflicted, has given rise to more than one legal wife. It could be vouched for with sufficient confidence that Venus in favourable positions is certain to assure marital felicity and success with a single wife. The marriage aspect would be most important to the Hindus among whom the dangerous contagion of divorce has not spread as in the Western nations. Considerable attention has been bestowed upon this subject by the ancient writers. When Venus occupies the house of Jupiter or that of the lord of the 1st or the 9th, either in the Rasi or Navamsa, the native will have a chaste, loving and happy wife. The 7th house should not be occupied by any planet save a benefic. In the case of a woman, the Moon must occupy the navamsa of Jupiter to make her loyal and chaste and should not fall in the navamsa of Saturn or Mars. Mars in the 8th house causes widowhood provided there are no other counteracting factors.

Lords of the 3rd, the 6th and the 11th play an important part in causing debts, diseases and ill-health. The best feature in a horoscope would be that those lords of the 3rd, the 6th and the 11th remain isolated and unassociated with any other planet. The lord of the 3rd causes debts and diseases in a sudden spurt; ill-timed courage and head-long spirit work much in the native. Egotism and misanthrophy are marked by the lord of the 6th, in exercising discretion, who has special control over debts and diseases. Anarchic qualities would result if the lord of the 11th is very powerful. Delicate circumstances involving life and honour for the sake of debts and diseases can be overcome but for Mars and Saturn who, if they occupy unfriendly signs, give rise to excess of evil.

The Sun governs father, and the 9th house indicates father. Jupiter has control over children as he is called *Putrakaraka* and the 5th house is *Putrasthana* or the house of children. The fourth represents mother and the Moon governs her. When the lords of the 4th, the 5th and the 9th and the Moon, Jupiter and the Sun are well situated, and occupy favourable and friendly navamsas prosperity for father, mother and children is invariably indicated. An examination of a number of horoscopes has revealed that the Moon, Jupiter or the Sun in the 4th, the 5th or the 9th with Saturn has caused death to mother, children or father respectively, early in life. Moon with Saturn without any favourable aspect has caused death to the mother within one year of the birth of the child. Mercury and Mars in the 5th house make the children short-lived. Jupiter in the ascendant is the best gift in a horoscope and the native gets dutiful children and long-lived parents.

Long life for an individual may be predicted if the lords of the 1st and the 8th and Saturn are in good positions and have the aspect of Jupiter.

This important and final event is elaborately dealt with in a separate chapter and the readers must study the principles contained in it very carefully.

CHAPTER XVII

Key-planets for Each Sign

As soon as the Dasas and Bhuktis are determined, the next step would be to find out the good and evil planets for each ascendant so that in applying the principles to decipher the future history of man, the student may be able to carefully analyse the intensilty of good or evil combinations and proceed further with his predictions when applying the results of Dasas and other combinations.

It the ascendant is :

Aries.—Saturn, Mercury and Venus are ill–disposed. Jupiter and the Sun are auspicious. The mere combination of Jupiter and Saturn produces no beneficial results. Jupiter is the Yogakaraka or the planet producing success. If Venus becomes a maraka, he will not kill the native but planets like Saturn will bring about death to the person.

Taurus.—Saturn is the most auspicious and powerful planet. jupiter, Venus and the Moon are evil planets. Saturn alone produces Rajayoga. The native will be killed in the periods and sub-periods of Jupiter, Venus and the Moon if they get death-inflicting powers.

Gemini.— Mars, Jupiter and the Sun are evil. Venus alone is most beneficial and in conjunction with Saturn in good signs produces and excellent career of much fame. Combination of Saturn an Jupiter produces similar results as in Aries. Venus and Mercury, when well associated, cause Rajayoga.

The Moon will not kill the person even though possessed of death-inflicting powers.

Cancer.—Venus and Mercury are evil. Jupiter and Mars give beneficial results. Mars is the *Rajayogakaraka* (conferor) of name and fame). The combination of Mars and Jupiter also causes Rajayoga (combination for political success). The Sun does not kill the person although possessed of maraka powers. Venus and other inauspicious planets kill the native. Mars in combination with the Moon or Jupiter in favourable houses especially the 1st, the 5th, the 9th and the 10th produces much reputation.

Leo.—Mars is the most auspicious and favourable planet. The combination of Venus and Jupiter does not cause Rajayoga but the conjunction of Jupiter and Mars in favourable houses produce Rajayoga. Saturn, Venus and Mercury are evil. Saturn does not kill the native when he has the maraka power but Mercury and other evil planets inflict death when they get maraka powers.

Virgo.—Venus alone is the most powerful. Mercury and Venus when combined together cause Rajayoga. Mars and the Moon are evil. The Sun does not kill the native even if he becomes a maraka but Venus, the Moon and Jupiter will inflict death when they are possessed of death-inflicting power.

Libra.—Saturn alone causes Rajayoga. Jupiter, the Sun and Mars are inauspicious. Mercury and Saturn produce good. The conjunction of the Moon and Mercury produces Rajayoga. Mars himself will not kill the person. Jupiter, Venus and Mars when possessed of maraka powers certainly kill the native.

Scorpio.—Jupiter is beneficial. The Sun and the Moon produce Rajayoga. Mercury and Venus are evil. Jupiter, even if he becomes a maraka, does not inflict death. Mercury and other evil planets, when they get death-inflicting powers, do not certainly spare the native.

Sagittarius.—Mars is the best planet and, in conjunction with Jupiter, produces much good. The Sun and Mars also produce good. Venus is evil. When the Sun and Mars combine together they produce Rajayoga. Saturn does not bring about death even when he is a maraka. But Venus causes death when he gets jurisdiction as a maraka planet.

Capricorn.—Venus is the most powerful planet and in conjunction with Mercury produces Rajayoga. Mars, Jupiter and the Moon are evil.

Aquarius.—Venus alone is auspicious. The combination of Venus and Mars causes Rajayoga. Jupiter and the Moon are evil.

Pisces.—The Moon and Mars are auspicious. Mars is most powerful. Mars with the Moon or Jupiter causes Rajayoga. Saturn, Venus, the Sun and Mercury are evil. Mars himself does not kill the person even if he is a maraka.

CHAPTER XVIII

Results of Ascending Signs

As soon as the map is cast and the ruling planet, constellation and the balance of the Dasa period are decided, the next step would be to find out the probable results of the ascendant or Lagna falling in any of the 12 signs. This gives us a clue to the determination of one's physical features, stature, marital disposition and other peculiarities.

The following details are only general in nature and should not be applied hastily. The strength of the rising sign, its ruler, the planets aspecting the ascendant, the peculiarities attending on the ascendant and its lord both in Rasi and Navamsa should be carefully considered before any predictions are ventured.

Aries.—Persons born in Aries will have a certain amount of independent thinking and reasoning faculty. They will be capable. They may not be strict followers of convention. They are lovers of scientific thought and philosophy; have their own ideas of right and wrong and are strongly bent upon educational pursuits. As the Ram rules them, they are rather stubborn but often frank, impulsive and courageous. They are more gossipers than practical men. They sometimes require a certain amount of cajolery and sycophancy to raise them to action. They become pioneers. As Mars is the lord of Aries, they will be martial in spirit. Their constitution will be hot, and they are occasionally subject to hot complaints, piles and the like, and must avoid enterprises obviously

involving any serious risks. They love beauty, art and elegance.
The diseases they suffer from will be mostly those of the head
and unpleasant sight-seeing may often lead to mental affliction
and derangement of brain. Their build will be slender and
females generally possess fairly perfect contours. One
peculiarity is craning the neck.

Taurus.—The stature of the persons born in this sign will
be medium or short and often inclined towards corpulence,
lips thick, complexion swarthy, square face, well-shaped lips
and dark hair are prominent features. Women are generally
handsome. They generally resemble the bull in their behaviour
towards new people if they are not listened to properly. They
have their own principles and ways. Often they have a piercing intellect. They shine well as authors, book dealers and
journalists. They are not bound by sentimentality but appreciate truth. They are remarkable for their ability to commit
to memory. Their physical and mental endurance are noteworthy. They have much business knack and good intuition.
They often think they are born to exercise authority over
others and in a sense they are right. They are sensitive to
physical influences. They are often liable to extremes,
zealous and easily accessible to adulteration. They generally
suffer from nervous complaints after their fiftieth year but their
memory and powers of imagination will never deceive them.
They are slow to anger, but when provoked, furious like the
bull. They are passionate and may become preys to sexual
diseases in their old age unless they moderate their pleasures
and learn to exercise self-control.

Gemini.—Persons born when Gemini is rising have a
wavering mind, often tall and straight in nature and active in
motion, forehead broad, eyes clear and nose, a bit snub. They
are active and become experts in mathematical sciences; and
mechanical sciences provided Saturn has some strong influence
over them. They will be "a jack of all trades but master of

none". They are vivacious, but liable to be inconstant. They will have sudden nervous breakdowns and must exercise a certain amount of caution in moving with the opposite sex ; a habit of self-control must be cultivated. Their mind will be often conscious of their own faults. They are liable to fraud and deception. If evil planets are found in Gemini, trickery and deceit will characterise their nature. Many of these traits can be corrected by training.

Cancer.—Persons born under Cancer have a middle-sized body, face full, nose snubbed to some extent and complexion white. They often have a double chin. They are very intelligent, bright and frugal and equally industrious. Their frugality often takes the form of miserliness. They are sympathetic but moral cowardice will be present. They will be much attached to their children and family. Their extreme sensitiveness renders them nervous and queer. Their minds will be bent upon schemes of trade and manufacture. The often meet with disappointments in marriage and love affairs. They are very talkative, self-reliant, honest and unbending. They have reputation for love of justice and fairplay. Saturn's situation in the ascendant is not desirable.

Leo.—Persons born under Leo will be majestic in appearance, broad shoulders, bilious constitution and bold and respectful in temperament. They possess the knack to adapt themselves to any condition of life. They are rather ambitious and sometimes avaricious too. They are independent thinkers. They stick up to orthodoxical principles in religion but are perfectly tolerant towards others' precepts and practices. They are lovers of fine arts and literature and possess a certain amount of philosophical knowledge. They are voracious readers. If the ascendant or the tenth house is afflicted, they may not succeed in life as much as they expect. They put forth much struggle. Their ambitions remain unfulfilled to some extent unless the horoscope has certain definite Raja-yogas. They are capable of non-attachment and contentment. As Saturn happens to be lord of the 7th, they must resist the temptation of yielding much to their wives or husbands if domestic happiness is to prevail.

Virgo.—People born when Kanya or Virgo is rising will exhibit their intelligence and memory when quite young. They will be middle-sized persons and exhibit taste in art and literature. Their chest will be prominent and when afflicted, very weak also. They are discriminating and emotional and are carried away by impulses. As authors, they make real progress especially in *Bhouthika Sastras* and *Rasayana Sastras* (Physical and Chemical Sciences) and can judge things at a glance. They love music and fine arts and acquire much power and influence over other people. They are liable to suffer from nervous breakdowns and paralysis when the sign is afflicted. Other combinations warranting they can become great philosophers or writers. They are generally lucky in respect of their wives or husbands.

Libra.—The complexion of persons born in this sign will be fair, their stature middle-sized, face broad, eyes fine, chest broad and light, appearance handsome, constitution rather phlegmatic, sensual disposition and keen observation. They have keen foresight and reason out things from the stand-point of their own views. Firm in conviction and unmoved by mean motives they are somewhat susceptible to the feelings of others' minds. They are more idealists than realists or practical men and often contemplate upon schemes like building castles in the air. They are not sensitive to what others say of them. But as political leaders and religious reformers they exert tremendous influence over the masses and some-times their zeal and enthusiasm go to such a high pitch that they force their views upon others of opposite thought not realising the baneful after-effects of such procedure. They love excitement and have the power of intuition upon which they often rely for their own guidance. They are not easily amenable to reason. They are great lovers of music. They have a special liking for truth and honesty and do not hesitate to sacrifice even their lives at the altars of freedom and fairplay. Their domestic life may be crossed by frequent tension.

Scorpio.—Those born under this sign have youthful appearance, a generous disposition and fierce eyes. They are fickleminded and love much excitement. They are inclined to sensual things in reality while they will not hesitate to philosophise upon the merits of controlling sensual pleasures. Even females born in this sign will have more of masculine tendencies. They are good correspondents and invite friendship from among people throughout the world. They can become expert musicians if they care to practise that art. They are proficient in fine arts, dancing and the like and no doubt they have a philosophic disposition. They set at naught conventional habits and customs. They vehemently uphold their own views but nevertheless will not clash with those holding opposite ones. Their constitution will be hot and they are liable to suffer from piles after their 30th year. They are silent and dignified and never speak before weighing each and every word. They are good conversationalists as well as writers and often rely too much on their own intelligence. Married life may not be quite happy not only due to temperamental differences but also due to illness affecting the generative system of the partner, unless there are other compensating combinations.

Sagittarius.—Jupiter rules this sign and persons born under this sign will generally be inclined towards corpulence. They possess almond eyes and their hair is brown. They are of a phlegmatic temperament. They are somewhat conventional and sometimes businesslike also. They are prompt

and uphold conservative views. They will be attracted towards the study of occult philosophy and sciences. In these
departments of knowledge they can acquire mastery. They
are too callous and enthusiastic. They hate all external show.
They are God-fearing, honest, humble and free from hypo-
crisy. They never think of schemes which are calculated to
disturb the progress of others. They generally exercise control
over their food and drinks but in regard to their relationship
with the opposite sex restraint is called for. They are
brilliant, their manners affable, winning and hearts, pure.
They are prone to be misunderstood unintentionally by others
on account of their hastiness in conversation. In their later
years they must be careful about their lungs as they are liable
to suffer from rheumatic pains and the like. Combinations
for political power warranting, persons born in this sign will
exercise power with firmness and justice and without yielding
to corruptive influences.

Capricorn.—Persons born in this sign will be tall, reddish-
brown in colour with prominent hair on the eye-brows and
the chest. Women will be handsome and youngish in appearance. They have large teeth sometimes protruding outside
the lips and presenting an uncouth appearance if the 2nd
house is afflicted. Their lips are flushy and ladies have an
inviting appearance. They have the knack of adopting themselves to circumstances and environments. They have great
aspirations in life and cannot economise funds even if they
were to be under the influence of adversity. They are modest,
liberal and gentlemanly in business transactions. They are
noted for their perseverance and strong-mindedness. In fact
they are stoical to the miseries of life. They are possessed of
sympathy, generosity and philanthropy and take great interest
in literature, science and education. Sometimes they are
vindictive. When Saturn is badly posited, they are possessed

of bigotry. God-fearing and humble they make good husbands or wives. Depending upon the disposition of the 9th house they can become philosophically minded or develop social consciousness.

Aquarius.—This "Water Bearer" sign in which the birth of an individual is condemned as the birth lord becomes the lord of the house of loss, has to its credit some of the greatest philosophers and seers. Those born under this sign will be tall, lean, fairly handsome, manners winning, appearance attractive, disposition elegant. Their lips are flushy, cheeks broad with prominent temples and buttocks. They are highly intelligent and make friends of others very soon. They are peevish and when provoked, rise like a bulldog but their anger is very soon subsided. They are pure in heart and always inclined to help others. They shine very well as writers and good spokesmen. They are at times timid. They feel shy to exhibit their talents but their conversation will be most inte-resting and highly instructive. They will specialise in subjects like astrology, psychology and healing arts, etc. Their literary greatness will come before the world when they are quite young and they themselves will not be able to estimate their capacities well, while others find in them something remark-able and extraordinary. They are intuitive and good judges of character. They have no organising capacity and are capable of acquiring very fine education. They will be much devoted to their husbands or wives and never betray the interests of even their enemies, when trust is placed in them. They are liable to suffer from colic troubles and must take special precautions to safeguard themselves against diseases incidental to exposure to cold weather. On the whole Aquarius people have something subtle in them which endears them to all they come in contact with.

Pisces.—Persons born in this sign will be fair, stout and moderately tall. They are reserved in their manners and are liable to draw premature conclusions on any matter. They are God-fearing. They are generally superstitious and religious, rigid in the observance of orthodoxical principles and can forego anything but their orthodoxy ; or they can be exactly the opposite. They are somewhat stubborn, rather timid, and ambitious to exercise authority over others. They are true friends and are proud of their educational and other attainments. If the lord of the 7th is badly afflicted, they will have double marriage. They are restless and fond of history, antiquarian talks and mythological masterpieces. They are frugal in spending money and though generally dependent upon others throughout their life still bear a mark of independence. They are just in their dealings and fear to transgress the laws of truth. With all this, they lack self-confidence.

CHAPTER XIX

Judgment of Bhavas (Houses)

The twelve bhavas or houses represent the entire history of the individual. By a careful scrutiny of the planetary combinations and aspects in the twelve houses, the whole life of a person can be predicted with sufficient accuracy. The combinations given below are not chosen at random but are chosen from a study of the horoscopes of persons of various ranks and eminences. Many have been gathered from the best and the most standard works on Hindu astrology. In applying these rules to practical horoscopes, the student must definitely bear in mind that they are merely for his guidance. In addition to this, he must also exercise discretion and common sense coupled, of course, with a certain amount of intuition. For instance, the astrological principles say that if the 4th house is occupied by benefics and its lord well situated, the native gets high education. This is quite sufficient for an intelligent student to anticipate certain other things not mentioned here. In fact they strike themselves to the student. In a horoscope, a benefic may be found in the 4th—which may be his house of exaltation, debilitation, or enmity or a friend's sign. Even though a benefic may be in the 4th, the results it gives apparently vary according to its disposition towards the lord of that sign. If Jupiter is in exaltation in the 4th house, religious learning may be predicted. If he is in debilitation, in the 4th house, the kind of education must necessarily differ. Still in both cases, it is Jupiter that occupies the 4th house. Similarly, with regard to other combinations one must consider all these problems carefully and then venture a prediction. The relations and interrelations of planetary placements must be carefully scrutinised and then predictions ventured. Deterministic interpretation of the combinations should not be given.

First Bhava (House).—The first house represents the beginning of life, childhood, health, environment, personality, the phycial body and character aud the general strength of the horoscope.

If the lord of the birth or 1st house is exalted, well associated, strongly placed, occupies quadrants, has the aspects of good planets, the person will have health, good appearance, and a generally happy future.

If the lord of the birth is in conjunction with an evil planet and occupies the 8th house, the health will suffer.

If the birth lord is in conjunction with the lord of the 6th, the 8th and the 12th, the body will suffer from constant complaints. If the lord of birth is in the 6th, the 8th or the 12th, the native has a sickly constitution.

If the birth lord is conjoined with an evil planet, and Rahu or Saturn occupies the Lagna, the person fears from deception from thieves and swindlers.

Urinary and bladder troubles and swelling of testicles are likely if Rahu, Mars and Saturn are in Lagna.

The body of the native will be emaciated if Lagna is occupied by planets like Mars, the Sun and Saturn.

Birth in watery signs make the person corpulent.

The native suffers from asthma and consumption if the Sun (Ravi) is in Lagna and Mars aspects him.

Many evil planets in the birth indicate either misery or a checkered career.

Venus in the first half of the Lagna makes the person happy in the beginning. Venus in the second half with evil planets in the 4th and the 5th houses makes the person miserable in the end.

Second Bhava (House).—Second house represents family, face, speech, right eye, food, wealth, literary gift; manner and source of death, self-acquisition and optimism.

If the lord of the 2nd is exalted and is aspected by Jupiter, the native will be a man of considerable wealth.

If the lord of the 2nd is exalted and quadrants are aspected by benefics, the eye-sight will be good and the facial expression charming.

One becomes an orator and wealthy if Jupiter is with the lord of the second or the latter is aspected by Mercury, or Venus occupies favourable positions.

Poverty will attack the native if the lord of the second is weak, debilitated or aspected by malefics.

If the lord of the 2nd is in quadrants aspected by malefics, the person will look ugly and grotesque.

If the lord of the 2nd is a watery planet and combines with or is aspected by the lord of the *navamsa* of the 2nd house-lord, and if the Ascendant falls in a watery sign, the person will be an international trader and the source of his income will be mostly from beyond the confines of his motherland.

Defective speech can be predicted if malefics are with the lord of the second or aspects it.

Mercury in a quadrant and the lord of the 2nd powerfully situated make one proficient in occult sciences, especially astrology.

Confiscation of property and penal action by Government is likely if the Ascendant is weak and its lord joins malefics and the lord of the 2nd is in conjunction with the Sun in the 12th house.

If the lord of the 12th joins the 2nd and the lord of the 11th joins the 12th with the lord of the 2nd in the 6th, the 8th or the 12th, one has to pay fines to the Government.

Loss of wealth by thieves and rulers can be foretold if the lord of the 2nd is aspected by or combined with Mars in debilitation or in cruel navamsa.

The occupation of the 2nd by malefics indicates that the person becomes showy and the period must be predicted under the Dasa of such planets.

If the 7th house occupied by the lord of the 10th has the beneficial aspects of Jupiter and Venus, the native earns a substantial amount during the periods of such planets.

If the lord of the ascendant is in the 2nd and lord of the 2nd is in the 11th with the lord of the 11th in the 1st, the native may come across hidden treasures.

If the lord of the 2nd is debilitated and is in conjunction with evil planets, the person contracts hopeless debts.

Third Bhava (House).—The third house represents brothers and sisters and intelligence, shorts journeys, neighbours, immediate relations and letters and writings. It also denotes courage, right ear and breast.

If a malefic planet is in the 3rd or the 3rd is between two evil planets, one will not have brothers; or all the brothers may pass away.

If the lord of the 3rd or Mars occupies the 8th, the 6th or the 12th and has no beneficial aspects, prosperity to brothers is rarely to be predicted.

If the lord of the 3rd occupies a beneficial navamsa and Mars is well posited, the native will be courageous and will have thriving brothers.

If the lord of the 3rd is in the 12th and is aspected by evil planets, the person will be funky and henpecked.

If the lord of the 3rd is in conjunction with the Sun, the native will be bold in mind, and stubborn and angry.

The number of brothers may be approximately known by
the navamsa the 3rd house falls in or by the number of the
navamsa the lord of the 3rd or the karaka for the brothers
falls in.

Fourth Bhava (House).— Peace of mind and happiness,
mother, home life, relatives, house, self-prosperity, enjoyments, conveyances, landed and ancestral property, general
happiness, education, vehicles and the general build of the
neck and shoulders.

If the lord of the 4th is with the lord of the 1st occupying
a good place or if the 4th lord occupies trines or quadrants,
the person possesses many houses.

If the lord of the 4th is with powerful Jupiter and Mercury
and occupies quadrants, the person will have an aristocratic
disposition and commands respect, conveyance and name.

If the lord of the 9th is in quadrants and the lord of the
4th well situated, the person will have a good taste for artistic
furniture.

If Mercury is in the 3rd, and the lord of the 4th is well
placed, the person possesses an attractive house or houses.

If the lord of the 4th occupies the 12th, loss of ancestral
property is to be feared.

If the 4th is occupied by Saturn with the Moon in exaltation and Jupiter aspecting it, the person will be an author in
his early age and have much education but the mother dies
early.

If the lords of the Ascendant and the 4th are in the 11th
and the lord of the 2nd is in the 12th with the Sun, the person
possesses limited education but good landed property. These
results have to be applied taking into consideration of other
conditions.

Jupiter in exaltation in the 4th house and the lord of the
4th in his own sign makes the person get high legal education.

If Lagna is Sagittarius and its lord and Saturn are in the same house, the person will acquire high education.

If Venus or the Moon occupies the 4th without any aspects from any malefics, the person will be a voracious eater.

If lord of the 4th is debilitated and joins evil planets, the native becomes sinful and licentious.

If the Moon and Venus are in quadrants occupying evil navamsas and aspected by or joined with evil planets, one becomes guilty of improper relations with close relatives of the opposite sex.

If the lord of the 4th is badly situated and is aspected by malefics, the person's private life will be questionable.

If the Moon occupies birth with Rahu or Ketu, the mother's character cannot be above board.

Saturn in conjunction with the lord of the 4th or with the Moon will kill the mother early.

The person becomes dishonest and indulges in fraudulent schemes if the 4th is combined with Saturn, Rahu and Ketu.

Fifth Bhava (House).—Intelligence, father, atman, discriminating power, children, fame and position should be predicted from the 5th house.

If the lord of the 5th occupies the 3rd, the 6th or the 12th and is aspected by malefics, the person's children die early.

If the Sun is in the 5th house and is badly placed, the father will die. If the lord of the 5th house joins favourable planets, the person gets many issues.

If Jupiter becomes lord of the 5th and being powerful is aspected by the lord of the birth, the person will have children.

If the 5th as well as its lord are placed between evil planets and Jupiter is in company with malefics, there will be loss of children.

If all the malefics occupy the 4th or if all of them occupy the 12th, the 5th, the 8th and the 1st, the person's family becomes completely extinct.

The person will have a piercing intellect if the 5th house is between beneficial planets.

If Saturn is in the 5th, or aspects the lord of birth or Jupiter, there will be brain derangement.

If Mercury and Saturn have major influence on the child at birth, the child born will be impotent.

If the 5th house falls in a sign of Mercury or Saturn and its lord combines with Saturn the person will have an adopted son.

If the lord of the 5th is masculine, joins a masculine sign, and combines in a masculine navamsa, the first-born child to the native will be a male.

If the lord of the 5th joins a female sign with a feminine planet and combines in a feminine navamsa, the first born baby will be a female.

Sixth Bhava (House).—Represents enemies, thieves, cuts and wounds in the body, disappointments, miseries, sorrows, debts, illness, paternal relations, sinful deeds, battle and diseases.

Two or more malefics in the 6th make the native a prey to complicated diseases and a malefic aspect will practically confine the person to bed.

If the lord of the 6th occupies the 1st or the 8th with evil associations and with no beneficial aspects, the native will have many sores.

If the Moon, Venus and the lord of birth combine with the Sun or Rahu, the person may suffer from syphillis.

If the lord of birth and the 6th are in conjunction with the Moon, water accidents occur, and if Mars joins the birth lord, danger in violent fights or battles is indicated.

If the lord of the 6th and birth conjoin Saturn and occupy quadrants and trines, imprisonment is indicated. If Saturn is lord of Lagna, this result should not be predicted.

If Saturn is in the 9th, Jupiter in the 3rd and the Moon in the 7th or the 8th, the person's hands will become deformed.

If the 10th house is occupied by Rahu, Saturn and Mercury, the native's hands may be amputated.

Venus in conjunction with the lord of the 6th, and Saturn or the Sun with Rahu in cruel amsas, indicate capital punishment. Neutralising factors should be carefully considered.

When the Moon occupies the 6th, the 8th or the 12th aspected by the lord of Lagna and conjoined with Saturn and Rahu, the person may meet with accidents.

If the lord of the 6th or the 8th or Mars joins the lord of the 3rd, and Saturn and Rahu are in cruel navamsas, the person dies in a battle or fight.

If the lord of the 6th be a malefic and conjoins Mercury, who is in debilitation, the person suffers from toothache early in his life.

Mercury in the 6th, debilitated with Saturn and Mars, will render the person an invalid throughout life.

If the lord of the Ascendant joins the 6th aspected by the lord of the 6th, the person will suffer much from the machinations of his close relatives.

If the lord of the 9th joins the 6th aspected by the lord of the 6th and the lord of the 6th has the conjunction of Saturn and Mars, the person will suffer from fires, thieves and swindlers.

Seventh Bhava (House).—Represents wife, husband, marriage, urinary organs, marital happiness, sexual diseases, trade and speculation, desire, diplomacy and honour, travels, business tact and the latent energies.

If the lords of the 2nd and the 6th have evil conjunctions and occupy the 6th house or if the afflicted lord of the 7th joins the birth, the moral character of the person will be questionable.

If the lord of the 7th joins Rahu or Ketu and is aspected by Mars or Saturn, and Venus is ill-placed, one becomes loose in morals in his early years.

If evil planets occupy the 1st and the 6th, the person will be licentious and indulges in clandestine pleasures.

If the weak Moon joins a malefic in the 7th, the person becomes immoral.

If Venus combines with the lord of the 2nd, the 7th and the 6th and occupies the Ascendant, the native's moral character will be questionable.

Venus in the 7th makes one passionate.

Afflicted Mercury and Venus in the 7th make the native inclined towards secret pleasures.

Mars, Mercury and Venus in the 7th aspected by no benefics render the person passionate and make him seek unnatural sources of gratification, unless Jupiter is in a kendra.

Jupiter in the 7th or the 10th with no malefic aspects will make the person principled and chaste in sexual matters.

If the lord of the 5th is in the 7th and the lord of the 7th is with malefics and Venus is weak, the wife dies during pregnancy.

If the lords of the 2nd and the 7th are in their own houses, the person will have only one wife.

If the lord of the 7th is powerful and exalted occupying birth, more than one wife must not be predicted.

If the 7th falls in an evil sign, if the lord of the 7th joins debilitation, two marriages may be indicated.

If the lord of the 7th and the 12th is Venus and he occupies the 9th aspected by Saturn, the person will have more than one wife.

If the lord of the 7th is in the 6th aspected by Rahu and with no beneficial conjunction, two marriages should be predicted.

If the lords of the 7th and the 10th exchange their houses and the lord of the 2nd occupies a beneficial navamsa. the person will have all marital happiness.

If the Sun is in the 7th one will have liaison with barren women.

If the Moon is in the 7th debilitated, sex-relations take place with maid-servants.

If Mars is in the 7th house with no aspects of benefics, intercourse occurs with unmatured girls.

If three quadrants are occupied by evil planets, happiness with wife is not indicated.

Eighth Bhava (House).—Indicates longevity, secret organ, death legacies and gifts and unearned wealth, cause of death, wills, disgrace and degradation, the place and surroundings of death, defeat or insult, sorrow, blame, servants and impediments.

If the lord of the 8th joins the 12th with a malefic, there will be short life.

Life will be short if the lord of the birth and the lord of the 8th join the 6th.

There will be long life if the birth lord occupies beneficial houses with the lord of the 8th.

If all malefics occupy the 8th, one will have short life.

If Saturn is in the 12th and the lord of the 8th is in the 2nd with a benefic, death occurs in the 21st year.

If the lord of the 8th is in the 5th in conjunction with malefics, and the lord of the 10th is in the 2nd aspected by malefics, the native dies in the 2nd year.

If quadrants are occupied by benefics and the lord of birth combines with a benefic planet aspected by Jupiter, long life may be predicted.

If the lords of the 8th, the 1st and the 10th combine with Saturn and occupy quadrants, life will be long.

When the lords of the 2nd and 6th combine with Saturn and occupy the 3rd, the 6th and the 12th, death will be due to asphyxiation.

If Saturn becomes the lord of the 6th and joins with Rahu or Ketu, death will be from the attack of beasts.

If in the same combination Jupiter has prominence, danger arises from elephants.

If Saturn joins the Sun and occupies or aspects the 8th, death will be from canine bites.

If the weak Moon occupying the 8th with Rahu joins malefics, the person dies by the troubles of apparitions and spectres.

If the 6th house is occupied by its lord and the lord of the 8th is with Rahu, and Saturn with Ketu aspected by Mars, the person will be killed by weapons.

If the Sun in debilitation occupies the 6th or the 8th aspected by a malefic, the father will die through the displeasure of the state.

If Mercury is not well situated and occupies an unfavourable position, death takes place from sudden heart failure.

If the 8th is favourably situated with the aspects of Mercury, Venus and Jupiter, the native will bequeath vast legacies to his successors.

If the 8th is occupied by Saturn, and Mars aspects it with his special aspects, the person will contract many debts and no redemption can be expected.

If the 8th becomes a moveable sign and its lord is also found in a moveable sign, death takes place in a foreign country.

If the 8th and its lord are in a fixed sign and Saturn is similarly placed, the person dies in his own house.

If the 8th house falls in a common sign and its lord also occupies a common sign, death will occur while travelling.

If Mars gets prominence and the combinations are placed as above, death takes place in automobiles and aeroplanes. Accidental deaths are always due to Mars.

Mercury kills the native in balloons and airships. Brain fever, anaemia, neuritis and paralysis bring about death when Mercury is afflicted in the 8th.

The Moon causes death through watery diseases, cholera and lung troubles.

Jupiter brings about death by diabetes, dropsy, liver and spleen trouble and swelling of the body.

Saturn inflicts death on water or by typhoid.

The Sun causes death through fire or heart trouble or by self-immolation for others' cause provided he is not debilitated.

Rahu indicates death by skin troubles, leprosy, poisoning, smallpox and drowning.

Ketu causes death by suicide and other unnatural causes.

Ninth Bhava (House).—Represents godliness, righteousness, preceptor, grandchildren, metaphysical studies, imagination and intuition, religious devotion, law, sympathy, philosophy, science and literature, lasting fame, leadership, charities, communication with spirits, ghosts and the like, long journeys, foreign travels and father.

If the weak Moon occupies the 9th in a debilitated state or Venus is bad and occupies evil conjunctions or if the lord of the 9th is debilitated, the native will be guilty of improper relations with his preceptor's wife.

If the 9th is occupied by benefics and the lord of the 9th combines with no malefics, the person rests content with his own wife.

If the lord of the 9th is in the 8th or any moveable sign, the child will be born when its father is not in the place.

If the lord of the 9th joins the navamsa of Jupiter, the person becomes righteously inclined and charitable in disposition.

If the 9th is occupied by Venus, Ketu and the Sun, proficiency in miscellaneous subjects is to be predicted; Ketu in the 9th makes a man interested in mesmerism.

If the lord of the 9th is in the 4th aspected by Saturn, the person will be charitable in disposition, irritable in temperament and generally bigotted.

If the lords of the 1st and the 9th are powerful and the Sun is aspected by benefics, the native will be obedient and dutiful to his father.

If the lord of the 9th is in quadrants or in trines, the person becomes well acquainted with metaphysical lore provided such a combination has the aspect of Jupiter or Jupiter is in a kendra.

If Rahu and Saturn occupy the 9th and otherwise badly situated, the person will be cold-hearted, engaged in inflicting miseries and injuries on innocent people and quite unsympathetic.

Mars and Ketu in the 9th with Jupiter in the 2nd, and Mercury, the Sun and Venus in the 5th, the 6th and the 7th respectively, make the man very rich.

If the lord of the Ascendant joins the 9th and combines with the lord of the 5th, wealth may be predicted through children.

If Mercury is the lord of the 9th or aspects its lord and if Jupiter occupies an exalted position, the person will be highly learned in mystical philosophy. If the lords of the Ascendant and the 9th are combined or are in mutual aspect or in mutual kendras, one will have foreign travels.

Tenth Bhava (House).—Represents occupation, rank, temporal honours and success, respect, means of livelihood, self-respect, religious knowledge and dignity.

If the lord of the 10th is the Sun, who is well placed and powerfully aspected, income will be from inherited wealth, from drugs, medicines and chemical dealings.

If the Moon occupies the 10th house and Mars aspects it, the native will earn money by selling precious stones and dealings with aristocracy, women of questionable character and agriculture to some extent.

If Mars is the lord of the 10th or occupies it and is aspected by the Sun or the Moon, the person will be a respectable Commander-in-Chief; if by Saturn, a gang leader and a robber; if by Mercury, a doctor.

If the 10th is occupied by Mercury, the native will be a professor in religious philosophy, mathematical sciences, and earns his livelihood as such.

If Jupiter becomes the lord of the 10th or aspects it, livilihood might be predicted through being a preceptor, teacher. judge, etc.

Venus as the lord of the 10th house gets the native income from brokerage, as manager of art gallaries, cinemas, music houses and if afflicted, brothels and other mean associations.

If Saturn occupies the 10th or aspects it with no beneficial conjunction, earnings will be from being a municipal official, a scavenger, a factory worker, etc.

If Pisces becomes the 10th house and Mercury or Mars occupies it, the person will have *Mukti* or emancipation and will have dips in sacred waters.

If Jupiter joins Mercury or Mars, the person builds charitable institutions and performs meritorious deeds.

If the Moon occupies a quadrant and Jupiter aspects her, he will have pure reputation for his conduct and truthful nature.

If Mars and Saturn are in the 10th aspected by other malefics, the person will have communication with supernaturals or Uchchista Devatas.

If the 10th house is a watery sign and its lord occupies a moveable Rasi and Navamsa, the person will have foreign travels. If the Sun is also in the 10th, the travel will be on some political mission.

Eleventh Bhava (House).—Represents means of gains, accomplishment, friends, personality, ornaments, elder brother and freedom from misery and pain.

If the lord of the 11th is in exaltation and in a *kendra* (quadrant), and if Mercury becomes the lord of the 2nd, much gain will accrue from trade.

If the lord of the 11th is aspected by the lords of the 2nd and the 4th and combines with the lord of the 9th, the man becomes very rich and exercises frugality in expenditure.

If the lord of the 11th is a benefic and has beneficial aspects, the person will be attracted towards decent ornaments.

If Jupiter occupies the 11th and Mercury aspects it, the person gains much reputation as a philosopher and lecturer.

If the lord of the 11th is a benefic aspected by benefics and occupying favourable positions, the person will have perfect contours.

If the above combination is afflicted by Saturn or Mars, the person becomes deaf.

If the lord of the 11th and its occupants are powerful, the native will have powerful influence in society.

If the 11th is occupied by Saturn, Mars, Rahu and the Sun with no other benefics aspecting it, the person will be mentally miserable but financially well off.

Twelfth Bhava (House).—Indicates misery, loss, expenditure, waste, extravagance, sympathy, piety, divine knowledge and worship, *Moksha* (final emancipation) and the state after death.

If the lord of the 12th is aspected by the lord of the 7th and these two are powerful, the native's money and influence will be wasted through the agency of his wife.

If the 12th is occupied by a malefic and its lord is an evil planet, money will be spent on immoral purposes.

If the powerless lord of the 12th occupies unfavourable positions in the navamsa, the native will have deformed limbs.

If the lord of the 12th is Jupiter and has no malefic influences or aspects, the person will die in divine contemplation.

If the lord of the 12th is Mars and Saturn occupies the 12th, death takes place on account of piles and other bloody diseases.

If the lord of the 12th is weak and is seen by the lord of the 6th, money will be spent on useless litigation.

If the Sun and the Moon are in the 12th without any favourable aspects, the native will be a simpleton.

If benefics occupy the 12th or its lord joins with them, the person will have close relations surrounding him at his death.

For a detailed discussion of each Bhava reference may be made to the author's *How to Judge a Horoscope*.

CHAPTER XX

Some Special Yogas

Yogas in Sanskrit astrological nomenclature mean special planetary combinations for the production of high political power and influence, great wealth, philanthropy, asceticism, misery, debts, demoralisation and curruption. In all horoscopes, these yogas must be properly scrutinised along with the application of the usual astrological rules. These important yogas make or mar a man for, if special *arishtas* or misfortunes are found in a horoscope, the person will be always miserable, even though according to ordinary astrological rules, such a horoscope is a promising one. The word Yoga is quite indigenous and such a system cannot be found in the astrological principles of other nations. These reveal a flood of information to the astrological student, when properly studied and applied. The Western reader must clearly comprehend the technicalities involved in the application of these yogas and try to understand their significance thoroughly.

There are different types of yogas—*Rajayoga*—producing high political power; *Dhanayoga* or combination for great wealth; *Gnanayoga* or combination for real higher knowledge and renunciation of the world; and *Arishtayoga*—series of misfortunes of the most baneful nature. There are thousands of such yogas given in the original Sanskrit works and their reproduction here would mean firstly a great strain on the comprehending powers of the reader and secondly, increase of the bulk of the book beyond proportion. The results ascribed to each yoga will completely manifest themselves if the *yogakarakas* (planets producing such yogas) are not afflicted. For more detailed information I would refer my readers to my book *Three Hundred Important Combinations*.

I shall now briefly sketch some favourable yogas and their probable results.

1. *Chamara Yoga.*—This is produced when the lord of the Ascendant is exalted and occupies a quadrant and has the powerful aspect of Jupiter ; or two benefics in the Ascendant, the 7th or the 10th also cause the same yoga.

The person will be greatly respected by rulers and the aristocracy, good conversationalist, a profound scholar and lives more than 70 years.

2. *Shankha Yoga.*—When the lord of the 10th or Ascendant occupies moveable signs like Aries, Cancer, etc., and the lord of the 9th is powerful, this yoga is caused. If the lords of the 5th and the 6th are in mutual quadrants from each other and the ruler of the rising sign powerful, this yoga is caused.

Fond of pleasures, learned in sciences and philosophy, philanthropic, agreeable family surroundings, charitable disposition and long life upto 80.

3. *Sreenatha Yoga.*—When the exalted lord of the 7th occupies the 10th and the lord of the 10th combines with the lord of the 9th— Great respect, reputation, honourable living, much wealth and nice surroundings.

4. *Bheri Yoga.*—Lord of the 10th powerful with three planets in the 12th, the 2nd, the 1st and the 7th houses ; or lord of the 9th is powerful and Venus and lord of Ascendant are in quadrants from Jupiter—Landed estates, free from encumbrance, high family traditions, exalted soul, courageous, expert in sciences and arts, long lived, free from any kind of diseases.

5. *Sarada Yoga.*— Jupiter in a trine from the Moon, and Mars in trine to Mercury or Jupiter in the 11th from Mercury or lord of the 10th occupies the 5th, Mercury in a quadrant and the Sun in his own sign—Attracted by fair ladies, respector of preceptors and religiously inclined, praised by the royalty and aristocracy, saintly disposition and a patron of fine arts and sciences.

6. *Matsya Yoga* (Fish combination).—Malefics in birth and the 9th, benefics and malefics in the 5th and malefics in the 4th and the 8th—Lover of astrology, sympathetic temperament and religious nature.

7. *Kesari Yoga.*—The Moon and Jupiter in quadrants to each other—Respected by relations and friends, Municipal Comm ssioner or Manager of a big corporation, name goes to posterity, possession of all worldly enjoyments.

8. *Adhi Yoga.*—Benefics in the 6th, the 7th and the 8th from the Moon—Commander, Minister or a king or eqaul to him, foeless, long-lived and free from diseases.

9. *Anapha Yoga.*—Planets in the 12th from the Moon—Man of commanding and majestic appearance, healthy, moral, free from mental sorrow, renowned, fond of sense pleasures and renunciation of worldly concerns later on in life.

10. *Sunapha Yoga.*—Planets in the 2nd from the Moon—Self-made man, self-acquired wealth, intelligent and reputed.

11. *Durdhura Yoga.*—Planets in the 2nd and the 12th from the Moon—Enjoyment of all pleasures, conveyances, liberal and generous and commanding, dutiful and faithful children.

12. *Kahala Yoga.*—The lord of the 4th and Jupiter in mutual quandrants, and the lord of the Ascendant powerful—Stubbornness, courageous and adventurous, commanding infantry, cavalry, artillery, etc., and ruling towns and cities.

13. *Vasi Yoga.*—Planets in the 12th from the Sun—Influential, rich and wealthy.

14. *Vesi Yoga.*—Beneficial planets in the 2nd from the Sun—Good conversationalist, fluent speaker, wealthy, courageous and extremely charitable.

15. *Obhayachari Yoga.*—Benefics in the 2nd and the 12th from the Sun—Equal to a king, good, sympathetic and philanthropic.

16. *Mridanga Yoga.*—The lord of the navamsa occupied by an exalted planet in a quadrant and himself exalted, in his own sign or in a friendly house and the lord of the Ascendant powerful—Healthy throughout life, attractive personality, great influence among the people.

17. *Koorma Yoga.*—Benefics in the 5th, the 6th and the 7th in the Rasi and exalted and in friendly and own navamsa—Royal enjoyments, charitable disposition, courageous, happy and philosophical.

18. *Khadga Yoga.*—Lord of the 2nd in the 9th, and the lord of the 9th in the 2nd and the lord of Ascendant in a quadrant or a trine—Religiously inclined, courage, strong, penetrating intelligence.

19. *Lakshmi Yoga.*—Lord of the 9th in a quadrant, *moolatrikona* or in deep exaltation or lord of Lagna in conjunction with the 9th lord—Extremely handsome appearance, noble qualities and virtues, possessed of high reputation for honesty and honoured by aristocracy.

20. *Kusuma Yoga.*—Venus in a fixed sign, in a quadrant, a weak Moon in a trine and the Sun in the 10th house—Extremely liberal, war-like and possessed of unsullied reputation and good enjoyment.

Bad Yogas

21. *Kemadruma Yoga.*—No planets in the 2nd and the 12th houses from the Moon at birth—Misery and poverty

throughout life and generally capable of neutralising all beneficial yogas.

22. *Rajju Yoga.*—All planets in moveable signs—Resident in foreign country, unjust.

23. *Brihadbija Yoga.*—Rahu with Mars and Saturn in the Ascendant or the lord of the Ascendant in the 8th with Rahu and malefics—Testicles swelling and venereal complaints.

24. *Daridra Yoga.*—Lord of the Ascendant in the 12th and *vice versa*—Loss of wealth, generally poor and mean motives.

25. *Asatyavadi Yoga* —If the lord of the house occupied by the lord of the 2nd is Saturn—Likes falsehood and indulges in fraudulent schemes.

Gnana Yoga

Gnana means knowledge which may mean for the acquisition of power and wealth or the kind of knowledge which makes a man "know thyself" as Socrates says. In acquiring knowledge there are two aspects to be considered. One is scholarship, culture, literary power and imagination and the other is spiritual knowledge and the realisation of Self.

Literary power and scholarship are obtained from the position of Venus and Mercury and this is also controlled by Jupiter.

When Jupiter is powerful, well aspected and occupies a Vargottama (occupying the same sign in Rasi and Navamsa), the person becomes a great lecturer and orator.

When Mercury is in a kendra, Venus in the 2nd, the Moon or Jupiter in the 3rd, it makes the native a great astrologer.

Mars strongly posited in the 2nd with Mercury and the Moon or the Moon, Mars and Mercury in a quadrant makes a person a great mathematician.

Jupiter or Venus becoming lord of the 2nd and aspected by Mars and the Sun in exaltation or *moolatrikona*, the person becomes a great logician and psychologist.

Jupiter and the lord of the 2nd powerful and Jupiter in conjunction with the Sun produces a man extraordinarily well-versed in grammar and prosody.

A man becomes a versatile genius if Jupiter and Venus are in quadrants and Mercury becomes the lord of the navamsa occupied by the lord of the 2nd.

A person becomes a great philosopher when the lord of the 2nd, Mercury, is in deep exaltation and Jupiter is in the navamsa of Leo.

Dhana Yoga.—The Moon, Jupiter, lords of the 2nd, the 4th, the 9th and the 11th houses control wealth. The favourable position of these planets in the Rasi or in the Navamsa invariably leads to great wealth. The lords of the 2nd, the 4th and the 9th should be aspected by the Moon and be disposed friendly towards it. The lord of the 2nd with the lord of the 9th occupying the 11th with the Moon and Jupiter will make the person a millionaire.

CHAPTER XXI

Planets in Different Bhavas or Houses

THE SUN : In the first house.—Righteous-minded, healthy,
bilious, eye-disease, intelligence, good morals, political
success, stately appearance, humanitarian instincts, lazy in
work, fond of daring deeds, hot constitution, careless of
reputation, strong will, caprice, generosity, neglect of personal
credit or respect, good work, not combative or impetuous
and pioneering.

Second house.—Diseased face, ugly, losses from prosecu-
tions good earnings, inclined to waste, bright speech, enquiring,
well-educated, scientific, stubborn and peevish temper, danger
in the 25th year, will stammer.

Third house.—Courageous, liberal, adventurous, famous,
intelligent, wealthy, successful and restless.

Fourth house—Mental worry, meditative defective organs,
success in foreign countries, hatred of relations, keen-minded,
sensitive, good reputation, success after middle age, quarrels
without causes, weak constitution, introspective, unhappy,
philosophical, squanders paternal property.

Fifth house.—Intelligent, poor, few children, paternal
danger, corpulent, danger to father early, unhappy, disturbed
in mind, lover of fine arts, and tactful in decision.

Sixth house.—Defier of customs and castes, good administrative ability, few cousins and few enemies, bold and
successful, war-like, licentious, wealthy, gains from enemies,

clever in planning, terror to enemies, executive ability, colic troubles.

Seventh house. — Late marriage and rather troubled, loose morals and irreligious, hatred by the fair sex, fond of travelling, submissive to wife, wealth through female agency, fond of foreign things, discontented, wife's character questionable, subservient to women and risk of dishonour and disgrace through them.

Eighth house. — Long life, uncharitable, sickly constitution, sudden gains, complaints in eyes, sores in the head, poor and uneventful life, narrow and obscure.

Ninth house. — Well read in solar sciences, attracted by sublime phenomena, charitable, godly, lucky and successful, devoted, ordinary health, little patrimony, dutiful sons, a man of action and thought, self-acquired property, many lands, philosophical, glandular disease, lover of poetry and music, successful agriculturist, learned in esoteric and occult subjects, ambitious and enterprising.

Tenth house. — Bold, courageous, well known, famous, clever in acquiring wealth, superior knack, healthy, learned, adventurous, educated, quick decision, fond of music, founder of institutions, high position, dutiful sons, much personal influence, successful military or political career.

Eleventh house. — Learned, wealthy, stately and persevering, success without much effort, famous, many enemies, wealth through fair means, good reputation, profound insight, capacity to befriend, many political enemies, man of principles, great sagacity, great success and position.

Twelfth house. — Sinful, poor, fallen, thieving nature, unsuccessful, adulterous, neglected, long limbs, ceremonial-minded and lover of esoteric and occult knowledge, no happiness from children.

THE MOON : In the Ascendant.—Fanciful and romantic, moderate eater, an attractive appearance, inclined to corpulence, windy temperament, much travelling, disease in private organs and ears, capricious, licentious, sociable, easy going, educated, warring, loved by the opposite sex, shy, modest, stubborn, proud, fickle-minded and eccentric.

• *Second house.*—Wealthy, handsome, attractive, generous, highly intelligent, breaks in education, charming, poetical, great respect, sweet speech, persuasive, squint eyes and much admired.

Third house.—Sickly, dyspeptic and later on piles, mild, lean, disappointments, impious, many brothers, cruel, educated, consumption, famous, sisters, intelligent, unscrupulous, purposeless, miserly, fond of travelling and active-minded.

Fourth house.—Comfortable, fine taste, good perfumes and dress, polite and affable manners, high education, happy, licentious, helped by all, wealthy and successful, good mother, popular and death to mother early if in conjunction with malefics.

Fifth house.—Subtle, handsome wife, shrewd, showy, many daughters, intelligent, gains through quadrupeds, interrupted education, high political office.

Sixth house.—Submissive to the opposite sex, indolent, imperious, short-tempered, intelligent, lazy, slender body, weak sexual connection, widow-hunter, poor, drunkard, refined, tender, pilfering habits: stomach troubles, many foes, worried by cousins.

Seventh house.—Passionate, fond of women, handsome wife, mother short-lived, narrow-minded, good family, pains in the loins, social, successful, jealous and energetic in several matters.

Eighth house.—Unhealthy, legacy, capricious, mother short-lived, few children, bilious, slender bad sight, kidney disease, unsteady, easy acquisitions.

Ninth House.—Popular, educated, intelligent, well read, lover of fiction, builder of charitable institutions, wealthy, active, inclined to travel, godly, good children, immoveable property, religious, mystical, righteous, agricultural success, devotional, successful and good reputation.

Tenth house.—Persuasive, passionate, charitable, shrewd, adulterous, bold, tactful, ambitious, great position, active, trustee of religious institutions, obliging to good people, many friends, easy success, popular and able, wealthy, comfortable and long life.

Eleventh house.—Many children, powerful, philanthropic, polite, literary and artistic taste, helpful, influential, cultured, charitable, many friends, great position, reputation, good lands, easy success, liked and helped by the fair sex, giver of donations, man of principles.

Twelfth house.—Obstructed, deformed, narrow-minded, cruel, unhappy, obscure, powerless, deceived, solitary, miserable.

MARS : In the first house.—Hot constitution, scars in the body, pilfering habits, big navel, early danger to father, reddish complexion, active, adventurous, powerful and low-minded.

Second house.—Quarrelsome, extravagant, harsh speech, adulterous, short-tempered, wasteful, sharp-tongued, broken education, satirical, large patrimony, bad-tempered, aggressive, unpopular and awkward.

Third house.—Pioneering, few brothers, sex-morals weak, courageous, intelligent, reckless, adventurous, short-tempered, unprincipled, easy morals, unpopular.

Fourth house.—Sickly mother, quarrels, unhappy home life, danger to father, domestic quarrels and conveyances, uncomfortable, coarse, brutal, tyrannical, vulgar.

Fifth house.—Unpopular, no issues, ambitious, intelligent, persevering, unhappy, bold, unprincipled, decisive.

Sixth house.—Successful, good lands, rich success over enemies, intelligent, political success, powerful, worry from near relations.

Seventh house.—Two wives or friction with wife, dropsy, rash speculations, unsuccessful, intelligent, tactless, stubborn, idiosyncratic, peevish, passionate, tension in married life.

Eighth house.—Short life, few children, danger to maternal uncles, widower later, hater of relations, bad sight, extramarital relations.

Ninth house.—Unkind, worldly, successful trader, loss from agriculture, sickly father, naval merchant, dependent life, self-seeking, acute, stubborn, impetuous, logical.

Tenth house.—Founder of institutions and towns, energetic, adventurous, wealthy, active, healthy, famous, self-made man, good agriculturist, good profits, clever, successful, loved by relations, decisive.

Eleventh house. Learned, educated, wealthy, influential, property, crafty, happy, commanding.

Twelfth house.—Unsuccessful, poor, rotten body, unpopular, incendiary diseases, suffering, stumbling, active, fruitless, liable to fraud and deception, dishonest, unseen, impediments, deformed eyes.

MERCURY : In the First house.—Cheerful, humorous, well read, clever, many enemies, learned, fond of accult studies and astronomy, witty, influential, intellectual, respected, long-lived, love of literature and poetry.

Second house.—Learned in religious and philosophical lore, sweet speech, good conversationalist, humorous, clever, many children, determined, fine manners, captivating look, self-acquisition, wealthy, careful, thrifty, clever in earning money.

Third house.—Daughter, happy mother, clever, cruel, loved by fair sex, tactful, diplomatic, discretion, bold, sensible.

Fourth house.—Learned, agriculturist, good mother, unhappy, skilled in conjuring tricks, obliging, cultured, affectionate, popular, inclined to pursue literary activities.

Fifth house.—Showy, learned, quarrelsome, danger to maternal uncles, parents sickly, good administrative capacity, fond of good furniture and dress, respect from moneyed men, ministerial office, executive ability, speculative, scholar, vain, danger to father, combative.

Sixth house.—Respected, interrupted education, subordinate officer, executive capacity, quarrelsome, showy, dissimulation, losses in money, peevish, bigoted, troubles in the feet and toes.

Seventh house.—Diplomatic, interesting literary ability early in life and success through it, early marriage, wife handsome, dutiful and short-tempered, breaks in education, learned in astrology, astronomy and mathematics, success in trade, successful, dashing, gay, skilful, religious, happy mother and early death to her, cunning, adulterous, charitable, strong body.

Eighth house.—Long life, landed estate, easy access to anything desired, grief through domestics, obliging, few issues, many lands, famous, respected, ill-health.

Ninth house.—Highly educated, musician, many children, obliging, licentious, philosophical, lover of literature, creative mind, inquisitive, scientific-minded, popular, well known.

Tenth house.—Determined, fortunate, enjoyments in life, intelligent, bad sight, active, cheerful, charitable, able, philanthropic.

Eleventh house.—Wealthy, happy, mathematical faculty, good astrologer, many friends among famous men, many lands, logical and scientific, success in trade.

Twelfth house.—Philosophical, intelligent, worried, adulterous, obliging, capricious, wayward, narrow-minded, gifted, despondent, passionate, few children, lacking in opportunities, danger to mother.

JUPITER : In the First house.—Magnetic personality, good grammarian, majestic appearance, highly educated, many children, learned, dexterous, long-lived, respected by rulers, philologist, political success, sagacious, stout body, able, influential, leader.

Second house.—Wealthy, intelligent, dignified, attractive, happy, fluent speaker, aristocratic, tasteful, winning manners, accumulated fortune, witty, good wife and family, eloquent, humorous, and dexterous.

Third house.—Famous, many brothers, ancestors, devoted to the family, miserly, obliging, polite, unscrupulous, good agriculturist, thrifty, good success, energetic, bold, taste for fine arts and literature, loved by relatives.

Fourth house. – Good conveyances, educated, happy, intelligent, wealthy, founder of charitable institutions, comfortable, good inheritance, good mother, well read, contented life.

Fifth house.—Broad eyes, handsome, statesmanly ability, good insight, high position, intelligent, skilful in trade, obedient children, pure-hearted, a leader.

Sixth house.— Obscure, unlucky, troubled, many cousins and grandsons, dyspeptic, much jocularity, witty, unsuccessful, intelligent, foeless.

Seventh house.—Educated, proud, good wife and gains through her, diplomatic ability, speculative mind, very sensitive, success in agriculture, virtuous wife, pilgrimage to distant places.

Eighth house.—Unhappy, earnings by undignified means, obscure, long life, mean, degraded, thrown with widows, colic pains, pretending to be charitable, dirty habits.

Ninth house.— Charitable, many children, devoted, religious, merciful, pure, ceremonial-minded, humanitarian principles, principled, conservative, generous, long-lived father, benevolent, God-fearing, highly cultured, famous, high position.

Tenth house.—Virtuous, learned, clever in acquisition of wealth, conveyances, children, determined, highly principled, accumalated wealth, founder of institutions, good agriculturist, non-violent, ambitious, scrupulous.

Eleventh house.—Lover of music, very wealthy, statesmanly ability, good deeds, accumulated funds, God-fearing, charitable, somewhat dependent, influential, many friends, philanthropic.

Twelfth house.—Sadistic, poor, few children, unsteady character, unlucky, life lascivious, later life inclined to asceticism, artistic taste, pious in after-life.

VENUS : In the Ascendant.—Expert mathematician, very fortunate, ambitious, bold, long life, pioneering, fond of wife, strenuous, skilled in sexual science, successful, practical, scents, flowers, women skilled in fine arts, pleasing, vivacious, astrologer, much magnetic power, leader of people.

Second house.—Large family, happy, delicious drinks, luxurious meals, handsome, large fair eyes, charming wife, witty, brilliant, polite, educated, hating women, obliging, rapid in mind, clever in speech, agreeable, creative author, conservative, composer, economical, wealthy, logical, able.

Third house.—Lover of fine arts, prosperity to mother, wealthy, miserly, obliging, well placed, travelling, original.

Fourth house.—Intelligent, happy, affectionate, learned, affectionate mother, agriculturist, educated, scientific methods, peaceful life, protector of cattle, endeared by relations, fond of milk, famous, literary, successful, popular.

Fifth house.—Clever, intelligent, statesmanly ability, good counsel, danger to mother, commander, educated, able, sociable, kind-hearted, affable, good-natured, many daughters and few sons, affable manners.

Sixth house. – Licentious, foeless, loose habits, anger, low-minded, well informed, destruction to enemies, fond of other women.

Seventh house.—Passionate, unhealthy habits, happy marriage, sensual, inclined towards sex pleasure.

Eighth house.— Danger to mother, happy, given to bad habits, short-lived, famous, celebrated, unexpected legacies, trouble in mind, disappointment in love affairs, pious later in life.

Ninth house. – Selfish, religious, respect for preceptors, able, successful, commander, lover of fine arts, generous.

Tenth house.—Respect for divine people and parents, marriage, broken education, successful as a lawyer, popular, social, moderate eater.

Eleventh house. – Influential, learned, wealthy, good conveyances, successful, many friends, much popularity.

Twelfth house.—Meen-minded, fond of low women, miserly, obscure, licentious, unprincipled, weak eyes, fond of sexual pleasures, clever, liar, pretentious, unhappy love affairs.

SATURN : In the First house. – Foreign customs and habits, perverted mind, bad thoughts, evil-natured, tyrannical, unscrupulous, well-built thighs, strong-minded, cunning, thrifty, unclean, passionate, aspiring, curious, deformed, sickly, exploring, flatulence, licentious, addicted to low-class **women.**

Second house.—More than one marriage, diseased face, unpopular, broken education, weak sight, unsocial, harsh speech, stammering, addicted to wine.

Third house.—Intelligent, wealthy, wicked, loss of brothers, polite, adventurous, bold, eccentric, cruel, courageous, obliging, agriculturist.

Fourth house.—Danger to mother if with the Moon, unhappy, sudden losses, colic pains, narrow-minded, crafty, estates encumbered, good thinker, success in foreign countries, political disfavour, licentious, interrupted education.

Fifth house.—Narrow-minded, mediocre life, no children, perverted views, tale-teller, government displeasure. troubled life, clear-minded.

Sixth house.—Obstinate, sickly, deaf, few children, quarrelsome, sex diseases, clever, active, indebted.

Seventh house.—More than one wife, enterprising, sickly, colic pains, deafness, diplomatic, stable marriage, ambitious, political success, travelling, dissimulator, foreign honours, deputation.

Eighth house.—Seeking disappointments, big belly, few issues, corpulent, inclined to drinking, friendship with women of other castes, colic pains, defect in sight, seductive, clever, well-informed, impious, danger by poisons, asthma, consumption, etc., if with malefics, dishonest, ungrateful children, cruel, long life.

Ninth house.—Legal success, founder of charitable institutions, very miserly, thrifty in domestic life, scientific, irreligious, logical, ceremonial-minded, unfilial.

Tenth house.—Visits to sacred rivers and shrines, great worker, bilious, good farmer, sudden elevations and depressions, residence in foreign countries uncertain, later on in life an ascetic.

Eleventh house.—Learned, feared and respected, very wealthy, much landed property, broken education, conveyances, political success, influential, political respect.

Twelfth house.—Deformed, squint eyes, losses in trade, learned in occult science, poor, spendthrift, many enemies, dexterous, unpopular, attracted towards yoga in later life.

RAHU : In the Ascendant.—Obliging, sympathetic, abortion, courageous, sickly wife or husband.

Second house.—Poor and more than one wife if afflicted, dark complexion, diseased face, peevish, luxurious dinners.

Third house.—Few children, wealthy, bold, adventurous, courageous, good gymnastic, many relations.

Fourth house.—Liaison with women of easy virtue, subordinate, proficient in European languages.

Fifth house.—Childless, flatulent, tyrannical, polite, narrow-minded and hard-hearted.

Sixth house.—Enjoyment, venereal complaints, no enemies, many cousins.

Seventh house.—Wife suffering from menstrual disorders, widow or divorcee connection, diabetes, luxurious food, unhappy.

Eighth house.—Vicious, degraded, quarrelsome, narrow-minded, immoral, adulterous.

Ninth house.—A puppet in the hands of the wife, impolite, uncharitable, emaciated waist, loose morals.

Tenth house.—Intimacy with widows, taste in poetry and literature, good artist, traveller, learned.

Eleventh house.—Wealthy, influential among lower castes, many children, good agriculturist.

Twelfth house.—Deformed, few children, defective sight, very many losses, saintly.

KETU : In the Ascendant.—Emaciated figure, weak constitution, much perspiration, weak-hearted, slender, piles, sexual indulgence, diplomatic.

Second house.—Bad speaker, quiet, quick in perception, peevish, hard-hearted, thrifty and economical.

Third house.—Adventurous, strong, artistic, wealthy, popular.

Fourth house.—Quarrelsome, licentious, weak, fear of poisons.

Fifth house.—Liberal, loss of children, sinful, immoral if afflicted.

Sixth house.—Fond of adultery, good conversationalist, licentious, venereal complaints, learned.

Seventh house.—Passionate, sinful, connections with widows, sickly wife.

Eighth house.—Senseless, obscure, dull, sanguine complexion, piles and similar troubles.

Ninth house.—Short-sighted, sinful, untruthful, thrifty, many children, good wife.

Tenth House.—Fertile brain, happy, religious, pilgrimages to sacred rivers and places, fond of scriptures.

Eleventh house.—Humorous, witty, licentious, intelligent, wealthy.

Twelfth house.—Capricious, unsettled mind, foreign residence, attracted to servile classes, much travelling, licentious, spiritual knowledge.

CHAPTER XXII

Planets in Different Rasis or Signs

THE SUN: In Aries.—Active, intelligent, famous, traveller, wealthy, warrior, variable fortune, ambitious, phlegmatic, powerful, marked personality, impulsive, irritable, pioneering, initiative.

Taurus.—Clever, reflective, attracted by perfumes and dealer in them, hated by women, slow to action, musician, self-confident, delicious drinks, happy meals, tactful, original, sociable, intelligent, prominent nose.

Gemini.—Learned, astronomer, scholarly, grammarian, polite, wealthy, critical, assimilative, good conversationalist, shy, reserved, lacking in originality.

Cancer.—Somewhat harsh, indolent, wealthy, unh constipation, sickly, travelling, independent, expert astr

Leo.—Stubborn, fixed views, strong, cruel, indepe organising capacity and talents for propaganda, humanit frequenting solitary places, generous, famous.

Virgo.—Linguist, poet, mathematician, taste for liter well read, scholarly, artistic, good memory, reasoning fa effeminate body, frank, lucid comprehension, learned in religious lore, reserved, wanting adulation.

Libra.—Manufacture of liquors, popular, tactless, base, drunkard, loose morals, arrogant, wicked, frank, submissive, pompous.

Scorpio.—Adventurous, bold, fearing thieves and robbers,

reckless, cruel, stubborn, unprincipled, impulsive, idiotic, indolent, surgical skill, dexterous, military ability.

Sagittarius.—Short-tempered, spoils, reliable, rich, obstinate, respected by all, happy, popular, religious, wealthy, musician.

Capricorn.—Mean-minded, stubborn, ignorant, miserly, pushful, unhappy, boring, active, meddlesome, obliging, humorous, witty, affable, prudent, firm.

Aquarius —Poor, unhappy, stubborn, unlucky, unsuccessful, medium height, rare faculties, self-esteem.

Pisces.—Pearl merchant, peaceful, wealthy, uneventful, religious, prodigal, loved by women.

THE MOON : In Aries.—Round eyes, impulsive, fond of travel, irritable, fond of women, vegetable diet, quick to decide and act, haughty, inflexible, sores in the head, dexterous, fickle-minded, war-like, enterprising, good position, self-respect, valiant, ambitious, liable to hydrophobia if the Moon is afflicted, large thighs, popular, restless, idiosyncratic, versatile.

Taurus.—Liberal, powerful, happy, ability to command, intelligent, handsome, influential, fond of fair sex, happy in middle life and old age, great strides in life, beautiful gait, large thighs and hips, phlegmatic afflictions, rich patience, respected, love-intrigues, inconsistent, wavering mind, sound judgement, voracious eater and reader, lucky, popular, influenced by women, passionate, indolent.

Gemini.—Well read, creative, fond of women, learned in scriptures, able, persuasive, curly hair, powerful speaker, clever, witty, dexterous, fond of music, elevated nose, thought reader, subtle, long life.

Cancer.—Wise, powerful, charming, influenced by women, wealthy, kind, good, a bit stout, sensitive ; impetuous, unprofitable voyages, meditative, much immovable property, scientist, middle stature, prudent, frugal, piercing, conventional.

Leo.—Bold, irritable, large cheeks, blonde, broad face, brown eyes, repugnant to women, likes meat, frequenting forests and hills, colic troubles, inclined to be unhappy, haughty, mental anxiety, liberal, generous, deformed body, steady, aristocratic, settled views, proud, ambitious.

Virgo.—Lovely complxeion, almond eyes, modest, sunken shoulders and arms, charming, attractive, principled, affluent, comfortable, soft body, sweet speech, honest; truthful, modest, virtuous, intelligent, phlegmatic, fond of women, acute insight, conceited in self-estimation, pensive, conversationalist, many daughters, loquacious, astrologer and clairvoyant or attracted towards them, skilled in arts like music and dancing, few sons.

Libra.—Reverence and respect for learned and holy people, saints and gods; tall, raised nose, thin, deformed limbs, sickly constitution, rejected by kinsmen, intelligent, principled, wealthy, business-like, obliging, love for arts, far-seeing, idealistic, clever, mutable, amicable, losses through women, loves women, just, not ambitious, aspiring.

Scorpio.—Broad eyes, wide chest, round shanks and thighs, isolation from parents or preceptors, brown complexion, straight-forward, frank, open-minded, cruel, simulator, malicious, sterility, agitated, unhappy, wealthy, impetuous, obstinate.

Sagittarius.—Face broad, teeth large, skilled in fine arts, indistinct shoulders, disfigured nails and arms, deep and inventive intellect, yielding to praise, good speech, upright, help from wife and women, happy marriage, many children, good inheritance, benefactor, patron of arts and literature, ceremonial-minded, showy, unexpected gifts, author, reflective mentality, inflexible to threats.

Capricorn.—Ever attached to wife and children, virtuous, good eyes, slender waist, quick in perception, clever, active, crafty, somewhat selfish, sagacious, strategic, liberal, merciless, unscrupulous, inconsistent, low morals, niggardly and mean.

Aquarius.—Fair-looking, well-formed body, tall, large teeth, belly low, youngish, sensual, sudden elevations and depressions, pure-minded, artistic, intuitional, diplomatic, lonely, peevish. artistic taste, energetic, emotional, esoteric, mystical, grateful, healing power.

Pisces.—Fixed, dealer in pearls and fond of wife and children, perfect build, long nose, bright body, annihilating enemies, subservient to opposite sex, handsome, learned, steady, simple, good reputation, loose morals, adventurous, many children, spiritually inclined later in life.

MARS : In Aries.—Organising capacity, commanding, rich, social, scars in the body, sensual, dark, mathematician, active, powerful, inspiring. pioneering. able, statesmanly. frank, generous, careful not economical in domestic dealings, vague imaginations, combative tendencies, hard-hearted.

Taurus.—Influenced by women, timid, rough body, stubborn, sensual, liking for magic and sports, somewhat unprincipled, selfish, tyrannical, not soft-hearted, rash, emotional, animal instinct strong sensitive.

Gemini.—Loving family and children, taste in refinement, scientific, middle stature, well built, learned, ambitious, quick, rash, ingenious, skilled in music; fearless, tactless, peevish, unhappy, subservient, diplomate. humiliating, detective.

Cancer.—Intelligent, wealthy, rich. travels and voyages, wicked. perverted, love of agriculture, medical and surgical proficiency. fickle-minded, defective sight, bold, dashing, headlong, speculative unkind, egoistic.

Leo.—Tendency to occultism, astrology astronomy and mathematics, love for parents, regard and respect for elders and preceptors, independent thinking, peevish, liberal, victorious, stomach troubles, worried by mental complaints, generous, noble, author early in life, successful, combative, restless.

Virgo.—Imitable, explosive, trouble in digestive organs, no marital harmony, general love for the fair sex, revengeful, self-confident, conceited, affable, boastful, materialistic, ceremonial-minded, positive, indiscriminative, pretentious, deceptive, scientific enterprises.

Libra.—Tall, body symmetrically built, complexion fair and swarthy, ambitious, self-confident, perceptive faculties, materialistic, love for family, self-earned wealth, affable, warlike, foresight, business-like, deceived by women, sanguine temperament, kind, gentle, fond of adulation, easily ruffled, boastful.

Scorpio.—Middle stature, clever, diplomatic, positive tendency, indulgent, tenacious memory, malicious, aggressive, proud, haughty, great strides in life.

Sagittarius.—Gentlemanly, many foes, famous minister, statesman, open, frank, pleasure loving, few children, liable to extremes, conservative, indifferent, exacting, impatient, severe, quarrelsome, litigation troubles, good citizen.

Capricorn.—Rich, high political position, many sons, brave, generous, love for children, middle stature, industrious, indefatigable, successful, penetrating, bold, tactful, respected, generous, gallant, influential.

Aquarius.—Unhappy, miserable, poor, not truthful, independent, unwise, wandering, impulsive, controversial, combative, well-versed in dialects, free, quick in forgiving and forgetting, conventional, danger on water, morose, meditative.

Pisces.- Fair complexion, troubles in love affairs, few

children, passionate, restless, antagonistic, exacting, uncertainty of feeling, faithful, unclean, colic, indolent, wilful.

MERCURY : In Aries.—Evil-minded, middle stature, obstinate, clever, social, great endurance, materialistic tendencies, unscrupulous, wavering mind, antagonistic, fond of speculation, impulsive, greedy, dangerous connections, deceitful, swerving from rectitude.

Taurus. — High position, well built, clever, logical, mental harmony, many children, liberal, persevering, opinionative, wealthy, practicable, friends among women of eminence, inclination to sensual pleasures, well read, showy.

Gemini. Inclination to physical labour, boastful, sweet speech, tall, active, cultured, tactful, dexterous to mothers, indolent, inventive, taste in literature, arts and sciences, winning manners, liable to throat and bronchial troubles, musician, mirthful, studious.

Cancer.—Witty, likes music, disliked by relations, low stature, speculative, diplomatic, discreet, flexible, restless, sensual though religious, liable to consumption, strong parental love, dislike for chastity.

Leo.—Few children, wanderer, idiotic, proud, indolent, not fond of women, boastful, orator, good memory, two mothers, poor, early marriage, independent in thinking, impulsive, positive will, remunerative profession, likes travelling.

Virgo.—Learned, virtuous, liberal, fearless, ingenious, handsome, irritable, refined, subtle, intuitive, sociable, no self-control, morbid imaginations, dyspeptic difficulties, eloquent, author, priest, astronomer.

Libra.—Fair complexion, sanguine disposition, inclination to excesses, perceptive faculties, material tendencies, frugal, agreeable, courteous, philosophical, faithful, ceremonial-minded, sociable, discreet.

Scorpio.—Short, curly hair, incentive to indulgence, liable to disease of the generative organ, general debility, crafty, malicious, selfish, subtle, indiscreet, bold, reckless.

Sagittarius.—Taste in sciences, respected by polished society, tall, well built, learned, rash, superstitious, vigorous, executive, diplomatic, cunning, just, capable.

Capricorn.—Selfless, business tendencies, economical, debtor, inconsistent, low stature, cunning, inventive, active, restless, suspicious, drudging.

Aquarius.—Middle stature, licentious, proud, quarrelsome frank, sociable, rapid strides in life, famous, scholar, cowardly, weak constitution.

Pisces.—A dependent, serves others, dexterous, peevish, indolent, petty-minded, respect for gods, and Brahmins.

JUPITER · In Aries.—Love of grandeur, powerful, wealthy, prudent, many children, courteous, generous, firm, sympathetic, happy marriage, patient nature, harmonious, refined, high position.

Taurus.—Stately, elegant, self-importance, liberal, dutiful sons, just, sympathetic, well read, creative ability, despotic, healthy, happy marriage, liked by all, inclination to self-gratification.

Gemini.—Oratorial ability, tall, well-built, benevolent, pure-hearted, scholarly, sagicious, diplomatic, linguist or poet, elegant, incentive.

Cancer.—Well read, dignified, wealthy, comfortable intelligent, swarthy complexion, inclined to social gossip, mathematician, faithful.

Leo.—Commanding apperance, tall, great, easily offended, ambitious, active, happy, intelligent, wise, prudent, generous broad-minded, literary, harmonious surroundings, likes hills and dales.

Virgo.—Middle stature, ambitious, selfish, stoical, resignation, affectionate, fortunate, stingy, lovable, a beautiful wife, great endurance, learned.

Libra.—Handsome, free, open-minded, hasty, attractive, just, courteous, strong, able, exhaustion from over-activity, religious, competent, unassuming, pleasing.

Scorpio.—Tall, somewhat stooping, elegant manners, serious, exacting, well built, superior airs, selfish, imprudent, weak constitution, sub-servient to women, passionate, conventional, proud, zealous, ceremonious, unhappy life.

Sagittarius.—Pretty inheritaner, wealthy, influential, handsome, noble, trustworthy, charitable, good executive ability, weak constitution, artistic qualities, poetic, open-minded, good conversationalist.

Capricorn.—Tactless, good intention, disgraceful behaviour, generous, unhappy, irritable, inconsistent, avaricious, unmanly, jealous.

Aquarius.—Learned, not rich, controversial figure, philosophical, popular, compassionate, sympathetic, amiable, prudent, humanitarian, melancholic, meditative, dreamy, dental troubles.

Pisces.—Good inheritance, stout, medium height, two marriages if with malefics, enterprising, political diplomacy, high position.

VENUS : In Aries.—Extravagant, active, mutable, artistic, dreamy, idealist, proficient in fine arts, licentious, sorrowful, fickle-minded, prudent, unhappy, irreligious, easy going, loss of wealth due to loose life.

Taurus.—Well built, handsome, pleasing countenance, independent, sensual, love of nature, fond of pleasure, elegant taste in dancing and music, voluptuous.

Gemini.—Rich, gentle, kind, generous, eloquent, proud, respected, gullible, love of fine arts, learned, intelligent, good logician, just, dual marriage, tendencies towards materialism.

Cancer.—Melancholy, emotional, timid, more than one wife, haughty, sorrowful, light character, inconsistent, unhappy, many children, sensitive, learned.

Leo.—Money through women, pretty wife, wayward, conceited, passionate, fair complexion, emotional, zealous, licentious, attracted by the fair sex, premature in conclusions, superior airs, unvanquished by enemies.

Virgo.—Petty-minded, licentious, unscrupulous, unhappy, illicit love, agile, loquacious, rich, learned.

Libra.—Statesman, poet, intelligent, generous, philosophical, handsome, matrimonial felicity, successful marriage, passoinate, proud, respected, intuitive, sensual, wide travels.

Scorpio.—Broad features, quarrelsome, medium statured, independent, artistic, unjust, proud, disappointed in love, haughty, not rich.

Sagittarius.—Medium height, powerful, wealthy, respected, impertinent, generous, frank, happy domestic life, high position, philosophical.

Capricorn.—Fond of low class women, imprudent, ambitious, unprincipled, licentious, boastful, subtle, learned, weak body.

Aquarius.—Liked by all, middle stature, handsome, affable, persuasive, witty, timid, chaste, calm, helpful and humanitarian.

Pisces.—Witty, tactful, learned, popular, just, ingenious, caricaturist, modest, refined, powerful, exalted, respected, pleasure-seeking.

SATURN : In Aries.—Idiotic, wanderer, insincere, peevish, resentful, cruel, fraudulent, immoral, boastful, quarrelsome, gloomy, mischievous, perverse, misunderstanding nature.

Taurus.—Dark complexion, deceitful, successful, powerful, unorthodox, clever, likes solitude, voracious eater, persuasive.

cool, contagious diseases, many wives, self-restraint, worried nature.

Gemini.—Wandering nature, miserable, untidy, original, thin, subtle, ingenious, strategic, few children, taste for chemical and mechanical sciences, narrow-minded, speculative, logical, desperado.

Cancer.—Poor, weak teeth, pleasure-seeking, few sons, cheeks full, slow, dull, cunning, rich, selfish, deceitful, malicious, stubborn, devoid of motherly care.

Leo.—Middle stature, severe, obstinate, few sons, stubborn, unfortunate, conflicting, hard worker, good writer, evil-minded.

Virgo.—Dark complexion, malicious, poor, quarrelsome, erratic, narrow-minded, rude, conservative, taste for public life, weak health.

Libra.—Famous, founder of institutions and the like, rich, tall, fair, self-conceited, handsome, tactful, powerful, respected, sound judgment, antagonistic, independent, proud, prominent, charitable, sub-servient to females.

Scorpio.—Rash, indifferent, hard-hearted, adventurous, petty, self-conceited, reserved, unscrupulous, violent, unhappy, danger from poisons, fire and weapons, wasteful, unhealthy.

Sagittarius.—Pushful, artful, cunning, famous, peaceful, faithful, pretentious, apparently generous, troubles with wife, courteous, dutiful children, generally happy.

Capricorn —Intelligent, harmony and felicity in domestic life, selfish, covetous, peevish, intellectual, learned, suspicious, reflective, revengeful, prudent, melancholy, inheritance from wife's parties.

Aquarius.—Practical, able, diplomatic, ingenious, a bit conceited, prudent, happy, reflective, intellectual, philosophical, vanquished by enemies.

Pisces.—Clever, pushful, gifted, polite, happy, good, wife trustworthy, scheming, wealthy, helpful.

Rahu and Ketu are *aprakasha* grahas or lustreless planets and they give the results of the lords of the house they occupy.

In the above description of the characteristics of the persons born when the different planets are in different signs, the qualities ascribed hold good only when a particular planet is not either glorified or afflicted. Results must be duly modified or qualified according to the affliction or otherwise of the planets concerned.

Leo.—Heart of Kalapurusha, inaccessible peaks and rocks, jungles and thick forests frequented by ferocious beasts, deep forests, forts, palaces, extensions, fortifications, smelters, government institutions, caves and mountains, chemical laboratories, explosives and factories, hunting places, glass factories and localities infected with beasts and birds of prey.

Virgo.—Stomach of Kalapurusha, arts, sciences, literature, meadows, grassy plains, banks, exchange places, large manu-

CHAPTER XXIII

Characteristics of the Signs and Planets

The following information will be of much use in Horary Astrology, when it is a question of ascertaining the nature of the lost goods or articles, their location, how, when, where and by whom such things were stolen or robbed, the person involved in the crime and so on. It will also assist one to obtain a clear insight into the study of Mundane and Medical Astrology.

SIGNS : Aries governs —Lands frequented by sheep and goats, jungles, caves, mountains, forests, cattlesheds, mines and places worked up by internal fires, head of *Kalapurusha* (Zodiacal Man or Time Personified).

Taurus.—Neck of the *Kalapurusha*, pastoral and cultivated fields, projecting rocks, lively tracts, wilderness, mountains, lands frequented by cattle and jungles abounding in elephants.

Gemini.—Musical and entertainment halls, brothels, dens frequented by fair girls and debauchees, shoulders of *Kalapurusha*, carpenters, parks, gambling houses, cinemas, theatres, countries, noted for special manufactures and tracts where vice is largely found, libraries, granaries, store-houses, aeroplanes.

Cancer.—Chest of *Kalapurusha*, watery places, tanks, rivers, pearls, lands, and fields of wet cultivation, canals, reservoirs, marshes, holy places, picturesque localities and sandy places.

Leo.—Heart of *Kalapurusha*, inaccessible peaks and rocks, jungles and thick forests frequented by ferocious beasts, deep forests, forts, palaces, extensions, fortifications, smelters, government institutions, caves and mountains, chemical laboratories, explosives, manufacturing places, hunting places, glass factories and localities infected with beasts and birds of prey.

Virgo.—Stomach of *Kalapurusha*, arts, sciences, literature, meadows, grassy plains, banks, exchange places, large manufacturing cities, secret organisations, industries, brothels, oceanic surface, nurseries and gambling rendezvous.

Libra.—Racing and gambling centres, abdomen, navel of *Kalapurusha*, roads, commercial places, betting places, streets, exchanges, byeways, thoroughfares, forests, planes.

Scorpio.—Sexual organ of *Kalapurusha*, natural crevices, dark retreats, caves, openings in the earth, dens, kitchens, vaults, vineyards, underground cells or constructions, strategic fortifications, molehills, places abounded by serpents, vermin and reptiles, wilderness containing anthills, orchards, stagnant pools.

Sagittarius.—Camping grounds, military retreats, chariots, armouries, cavalry, stables, army barracks, battlefields, infantry, battery lines, magazines, places of offence and defence, ammunition depots, war implements, racing grounds, sacrificial places, military stores.

Capricorn.—Rivers, forests, lakes, caves, church yards, temple precincts, tombs, sepulchres, arsenals, jungles, marshy places, waters abounding in whales and crocodiles.

Aquarius.—Marshy places, inferior grains, rendezvous of debauchees, prostitutes and vulgar folk, toddy shops, intoxicating drinks, gambling dens, mines, aeronautic machinery, drunkard localities, infamous houses, vineyards, caves.

Pisces.—Feet of *Kalapurusha*, holy shrines, altars, sacred places and rivers, tanks, all oceans, hermitages, fountains, sacred pagodas, localities frequented by *mahatmas*, pumps, cisterns, fish ponds and excessive watery tracts.

PLANETS : The Sun represents.— Soul, father, personal magnetism, patrimony, self-reliance, psychic development, political power, *Satwa guna*, Godliness, nobility, fires, windy and bilious temperaments, pomp, despotism, positions of authority, temples and places of worship, *Greeshma Ruthu*, hot and pungent tastes, goldsmiths, money-lenders, chemists, druggists, sacrificial places, coronation chambers, courage, bones, doctoring capacity.

The Moon.—Mind, mother, clothes, water, women, cultivation, seamen, travelling agents, navigators, pearls, milk, gems, vegetation, politeness, manners, juicy articles, spirit mediums, white umbrellas, fishermen, jollity, salt, watery places, bath-rooms, springs, mental happiness, blood, *Satwa guna*, stubbornness, strength of mind, the psycho-physiological consciousness, moral and religious acts, vision, water journeys, feminine tendencies, human fancies, romances, popularity and human responsibilities.

Mars.—Brothers, sisters, bile, heir-apparents, endurance, physical strength, *Thamasa guna* (mild-nature), mental power, poisonous gases, fires, firemen, warriors, stifes, scars and wounds, human impetuosity, earthquakes, military operations, weapons of offence and defence, extravagance, treasures, catastrophes, caprice, litigation, red woollen shawls, blood, deserts, mountains, forests, fortifications, cannon, sulphur, courage, southern directions, zeal and enthusiasm, prowess, manliness, chemists, druggists, gold, copper, surgeons, sapphire, corals, beasts, burning gases, dentists, fire places, brokers, burnt clothes, engineers, butchers, engines, cookrooms, iron and steel, chemical laboratories.

Mercury.—Mercantile activity, trade and trading association, wisdom, intelligence, cunning, dexterity, journalists, hawkers, accountants, mathematicians, orators, public speakers, shrewdness, ambassadors, booksellers, publishers, brokers, sexual intercourses and enjoyments, putrified and rotten things, commerce, aerial and land journeys, imports and exports, industries, poets, architecture, weaving, vegetation, beauty, elegance, inferior or base metals, wit, humour, green colour, northern direction, psychological development, refined taste, *Rajasa guna*, betel leaves, nuts and limestone.

Jupiter.—Vedas, Vedanta, preceptor, faith, devotion, honours, legal affairs, diplomacy, religiousness, guardianships, truthfulness, proficiency in arts and sciences, power of discussion, religious institutions, morality, shrines, temples, progeny, fairness, *Satwa guna*, ministers, lawyers, philosophical wisdom, asceticism, bankers, philanthropists, silver, ordinary clothes, merchants, mental calibre, corpulence, manliness, restaurants and hotels, north-eastern direction, devotion, faith, charity, respect astrology and reputation.

Venus.—Poetical, faculty, attachments, wife, children, love affairs, singers, musicians, sexual pleasures, dress, fine arts, family bliss, actors, artists, botanists, feminine grace, venereal complaints, lustre in the eyes, scandals, adulation, indolence, sycophancy, sexual intercourse, toilets, marriage, pearls, meats and intoxicating drinks, authorship, rains, bedrooms, dens of prostitutes, harems, dancing, passions, environments, south-eastern direction, lakes, foresight, variegated colours, learning, amiability, kindness, perseverance and vitality.

Saturn.—Stubbornness, impetuosity, servitude, idiosyncrasies, impediments, despondency, defects, imprisonment, obstructions, demoralisation, bondage, servants, windy diseases, evil purposes, sorrows, injuries, risks, mean acts, jails, thieves, miners, brick layers, base-tricks, negroes, drunkenness, gambling, oils, seeds, pots, woollen fabrics, architectural skill, iron, lead, inferior orders, cereals, western direction, atmosphere, conservatives, whirl-winds and storms, *Thamo guna*, hair, teeth, houses, sinners, spoils and low people.

Rahu.—Serpents, diseases, scars, courage, adventures, Christians and Mohammedans, execution, venomous reptiles, stones, mud, travellers, inventors, lecturers, widowhood, litigation, duplicity, ant-hills, goldsmiths, aviators, pumps, cracks, crevices, astrologers, scientists, thieves, sepulchres, mole-hills, hunters, archers, buttock, spies, sediments of liquor, fevers, portentous evils, radio, aerial navigation, psychologists, metaphysical students, south-western direction, men of infamous characters, inflammable gases, renunciation, epidemics, violence and corruption, sudden accidents, political plots and exiles.

Ketu.—Religion, astrology, *moksha* or final emancipation, intrigues, spiritual initiation, religious resignation, sectarian principles, artistic taste, literary geniuses, pride, dissimulation, mendicancy, bankruptcy, miserliness, ascetics, quarrels, deception, biliousness, philosophers, selfishness, occultists, skulls, religious show, assassinations, friends, charms, amulets, vicious tendencies, secret intrigues and association, backbiting.

CHAPTER XXIV

Results of Dasas and Bhuktis
(Periods and Sub-periods)

We have already learnt the method of finding the ruling period (*Vimshottari Dasa*), its balance at the time of birth and how it is succeeded by subsequent *dasas* in a particular order (*vide* Chapter XII). *Dasas* are major periods in which the indications of the planets are realised.

Say, for instance when a man will have marriage, or issues or promotion in his position, has to be determined. For marriage, the 7th house is examined and then the most beneficial planet which assures all marital happiness found out. To determine the probable period of marriage, we must find out when that particular planet assumes control over the event in preference to others so that the time of realisation may be ascertained.

A number of combinations are given below which give the probable results a particular planet will produce during its Dasa. The student must be careful in applying these principles to practical horoscopes. He must bear in mind that these should not be applied *verbatim*. The results vary according to the strength and weakness of the Dasa (main period) lord, the Bhukti (sub-period) lord and the Antara (sub-sub-period) lord.

In predicting the events in a Dasa, a Bhukti or a still minor period Antara, the general results due to the planet should be carefully weighed and incongruous results, when

ver they occur, should be avoided. It is difficult to lay down
ny particular rules which will apply in all cases. Therefore,
e give some of the important rules by way of example. The
eader may draw similar canclusions, having all the time
egard to the strength and propensity of the planet. The
esult should be consistent with the person for whom it is
ntended, under the condition of life in which he is brought
p as well as the physical possibility at the time. For instance
olitical success may be predicted in the Dasa of the Sun, if
e is in Aries in the 10th house. This political success will be
t its maximum provided the Sun is not aspected by malefics
nd his position is equally strong in the Navamsa. If he is
spected by Saturn who may be in Aquarius, then in spite of
he Sun being in Aries, complete political success cannot be
nd ought not to be predicted.

The lord of the Dasa has a quality of his own stamped
pon him. This will again be modified by the nature of the
ouse, the nature of the sign, the nature of the aspecting
odies, the nature of the lord of the constellation the Dasa
ord is in, the favourable and unfavourable situation of the
ord of Dasa in the Navamsa and various other factors.

In general we may say :

1. The Dasa period of Saturn, if it happens to be the 4th
)asa, will be unfavourable.

2. The Dasa period of Jupiter will be unfavourable if it
appens to be the 6th Dasa.

If Saturn and Jupiter are strong and favourably disposed,
he evil effects get considerably modified.

3. The Dasa period of the lords of the 6th and the 8th
roduce harmful results unless they acquire beneficence
therwise.

4. The Dasa periods of planets in *Bhava sandhis* (junc-
ional points) will be unable to produce their full results.

5. In the course of a Dasa, a planet produces such results as it indicates by virtue of ownership, association, location and aspect. For instance, favourable position of the lord of the 2nd will give good income and wealth during his Dasa.

6. The Dasa results stand to be modified by the effect of *Gochara* or transiting planets.

7. When *Lagna* (Ascendant) is powerful, during the Dasa of lord of Lagna, favourable results can be expected to occur —such as rise in profession, good health and general prosperity.

8. Lord of the 2nd in his Dasa gives wealth.

9. Lord of the 3rd during his Dasa gives new friend. help to brothers, leadership, and physical pain (if afflicted).

10. If the lord is well placed as already explained above, he will do good regarding the house or houses with which he may have anything to do either by way of ownership or aspect or location during his period, while if the lord is weak and ill-placed, he will inflict misery.

11. The periods of lords of the 5th and the 9th are said to be good, so much so that the periods of planets, which are joined or otherwise related with them, are also supposed to give rise to good.

12. The general effect of the *Dasa* (major period) get modified by the planet that rules the particular *Bhukti* (sub-period). In such a case, however, the influences of both the planets are to be compounded and the relation between them taken into account

13. During the Dasa period of a malefic planet when the sub-period of a planet ruling the 3rd, the 5th or the 7th star (reckoned from the natal star) is in progress, the subject will have a period of trial and tribulation.

14. Unfavourable results will be realised when the sub-lord and the major lord are situated in the 6th and the 8th or the 12th and the 2nd from each other respectively.

15. The sub-period of the lord of the 5th in the major period of the lord of the 9th or *vice versa* is supposed to produce good effects.

These are all general principles and they should not be applied *verbatim*. No Dasa can prove exclusively beneficial or exclusively harmful. For a fuller appreciation see *How to Judge a Horoscope*. I give below general results produced during the Dasas and Bhuktis of different planets.

The Sun's Dasa—6 years

The Dasa of the Sun in Aries in deep exaltation.—Sudden gains in cattle and wealth, much travelling in eastern countries, residence in foreign countries, quarrels among friends and relations, pleasure trips and picnic parties and company of beautiful women. *Moolatrikona.*— Birth of children, much respect from high personages, gains in cattle and money, acquisition of power and political success. *Taurus.*—Increase in landed properties, fame among relations and friends, cultivation of love and reverence for holy people and saints. *Gemini.*—Much wealth, education, inclination to interest oneself in music and such other fine arts, and generally happy and cheerful. *Cancer.*—Political success, always gay and happy, travelling in foreign countries and increase in lands, houses and wealth. *Leo.*— Respect from kings and noble personages, righteous conduct, birth of children and respect among children. *Virgo.*—Suffering off and on from physical complaints, loss of cattle, wealth and house and misunderstandings with close relatives and friends. *Libra.*—Reduced to poverty, troubled by enemies, failure in undertakings, death of brothers and friends and miserable and complicated life. *Scorpio.*—Starting new schemes and enterprises, realisation of many ambitious things, travelling in hilly tracts and countries. *Sagittarius.*—Happiness, success

in undertakings, good health, destruction of enemies, satis-
faction in every way. *Capricorn.*—A wandering life, loss of
patrimony, self-respect and good name, misunderstanding
among his own people. *Aquarius.*— Mental worries, loss or
illness to wife, loss of property and wealth. *Pisces.*—Gains
in wealth, auspicious celebrations, respect among relations,
increase in family members and smooth sailing in every way.
Sthanabala (Positional Strength).— Gains from cultivation
lands, conveyances, general happiness, good reputation and
meritorious work and pilgrimages to holy shrines. *Digbala
(Directional Strength).*—Respect from many directions, happiness, power and pecuniary success. *Kalabala (Temporal
Strength).*—Respect among rulers, success in lands and cultivation. *Naisargikabala (Natural Strength).*—Unsolicited
pleasures and enjoyment of articles of comfort, pleasure trips
and excursions and much respect. *Chestabala (Motional
Strength).*—Birth of children, felicity and harmony in married
life, financial gains and success in speculation.

Bhuktis or Sub-periods in Sun's Dasa

The Sun's sub-period—3 months, 18 days.

Unpleasantness with relatives and superiors, anxieties,
headache, pain in the ear, some tendency to urinary or kidney
troubles, sickness, fear from rulers and enemies, fear of death,
loss of money, danger to father if the Sun is afflicted, stomach-
ache and travels, gains through religious people, mental
sufferings, a wandering life in a foreign country.

The Moon's sub-period—6 months.

Winning favour from superiors, increase in business, fresh
enterprises, troubles through women, eye troubles, many
relatives and friends, indulgence in idle pastimes, jaundice
and kindred ailments, new clothes and ornaments, will be
happy, healthy, good meals, respect among relatives.

Mars' sub-period—4 months, 6 days.

Rheumatic and similar troubles, quarrels, danger of enteric fever, dysentery, troubles to relatives, loss of money by thefts or wasteful expenses, failures, acquisition of wealth in the form of gold and gems, royal favour leading to prosperity, contraction and transmission of bilious and other diseases, mental worries, danger from fire, ill-health, loss of reputation, sorrow.

Rahu's sub-period –10 months, 24 days.

Many troubles, changes according to the position of Rahu, family disputes, journeys, pang of death, trouble from relatives and enemies, loss of peace or mental misery, loss of money, sorrows, unsuccessful in all attempts, fear of thieves and reptiles, scandals.

Jupiter's sub-period—9 months, 18 days.

Benefits from friends and acquaintances, increase in education, employment in high circles, association with people of high rank, success through obstacles, birth of a child, wealth got through sons (if there is a son), honour to religious people, virtuous acts, good traditional observances, good society and conversations, reputation, gains and court-honours.

Saturn's sub-period—11 months, 12 days.

Constant sickness to family members, new enemies, some loss of property, bodily ailments, much unhappiness, displacement from home accidents, quarrels with relatives, loss of money, disease, lacking in energy, ignoble calls, mental worries, loans, danger from thieves and rulers.

Mercury's sub-period—10 months, 6 days.

Gain in money, good reputation, acquisition of new clothes and ornaments, new education, trouble through relatives, mental distress, depression of spirits, waste of money and nervous weakness, no comforts, friends becoming

enemies, much anxiety and fears, health bad, children ungrateful, disputes and trouble from ruler or judge, suffer
disgrace, many short journeys and wanderings.

Ketu's sub-period—4 months, 6 days.

Loss of money, affliction of mind with troubles, faintings
or nervous exhaustion, mind full of misgivings, a long journey
to a distant place, change of house due to disputes, troubles
among relatives and associates, throat disease, mental anguish,
ophthalmia, serious illness, fear from kings or rulers and
enemies, diseases, cheated by others.

Venus' sub-period—1 year.

Gain of money, respect by rulers and gain of vehicles,
likelihood of marriage, increase of property, illness, does
many good works, acquisition of pearls or other precious
stones, fatigue, addiction to immoral females and profitless
discussions.

The Moon's Dasa—10 Years

The Moon in Aries.—Physical and mental happiness,
gains in wealth and perfect contentment. *Taurus.*—Increase
in fame and name, collection of enormous wealth, mental and
physical happiness. *Gemini.*—Progress in education and
acquiring of much immovable and movable properties. *Cancer*.
—Addition in wealth, success in litigation, unexpected findings
of treasure, travels. *Leo.*—Progress in education, much gains
from unexpected sources. *Virgo.*—Death of serious illness to
mother, worries from enemies and swindlers, mental and
physical restlessness. *Libra.*—Gains in wealth, increase in
friends, visits to holy places and shrines, realisation of
schemes and destruction of enemies. *Scorpio.*—Fear from
political heads, destruction of relatives, disappointments in
every respect, loss of wealth, liberty and honour at risk and
much mental uneasiness. *Sagittarius.*—Domestic happiness

and felicity, celebration of happy functions, accumulation of wealth and undisturbed progress of normal private affairs. *Capricorn.*—Increase in lands and houses and wealth, success in every new enterprise, pilgrimages to holy places and success in litigation. *Aquarius.*—Destruction of property, fear from political authorities, mental worries from enemies, misunderstandings among relatives and friends. *Pisces.*—Taking charges of fresh office, reciting religious texts and moral codes and easy access to anything coveted without effort. *Ascendant.*—The Moon's Dasa produces charitable feeling and good friends. *Avaroha (moving from exaltation to debilitation).*—Losses and troubles to wife, mental worry and illness, displeasure of his own people, fear from rulers, wells, poisons and the like. *Neecha (debilitation).*—Losses and troubles from various sources and mental worry. *Moolatrikona.*—Respect among rulers, money gains, acquisition of landed property, much happiness and sexual enjoyment.

Bhuktis in the Moon's Dasa

The Moon's sub-period—10 months.

Devoted attention to learning, love or music, good clothings, company of refined society, sound health, good reputation, journey to holy places, acquisition of abandoned wealth, power, vehicles and lands; marriage, reletives, fortunate deeds, inclination to public life, change of residence, birth of a child, increase of wealth, prosperity to relatives.

Mars' sub-period—7 months.

Quarrels and litigation among friends and relatives, headlong enterprises, danger of disputes between husband and wife, between lovers or in regard to marital affairs ; disease, petulence, loss of money, waste of wealth, trouble from brothers and friends, danger from fever and fire, injury from instruments or stones, loss of blood and disease to household animals.

Rahu's sub-period—1 year, 6 months.

Distress of risks from falls and dangerous diseases, waste of wealth and loss of relatives and no ease to body, loss of money, danger of stirring up enemies, sickness, anxiety, enmity of superiors and elders, anxiety and troubles through wife, scandals, change of residence, diseases of skin, danger from thieves and poison, ill-health to father and mother, suffering from hunger.

Jupiter's sub-period—1 year, 4 months.

Increase of property, plenty of food and comforts, prosperous, benefits from superiors such as masters or governors, birth of a child, vehicles, abundance of clothes and ornaments and success in undertakings, patronage of rulers, gain of property, respect, learned.

Saturn's sub-period – 1 year, 7 months.

Wife's death or separation, much mental anguish, loss of property, loss of friends, ill-health, mental trouble due to mother, wind and bilious affections, harsh words, and discussion with unfriendly people, disease due to indigestion, no peace of mind, quarrels with relatives.

Mercury's sub-period—1 year, 5 months.

Acquisition of wealth from maternal relatives, new clothes and ornaments, settlement of disputes, pleasure through children or lover, increase of wealth, accomplishment of desires, intellectual achievements, new education, honour from rulers, general happiness, enjoyment with females, addiction to betting and drinks.

Ketu's sub-period—7 months.

Illness to wife, loss of relatives, suffering from stomach ache, loss of property, sickness of a feverish nature, danger from fire, subject to swellings or eruptions, eye troubles, mind filled with cares, public criticism or displeasure, dishonour, danger to father, mother and children, scandals among equals, eating of prohibited food, bad acts, bad company, loss of money and memory.

Venus' sub-period—1 year, 8 months.

Sudden gain from wife, enjoys comforts of agriculture, water products and clothing ; suffers from diseases inherited by mother, sickness, pain, loss of property, enmity, gain of houses, good works and good meals, birth of children, expenses due to marriage or other auspicious acts.

The Sun's sub-period - 6 months.

Feverish complaints, pains in the eyes, success or failure according to position of the Sun and the Moon, legal power, free from diseases, decadence of enemies, happiness and prosperity, jaundice, dropsy, fever, loss of money, travels, danger to father and mother, piles, weakness, loss of children and friends.

Mars' Dasa—7 years

Mars in Aries.—Acquisition of wealth, increase in reputation and respect, much gain. *Taurus.*—Destruction of enemies, success in all struggles, respect from elders and rulers and good produce from lands. *Gemini.*—Access to great wealth, precious stones and metals, agricultural success, general success in all undertakings. *Cancer.*—Danger from enemies, of honour and reputation, domestic disharmony and misunderstandings among brothers or close relatives. *Leo.*—Happy and successful all through the period of 7 years, taste in fine arts and material gains through them, increase of income from house and lands. *Virgo.*— Beneficial results, successful termination of educational pursuits, ability to address meetings and deliver lectures, and happiness from relatives and friends. *Libra.*—Most miserable life, misunderstandings with cousins and brothers, death of wife and children, loss of wealth and grains and mortgaging of landed property. *Scorpio.*—Increase in wealth, good earnings, friendship and intimacy with exalted personages, love for own people, always happy and active. *Sagittarius*.—Earnings from political or royal sources, courting their friendships, destruction of enemies and realisation of all hopes and desires. *Capricorn*.—Success in battles and respect for military skill, gains from quadrupeds and increase in wealth. *Aquarius*.—Great hardships and difficulties, misunderstandings with rulers and the immediate superiors in office, unpleasant relations with mother and servants. *Pisces*.—Much wealth, general success and happiness, bumper crops in lands, prosperity and acquisition of house and business, respect as a learned man, great reputation.

Bhukti's in Mars' Dasa

Mars' sub-period—4 months, 27 days.

Great heat, dislike of friends, annoyance from brothers and sisters, danger from rulers, failure of all undertakings, danger of hurts according to the sign held by *Kuja*, trouble with superiors and some anxiety through strangers, foreigners or people abroad and through warlike clan. Danger of open violence, quarrel with relations, loss of money, skin disease, consumption, loss of blood, fistula, and fissures in anus, loss of females and brothers, evil doings and boils.

Rahu's sub-period—1 year, 18 days.

Danger from rulers and robbers, loss of wealth, success in evil pursuits, suffering from poisonous complaints, loss of relatives, danger from skin diseases, change of residence, some severe kind of cutaneous disease, journey to a foreign country, scandals, loss of cows and buffaloes, illness to wife, loss of memory, fear from insects and thieves, falls into well, fear from ghosts, affection of gonorrhoea, fretting and litigation.

Jupiter's sub-period—11 months, 6 days.

Loss of wealth, enemies, end the unfortunate period, favour from superiors and persons in position, gain of money, birth of children, auspicious celebrations, acquisition of wealth through holy people, freedom from illness, public reputation, ascendancy and happiness.

Saturn's sub-period—1 year, 1 month, 9 days.

Loss of money, diseases, loss of relatives and danger from arms or operation, illness leading to misery, evil threatened by enemies and robbers, disputes with rulers, loss of wealth, quarrel, disputes, litigation, loss of property, cutaneous effects, loss of office or position and much anxiety.

Mercury's sub-period—11 months, 27 days.

Marriage or inclination to marriage, knowledge and fruits of knowledge, wealth, bodily evils disappear, slander, fear of insects, poisoned by animals and insects, gain of wealth by trade, abundance of houses, trouble from enemies and mental worries, service rendered to friends and relatives, new knowledge, success in litigation.

Ketu's sub-period—4 months, 27 days.

Enmity and quarrels with low people, loss of money due to evil works, commission of signs, great sufferings due to troubles from relatives and brothers and opposition of bad people, family disputes, troubles with one's own kindred, diseases, piosonous complaints, trouble through women, many enemies.

Venus' sub-period—1 year, 2 months.

Acquisition of property, gain of money, domestic happiness, successful love affairs, inclination towards religious observances and festivities, favourable associations, influenced by priests, skin eruptions, boils, pleasure from travelling, jewels to wife, clothings, money from relatives and brothers, odium.of females and their society, increase of intelligence, enjoyment of females and gain of money.

The Sun's sub-period—4 months, 6 days.

Gain of money in bad ways, destruction of enemies, good reputation, long journey to foreign lands and peace of mind, blame, odium of elders, quarrels with them, sufferings by diseases, heartache occasioned by one's own relatives, fever or other inflammatory affection, danger of fire, troubles through persons in position, many enemies.

The Moon's sub-period—7 months.

Profit, acquisition of wealth, house renovated or some improvements effected in it, comforts of wealth, heavy sleep, ardent passion, enjoyment by the help of women.

Rahu's Dasa—18 Years

Rahu in Aries.—Auspicious celebrations in the house, recitations of sacred texts, acquisition of tracts of land, perfect domestic happiness, respect from rulers and a life of harmony in every respect. *Taurus.*—Pilgrimages to shrines and holy places, increase in philosophical knowledge, entertainments, gains from cattle and dealings with quadrupeds. *Gemini.*—Multiplication of enemies, always peevish and short-tempered, fear from police and magistrates, sickness to wife and family, misunderstandings and disfavour. *Cancer.*—Serving the suffering, humanitarian propaganda, zeal and enthusiasm for national service, gains and increase in wealth, riches and honour and great reputation. *Leo.*—Fear of imprisonment of fraud and deception or misappropriation or political offences, destruction of property and mental worries distractions. *Virgo.*—Gain in wealth, general prosperity and success, acquisition of new lands, elevation to exalted positions, respect for learning, sexual happiness and domestic harmony, birth of children and sudden access to much wealth. *Libra.*—Destruction of property, loss of wealth, waste of agricultural products, loss of position, fear of imprisonment, residence in foreign countries—rather in exile, many miseries, hardships, business failure, litigation troubles and physical and mental sufferings. *Scorpio.*—Rahu is debilitated here and as such, causes great havoc to the native. The results in Rahu's Dasa will be :—abortion, loss of children, inclination to bid farewell to moral aspect of life, failure in business enterprises and mental discontentment. *Sagittarius.*—Acqisition of wealth, sudden and unexpected gain without effort, great success in any undertakings, loss of near and dear relatives and mental unrest. *Capricorn.*—Sudden promotions to higher positions, recognition of one's merits by the State and rulers, marriage festivities at home, increase of wealth and general prosperity. *Aquarius.*—Orphanage, disappointments, mental derangement and affection, sorrowful news, loss of wife or children, premature death and mean instincts. *Pisces.*—Great fear in life from thieves, swindlers and such people, inclination to matrimonial alliance, progress of education, some gains, ill health and mental uneasiness. Rahu in Pisces gives mixed results—his position, *viz.*, whether he is in a friendly or unfriendly sign, in the house of loss or gain, wife or children, etc., should be correctly determined. These results are merely general and are to be modified with reference to the planet's correct position and the exact nature of strength or weakness it has to its credit.

Bhuktis in Rahu's Dasa

Rahu's sub-period—2 years, 8 months, 12 days.

Disturbance in mind, anxieties, quarrels among relatives, death of partner, master or the head of the family, mental anxiety, danger of poisoning, transfer, all sorts of scandals and quarrels, fever, bites of insects or wounds by arms, death of ralatives, going to court as witness, quarrels with parents, diseases, illness to wife, failure of intellect, loss of wealth, wandering in far-off countries and distress there.

Jupiter's sub period—2 years, 4 months, 24 days.

Total disappearance of enemies and sickness, royal favour, acquisition of wealth, birth of children, increase of pleasure, gain through nobles or persons in power, benefits and comforts from superiors, success in all efforts, marriage in the house, increase of enemies, litigations and dips in sacred rivers.

Saturn's sub-period—2 years, 10 months, 6 days.

Scandal, danger due to fall of a tree, bad associations, divorce of wife or husband, incessant disputes and contests, rheumatism, biliousness, etc., throughout; disease due to wind and bile, distress of relatives, friends and well-wishers, residence in a remote foreign land.

Mercury's sub-period—2 years, 6 months, 18 days.

Many friends and relatives, wife and children, accession to wealth or royal favour. In the first 18 months of this period very busy, seriously inclined to marry. In the latter 12 months, enemies increase through his own action, happiness, birth of children, acquisition of vehicles, happiness to relatives and family, enjoyments with prostitutes, showy, gains through trade, fraudulent schemes.

Ketu's sub-period—1 year, 18 days.

Danger, disease in the anus, no good and timely meals, epidemic diseases, danger of physical hurts and poison, ill-health to children, some swellings in the body, troubles through wife, danger from superiors, loss of wealth and honour, loss of children, death of cattle and misfortunes of all kinds.

Venus' sub period—3 years.

Accession to vehicles and things of foreign land, troubles from foes, relatives and diseases, acquisition of wealth and other advantages, friendly alliances, wife a source of fortune and happiness, benefits from superiors or heads above in office, liable to deception, false friends, gain in land, birth of a child or marriage.

The Sun's sub-period—10 months, 24 days.

Hot fevers, giddiness, fear and enmity of people, quarrels in family, benefits from persons in good position, fear and suspicion in connection with wife, children and relatives, change of position or residence, love of charitable acts, contentment, cessation of all violence and outrage of contagious diseases, success in examinations, private life happy, much reputation and fame, but mental unrest.

The Moon's sub-period—1 year, 6 months.

Abundance of enjoyments, good crops, coming in of money and communion with kith and kin, loss of relatives, loss of money through wife, pains in the limbs, change of position or residence, danger of personal hurts, unstability of health, sea voyages, gain of lands and money, loss or danger to wife and children.

Mars' sub-period—1 year, 18 days.

Danger from rulers, fires or thieves and by arms, defeat in litigation, loss of money due to cousins, difficulties, sorrows, danger to the person due to malice of enemies, tendency to ease or dissolute habits, disputes and mental anxiety, combination of all possible calamities, bewilderment in every work and culpable failure of memory.

Jupiter's Dasa—16 Years

Jupiter in Aries.—Acquisition of landed property, general prosperity and success in all undertakings and litigations, elevation to a responsible office or appointment as a trustee and great respect from his or her own people. *Taurus.*—If a king or a president—access to new territories, fresh treaties and pacts, if an ordinary person—acquisition of wealth, establishment of business on a firm foundation, gains in trade and agriculture, increase in lands and cattle, respect from friends and foes. *Gemini.*—Death of wife if married or sweet heart, loss of children, brothers and cousins, deportation, fear from rulers and mental uneasiness. *Cancer.*—Jupiter is exalted here and gives all beneficial results such as much political success, promotions, exalted positions, humanitarian work, national service, acquisition of wealth from unexpected sources and without efforts, journalistic success, minister of education or lands and perfect harmony in domestic life. *Leo.*—Respect from rulers, gain of lands, much agricultural produce, and realisation of one's own desires and ambitions. *Virgo.*—Residence in foreign countries, destruction of wife and property, loss of wealth, misunderstandings among relatives, strife, body ill-health and symptoms of nervous troubles and diseases. *Libra.*—Residence in desolate places, dissolute and shameful life, active part in perverted social reform, selfish interests, great and unbearable difficulties and troubles, tendency to create factions in societies and families. *Scorpio.*—Mental calm and happiness, acquisition of new lands and estates, undisturbed progress and religious worship and philosophical discourses and triumph of spiritual influences over sensual passions, reputation at stake if aspected by malefics. *Sagittarius.*—Many sons, much wealth, success in every undertaking, increase in relations and family members, widespread fame and perfect happiness. *Capricorn.*—Death or illness of children, wife always ill, loss of property, reputation and self-respect, irreligious acts, sacrilegious attacks upon sacred institutions, predominance of mean motives, liable to prosecution and the upspringing of numerous enemies. *Aquarius.*—Consumption and fear from wild beasts, animals, bad luck, many hardships and loss of wealth. *Pisces.*—Much fame throughout this long period of 16 years, high education and gain from exhibition of knowledge, acquisition of property and general success and happiness.

Bhuktis in Jupiter's Dasa

Jupiter's sub-period—2 years, 1 month, 18 days.

Increase of property, domestic happiness, benefit from employment or occupation, birth of children, reputation, good meals, good deeds, health, royal favour, great diligence, success in all attempts, travels, dips in sacred rivers, pilgrimage, honour at stake if afflicted.

Saturn's sub-period 2 years, 6 months, 12 days.

A feeling of aversion, mental anguish, waste of wealth through sons, failure of business, increase of wealth and prosperity, pain in the body, rheumatic pains in limbs, trouble through wife or partners, failure in profit and credit, sorrows, fears, enmity of friends and relatives, adultery, unrighteous, a witness in court, quarrels in family, mental depression, funeral ceremonies for others.

Mercury's sub-period—2 years, 3 months, 6 days.

Increase of wealth, good and auspicious works in the house, communion with relatives, happy, increase of knowledge, acquisition of wealth through trade, favour from rulers, material comforts, perfect practice of hospitality, gain through knowledge in fine arts, birth of a well-favoured child, advantages from superiors.

Ketu's sub-period—11 months, 6 days.

Pilgrimages to holy shrines, increase of wealth, suffering for the sake of several seniors and rulers, death of partner if in business, change of residence, separation from relatives and friends, may forsake business, poisonous effects, loss of wealth, destruction of work, illness, boils.

Venus' sub-period—2 years, 8 months.

Appointment, wealth, reputation, gain of money, savings, development of sons and grandsons, jewels, good and delicious meals, marital happiness, auspicious works, reunion of the family, good success in profession or business, gain of land in the month of Taurus or Libra, much enjoyment, relatives, friends, peace of mind, acquisition of valuables, troubles from females and odium of public.

The Sun's sub-period - 9 months, 18 days.

Enemies, victory, ease, great diligence, coming in of wealth, royal favour and sound health, gain, good actions or fruits of good action, loss of bodily strength.

The Moon's sub-period—1 year, 4 months.

Increase of prosperity, gain of fame and fortune, acquisition of property, benefits through children, sexual intercourse with beautiful women, good meals and clothing, success and birth of a female child or marriage to some male member in the family, gain of money.

Mars' sub-period - 11 months, 6 days.

Disappointments and troubles of various kinds, loss by thefts, loss of near and dear relatives, inflammatory disease, transfer or leave, failure in hopes and business, wandering, high fever, great risks, loss of wealth and depression of mind, pilgrimage to temples, acquisition of wealth and fame, adventures.

Rahu's sub-period—2 years, 4 months, 24 days.

Income through low-caste people, apprehension of diseases, possibility of every possible calamity, deprivation of wealth.

Saturn's Dasa—19 Years

Saturn in Aries.—The worst period in a man's career, unexpected losses, disappointments in every undertaking, misunderstandings among relatives and friends and increase in the number of enemies. *Taurus.*—Success and gains in agricultural operations, much prosperity to the cattle and other domestic animals, great income, and access to things desired. *Gemini.*—Recognition of his services, great humanitarian work, profits in speculations and trade, respect from rulers, political success, reputation, fame and much general happiness.

Cancer.—Miseries and calamities, family strife, increase of enemies, trouble from relatives and physical diseases and mental affliction. *Leo.*—A period of uneasiness, distrust, disappointments and unrest, misappropriation of money and consequent prosecution if Saturn is afflicted powerfully, hatred by all and courting death as a source of relief from mental worries. *Virgo.*—Elevation to exalted positions, royal favour, business success and establishment of fame and reputation. *Libra.*—Travelling in countries inhabited by Christians and Moslems, establishment of fresh branches if proprietor of a business concern, acceptance of invitations for public lectures and great honour and respect throughout the long period of 19 years and perfect domestic happiness. *Scorpio.*—Odium of superiors, disliked and hated by all, loss of prestige, self-respect and fame and destruction and damage to property and possessions. *Sagittarius.*—Inclination to study philosophical and religious treatises and success in such studies, auspicious occasions like marriage ceremonies, etc., at home and happiness and mental peace throughout. *Capricorn.*—Increase in lands, gains in wealth and business, friendship with great and illustrious personages. *Aquarius.*—Great travelling in Western countries, success in litigation, mental happiness and acquisition of wealth. *Pisces.*—Pilgrimage to sacred shrines and holy places, indifference towards sectarian restrictions and observances, sorrows, misery and unrest.

Bhuktis in Saturn's Dasa

Saturn's sub-period— 3 years, 3 days.

Brings on diseases, troubles and torments, much mental anguish, capacity of kings and free-booters, loss of wealth, fear of poisonous effect to cattle, much sufferings to family, fever, wind or phlegm, bodily ailments and colic, body languishes, loss of money and children, serious enmities, dispute and troubles from relatives, blood and bilious complaints, quarrels in family, loss of money, mental derangement.

Mercury's sub-period—2 years, 8 months, 9 days.

Charitable works, gain of wealth, birth of children, increase of knowledge in some branch, prosperity to children, success to relatives, general prosperity, favours and approbation from superiors, increase of happiness, wealth and fame, benefits occurring from acts of piety and customary religious observances, agriculture and commerce.

Ketu's sub-period—1 year, 1 month, 9 days.

Rheumatism or sickness, danger of poison, danger from sons, loss of money, contentions and quarrels with vile and wicked people, dread of evil dreams, quarrels in family.

Venus' sub-period—3 years, 2 months.

Auspicious, general happiness, attentions and favours from others, gifts, profits in business, increase of family members, victory over enemies, success in life, goodwill of relatives, accession to wife's property and wealth.

The Sun's sub-period—11 months, 12 days.

Loss of wife and children, trouble from rulers or robbers, sinking of heart, danger of blood poisoning, haemorrhage of the generative system, chronic poisoning, intestinal swellings, affliction of the eyes, sickness even to healthy children and wife, body full of pain and disorders, danger of death, fear of death to father-in-law.

The Moon's sub-period—1 year, 7 months.

Increase in cattle, enmity of friends and relatives, cold affections, troubles and sickness, family disputes, loss of money and property, reduction to great need, mortgage of property and its recovery after a lapse of time, death of a near relative, sorrow, dislike of relatives, coming in of money, windy diseases.

Mars' sub-period—1 year, 1 month, 9 days.

Some disgrace, serious enmity, strife, much blame, wanderings from place to place, unsettled life, many enemies, loss of money by fraud or theft, change of residence, serious lness, distress to brothers and friends, hot diseases.

Rahu's sub-period—2 years, 10 months, 6 days.

Disease in every limb, loss of wealth by rulers, robbers nd foes, danger of physical hurts, various physical troubles, evers, enemies, increase of troubles.

Jupiter's sub-period—2 years, 6 months, 12 days.

Worship of gods and holy people, happiness to family, ncrease in bodily comforts, accomplishment of intentions by ne help of superiors, increase of family circles, attainment of ank.

Mercury's Dasa—17 years

Mercury in Aries.—Marriage, performance of religious and ocial work, charity, increase in religiousness and intelligence, avour of rulers, gains from cultivation, cattle, precious tones and conveyances and happiness through these. *Taurus.* -Great happiness, sexual contact with beautiful young omen, getting titles and name, ornaments and authority over en, acquaintance of sweet girls and their company and ractice of music and kindred sciences. *Gemini.*—Access to reat intellectual treasures, increase in knowledge, successful rmination of educational career, acquisition of fame and ealth, happiness from wife and children, marriage cere- onies and recitation of sacred scriptures. *Cancer.*—Degrada- on, change of residence, fines and imprisonments, penalties, onfinement in chains, hatred of relations, loss of lands, ailure of crops and enmity with all. *Leo.*—Good courage nd elevation, travelling in hilly and mountainous tracts,

acquisition of wealth from various countries, progress i
knowlenge, expeditions to mountains, caves and simila
places, marriage and great reputation. *Virgo.*—The mos
auspicious and happy period of life, favour of kings, admirer
and royal courts and great success in them, undisturbe
health, marriage in the house, increase in intelligence, rel
giousness, charitable foundings, and unexpected gains. *Libre*
—Great works published in the native's name, favour c
wealthy and educated people without effort, and leadershi
over men. *Scorpio.*—Loss of wife, children, riches, ment;
troubles, losses from merchandise, great hatred of people an
relations and loss of reputation and power. *Sagittarius.*-
Success in education, meeting with learned and religiou
people, worship of holy men, virtuous and charitable deed
travelling in Eastern countries, inclination for marital ente
prises and great exhilaration. *Capricorn.*—Success in trad
inception of new business-like trades in tanneries, leath
goods, glassware, etc., recitation of religious scriptures. God
contemplations, patronage of kings, destruction of foes ar
enemies and general success in life. *Aquarius.*—Acquisiti•
of paraphernalia, access to good and much wealth, indulgi•
in a pleasurely life and good fame and name. *Pisces.*—Troub
from thieves, dysentery, destruction of relations, litigatio
quarrels with relatives, mental derangement, nervous brea
down and failure in attempts.

Bhuktis in Mercury's Dasa

Mercury's sub-period.—2 years, 4 months, 27 days.

Acquisition of beautiful house and apparel. money throu
relatives, success in every undertaking, the birth of a brotł
or sister, increase in family, gain in business, good min
charitable acts, learning of mathematics and arts.

Ketu's sub-period—11 months, 27 days.

Sorrow, disease, loss of work and *Dharma*, bilious sickness, aimless wandering, loss of property, misfortune to relatives, troubles through doctors, mental anxiety, trouble from relatives, mental agony, loss of comfort, dread of enemy, failure in business.

Venus' sub-period—2 years, 10 months.

Observance of duty, conformable to religion and morality, acquisition of wealth, clothes and jewels, birth of good children, happiness in married state, relatives prosper, trade increases, knowledge gained, return from a long journey, if not married, betrothal in this period, health, ornaments, vehicles, house, money gained.

The Sun's sub-period—10 months, 6 days.

Pains in head and stomach, enmity of people, loss of respect, danger of fire, anxieties, sickness to wife, troubles from enemies, many obstacles, troubles through superiors, acquisition of wealth.

The Moon's sub-period—1 year, 5 months.

Loss of health, some swellings or hurts in the limbs, quarrels and troubles through women, many difficulties, gain of money through ladies and agriculture and trade, success, happiness, diseases, ill-will of enemies, miscarriage of every concern, risk from quadrupeds.

Mars' sub-period—11 months, 27 days.

Disappearance of all dangers diseases, or enemies, fame derived from acts of charity and beneficence, royal favour, danger from jaundice or bilious fever, affections of the blood, neuralgic pains and headaches, troubles through neighbours, sickness, wounds or hurts, quarrels, addiction to drinks, betting and prostitutes, boils and hurts of arms, travels in forests and villages, sorrows, royal disfavour, imprisonment.

Rahu's sub period—2 years. 6 months, 18 days.

Intercourse with servants and prostitutes, skin diseases, sufferings from hot diseases, bad company and dirty meals, change of present position, fear and danger through foreigners, disputes concerning property, failure in litigation, evil dreams, headaches, sickness and loss of appetite, wealth from friends and relatives, happiness, new earnings.

Jupiter's sub-period—2 years, 3 months 6 days.

Hatred of friends, relatives and elders, wealth, liable to diseases, acquisition of land and wealth, gain by trade, reputation, good happiness, good credit, benefits from superiors, birth of a child or marriage.

Saturn's sub-period—2 years, 8 months, 9 days.

Bad luck, stranger to success and happiness, severe reversal, enmity, pain in the part governed by Saturn, downfall or disgrace to relatives, mind full of evil forebodings and distress, fear from diseases, loans, loss of children, destruction of family, scandals, troubles from foreigners, earnings through evil ways, acts of charity and beneficence, acquisition of wealth, material comforts through petty chiefs, failure in agricultural operations.

Ketu's Dasa —7 years

Ketu in Aries.—Disgrace, troubles from relatives, loss of property, cattle and other domestic animals, constant travels in Eastern countries, great hardship, sudden quarrels, loss of mother and wife or their serious sickness, want of prudence and capacity in private matters. *Taurus.*—Many dangers, death of wife, acquisition of wealth through evil ways and means, sexual sorrows, visits to sacred shrines and holy waters, inclination to religious study and success in it, compunction and in the end appeasing sins by resort to foul stratagems. *Gemini.*—Good health, happiness, elevation to responsible and exalted positions, founding of sacred institutions, good food, advent of relations and in later years venereal troubles, death of near relation and loss of reputation and self-respect. *Cancer.*—Many dangers, disturbances from his place and a period of exile, serious sickness to wife, parents or children, and if badly afflicted, their death, quarrels with friends, initiation into the mysteries of philosophical knowledge. *Leo.*—Increase of lands, cultivation, progress in education, heated debates and discussions on philosophical and scientific subjects with great scholars and eminent people, attracted by females and company with them, travels in mountainous tracts and hilly countries to spread any righteous cause, and treated to great musical entertainment. *Virgo.*—Fear from fires, weapons and poisonous gases, beasts and reptiles, destruction of dear lives, properties and self-respect, unrighteous acts and nasty venereal complaints. *Libra.*—Happiness and prosperity to wife or husband, self and children, enmity of relations, gains from gold and precious stones, headache, heart disease, nervous breakdown, trouble in the anus and much discontent. *Scorpio.*—Living dependent on relations, sycophant acts, acquisition of much wealth, loss of few children, gains from lands, contraction of new friendship from among the members of the fair sex and liable to suffer from venereal complaints. *Sagittarius.*—Perfect domestic harmony and happiness, favour from aristocrats, progress in education, religious discussions, moral elevation and manifestation of a spirit of tolerance and equality. *Capricorn.*—Misappropriation of private and governmental funds and consequent prosecution, wife or husband catching consumption and such diseases, death of a few children, anxiety about everything, misunderstanding with relations and disgrace and disappointments. *Aquarius.*—Hating all and hated by all, incurring the displeasure of superiors, pessimistic about every hope, abject dependency and servile flattery; in the end, happiness and prosperity to wife and children. *Pisces.*—Learned discussions, general success, helping the suffering, mental depression, promotion, acquisition of fertile lands, favour of the superiors and moneyed people, moral and religious devotions, vigorous and clear understanding, travel on water to distant countries and respect there.

Bhuktis in Ketu's Dasa

Ketu's sub-period—4 months, 27 days.

Fear of death of wife or children, loss of wealth and happiness, mental troubles, separation from relatives, subject to some estrangement, restraint or detention, danger of poison.

Venus' sub-period - 1 year, 2 months.

Wealth and happiness, birth of a child, efforts crowned with success, in the end sickness, wife ill, illness to children, quarrels, loss of relatives and friends, fever and dysentery.

The Sun's sub-period—4 months, 6 days.

Disappointment, physical pain, exile in foreign country, peril and obstruction in every business, increase of knowledge, sickness in family, long journey and return, anxiety about wife's health.

The Moon's sub-period—7 months.

Disputes about "fair sex", trouble through children, gains and financial success, diseases of biliousness and cold, loss of relatives and money, destruction of wealth and distress of mind.

Mars' sub-period—4 months, 27 days.

Odium of sons, wife and younger brothers, loss of relatives, trouble from diseases, foes and bad rulers, path of progress obstructed, fear and anxiety, disputes and contests of different kinds, enemies arise, danger of disputes and destruction through females, sufferings from fever, fear of

obbers, death, imprisonment, urinary diseases, loss and diffi-
ulties and surgical operations.

Rahu's sub-period—1 year, 18 days.

Loss of lands, imprisonment, quarrel with friends, danger
f blood poisoning, danger of ruin, loss of property, fame
nd honour, fear of kings and robbers, sorrow, ruin of all
usiness, adultery with mean women.

Jupiter's sub-period—11 months, 6 days.

Exemption from ailments, acquisition of lands and birth
f children, profitable transactions, association with people of
good position, danger of poison, wife an object of pleasure,
f unmarried marriage takes place.

Saturn's sub-period—1 year, 1 month, 9 days.

Loss of wife, danger from enemies, imprisonment, loss of
wealth, indigestion, property in danger of ruin, heavy loss in
different ways, change of residence, some cutaneous diseases,
anxiety owing to sickness of partner misgivings in the heart,
mental anguish, difference of opinion with relations, exile in
foreign countries.

Mercury's sub-period—11 months 27 days.

Society of relatives, friends and the like, material gains
from knowledge, danger from relatives, anxiety on account of
children, failure in plans, deception, jealousy, falsehood, and
knowledge.

Venus' Dasa – 20 Years

Venus in Aries.—Residence in palatial buildings, acquaintance with noble personages, wearing good clothes, good
earnings, spread of fame, much respect, birth of child, happy
sexual relations and praised by friends and enemies. *Taurus*.—
A life of great ease and indulgence throughout the period of
20 years, enjoyment of much happiness, company of beautiful
girls and joy through association with them, travels on seas

to foreign countries particularly southern, all ambitions o
life fairly realised, redemption from debts, symptoms o
venereal troubles. *Gemini.*—Gain of territory. affordin
protection to brothers, sisters, cousins and paternal uncle
and aunts, gain of vehicles, increase of reputation, children
harmony with wife, mental peace and a check over inclinatio
to indulge in loose life. *Cancer.*—Paroxysms of grief and
terror, destruction of property, discontent with relations, in
crease of enemies, loss of wealth, disturbance to good work
and some mental ease in the end. *Leo.*—Mental disease and
sorrow, troubles from fires, poisons and hurts, evil women,
foul language and mental disorder, exile, and aimless wanderings in deserts and woods to evade detection by law, dangerous
sickness to the better half or a child, stigma on self-respect
due to mean fellows and inclination to conceal true identity.
Virgo—Quarrels with wife or husband and separation from
him or her, mortgage of all property, trouble in the generative
organ often leading to surgical operation, symptoms of
arthritis, troubles relating to nervous breakdown, mental
unrest, separation from relatives and friends and much grief
and sorrow. *Libra.*—Great reputation, gain of wealth from
royal patronage, comforts, good enjoyment of life, luxurious
invitations and worships of mammon and a period of extreme
sensuality. *Scorpio*—Hatred for all, many miseries and
troubles, serious risks, vengeance against relatives, loss of
wealth and property, mental affliction and imbalance. *Sagittarius.*—Much fame and name, religious and philosophical
studies, recitation of sacred writings, regard for holy people
and ascetics, success in any undertaking and general prosperity. *Capricorn.*—Travels in foreign lands, freedom from
domestic worries, discussion with learned people, progress
in general education, acquaintance with low class people,
development of perverted ideas of social or religious reform

and success in all endeavours. *Aquarius.*—Acquisition of fresh property, a good library, lands and houses, honours and unexpected gains, love for Christian or Islamic literature and its studies, stray intercourse with servile women, domestic happiness and harmony. *Pisces.*—High political power and great success, promotion to responsible office, acts of charity and generosity, exercise of prudence in official matters and perfect happiness in domestic life and smooth-sailing in every respect.

Bhuktis in Venus' Dasa

Venus' sub-period—3 years, 4 months.

Success, good servants and good many pleasures, money plentiful, disappearance of enemies, attainment of fame and birth of children.

The Sun's sub-period—1 year.

Anxious about everything, prosperity collapses, troubles with wife, children, land, family, disputes and quarrels, diseases affecting head, belly and eyes, damage in respect of agriculture.

The Moon's sub-period—1 year, 8 months.

Gains of females, education, knowledge, money, children and vehicles, worship of God, accomplishments of desires, troubles through wife, domestic happiness afterwards, pain and disease due to inflammation of nervous tissues and from lust and other passions of human nature.

Mars' sub-period—1 year, 2 months.

Flow of bile, disease of the eyes, great exertion, much income, acquisition of wealth, marriage, acquisition of lands, venereal diseases, danger from arms, exile in foreign places, atheistic tendencies, increase of property through the influence of females, negligence of duty, bent on pleasure and passion, temporary affection of eyes.

Rahu's sub-period—3 years.

Meditation, seclusion, quarrels among relatives and his people, entire change of surroundings, schemes of deception, miserliness, acquisition of lost property, dislike of relatives, evil from friends and injury by fire.

Jupiter's sub-period—2 years, 8 months.

Means of livelihood settled, gains from profession, benefits through superiors or employers or persons ruled by Jupiter, fame, anxiety, quarrels with saints and religious men, gain of knowledge, end of dependence, worship of certain inferior natural forces, happiness and health, marriages, sexual intercourse, increase of family reputation and good deeds, wealth, ultimate happiness, wife and children suffer in the end.

Saturn's sub-period—3 years, 2 months

Sexual intercourse with females advanced in age, accession to lands and wealth, disappearance of enemies, affection of excretory system, piles, etc., rheumatic pains in legs and hands, danger to eye sight, distaste for food, loss of appetite, physical condition poor, loss of money, wanderings, servitude, bolting and gambling, addition to liquor, bad company, etc., ill-health, loss of memory, impotence.

Mercury's sub-period—2 years, 10 months.

Association with prostitutes, enjoyments, knowledge, mathematical learning, success in litigations, inclination to learn music, piles and other hot ailments, pleasure through wife and children, increase of wealth, gain of knowledge in arts and sciences, wealth, royal favour, prosperity on a large scale and sound health.

Ketu's sub-period—1 year, 2 months.

Discordance, death of relatives, injury inflicted by enemies, misgivings in heart, deprivation of wealth, troubles through wife, danger from quadrupeds, illness to partner or a member of the family, accidental blood poisoning, delirious fits, weakness in body and mind, gradual loss of wealth, loss of relatives, bad company, abode in seclusion, manifold sorrows, but happiness in the end.

A careful study of my book *How to Judge A Horoscope* is also recommended.

of the family), accidental blood poisoning, delicious fits, weakness in body and mind, gradual loss of wealth, loss of
relatives, bad company, abode in seclusion, manifold sorrows,
but happiness in the end.

A careful study of .... to Judge A Horoscope is
also recommended.

CHAPTER XXV

Source and Nature of Death

Fatalists and atheists may indulge in the hallucinations
that death is accidental, that it is merely the resolution of the
component elements of the human body into their former
states and that it signifies an end to the activities of the soul
as it becomes incorporated with the general ethereal currents;
but in reality it does not seem to be so. There is much significance attached to this by the Hindus as well as other people
believing in the existence of a Creator without whose knowledge "not even a sparrow falls to the ground".

Death does not come all of a sudden; neither does birth
take place so. Man does not come from nothingness and
disappear into the regions of annihilation. Some mysterious
and subtle power seems to control regulate the various phases
of human existence, like birth, life and death, operating in a
definite order and often transcending reason, logic and commonsense. The presence and operation of this power is
demonstrable by everyday occurrences.

Here comes the importance of the laws of *Karma* and the
laws of continuity and evolution. The Hindus grant the
existence of worlds other than our own and the possibility of
the soul migrating into good or bad states of future existence
after death, according as the *Karma* done in this world is good
or bad. As Socrates puts it, death is either the cessation of
all human activities or the migration of the soul into a happier
region.

Philosophers say that death is a state of transition for the soul to enter into more subtle forms of existence and the duration of life in such states of existence depends upon the balance sheet of *Karma* at one's credit at the time of death here.

By ascertaining the length of life beforehand, carefully, and the nature and source of death, it may be possible to prevent many catastrophes and family strifes in this life. Some aver that it may also be possible to prolong the life, by recourse to yoga and other remedies prescribed by the ancient Maharshis. Many times the sudden death of a person leaves his widow, children and other dependents in a state of abject poverty. Adequate provision could have been made for these people if the period of death were previously ascertained.

The following information will be useful to find out the place, nature and source of death, the particular diseases which the native suffers from at the time of death, unnatural deaths by drownings, tortures, accidents, wild beasts, suicide, Murder, etc., which can be prevented, the period of unconsciousness before death, the nature of cremation or burial of the dead body, the nature of the past and future births and the possibility or otherwise of attaining *moksha* or emancipation.

The disease from which a person dies is predicted by the nature of the planet, which aspects the 8th house and the part of the body to be affected would be that represented by the 8th house in the division under *Kalapurusha* (see chapter on Medical Astrology for this division).

In other words, the humour belonging to the planet (which is given in p. 174) in the 8th house causes the particular disease which produces death. If many planets occupy the 8th house, the body will be subject to several attacks resulting from an excess of the various humours indicated by such powerful planets and death will ensue. If the Sun, the Moon, Mars,

Mercury, Jupiter, Venus or Saturn is in the 8th house, death will be due to fire, water, weapons, fever, chronic diseases, thieves or starvation respectively.

If the 8th house is a movable, a fixed or a common sign, death occurs in foreign place, own place or while travelling.

If the Sun aspects the 8th house, the disease will be developed by bile or heat; if the Moon by wind and bile; if Mars, bile or heat; if Mercury, by wind, phlegm and bile; if Jupiter, by phlegm; if Venus, by phlegm and wind; and if Saturn, by wind. If one or more of these planets occupy the 8th, disease prior to death will be from the above-mentioned sources — the sources indicated by the particular planet. If no planet occupies or aspects the 8th, then the lord of the 8th house must be considered and the nature of disease determined from the humours indicated by the particular planet.

First take the planet occupying the 8th; if no planet is there, consider the one that aspects the 8th; if no planet aspects it, then give preference to the lord of the 8th. In the illustration given below, the 8th from the Ascendant is Aries. The Sun and Venus are posited there and are powerfully

	Sun Venus		
		RASI	
Mars			
		Moon	Ascdt.

aspected by the Moon who is in the 2nd from birth and by Mars who is in the 5th. Now the diseases the native suffered from at his death must be ascertained. The Sun in the 8th—bile; Venus in the 8th—wind and phlegm; Moon aspecting the 8th—bile and wind; Mars aspecting the 8th—bile. Three planets indicated bile, two wind and one phlegm. Therefore, the native died on account of the disease caused owing to inflammation of excessive bile in the head (Aries represents head).

According to Ayurveda or the Hindu system of Medicine, the existence of these *tridoshas* (wind, bile and phlegm) in a state of harmony constitutes health and when some one or more among these *doshas* is or are increased and some others possessed of opposite attributes are diminished, the result is disease (*vide* my book *Ayurveda*, 4th Edition).

Each *dosha* (humour) causes certain diseases and the exact nature of the disease from which a person dies should be ascertained with reference to the humour attributed to the planet, ruling, posited in, or aspecting the 8th house in a horoscope.

The Sun indicates death by fevers, apoplexy, paralysis.

The Moon causes death by watery diseases, drowning, loose motions, diarrhoea, dysentery, blood impurities.

Mars brings about death by pneumonia, cholera, plague and such other epidemics, haemorrhage, bronchitis, abortion and consequent surgical operation, accidents incidental to gun-shots, etc.

Mercury makes a person die by fever of brain, smallpox, ague, nervous disorders, sleeping sickness, kala-azar, whooping cough and assaults.

Jupiter causes death by mental worry or by some unknown disease, pleurisy, liver disease, inflammation of the lungs, heart failure and sparms.

Venus indicates death by excessive thirst, fast, excessive heating, syphilis, gonorrhoea.

Saturn causes death by suffocation, burns, rheumatic fever, paralysis, melancholia and consumption.

Accidental death is caused by the following combinations. If the Sun and Mars occupy the 10th and the 4th at birth, death will be due to hurts and injuries received by stone-throwing. If Saturn, the Moon and Mars are in the 4th, the 7th and the 10th respectively, death occurs by drowning in a well or falling into it. The Sun and the Moon, in Virgo with or aspected by malefics, cause death by drinking poison or being poisoned by enemies.

Apart from the 8th house signifying the source and nature of death, certain other combinations at birth also indicate the kind of death.

When Mars and Saturn are afflicted, death occurs by suffocation. Saturn in Taurus in conjunction with a malefic indicates death by hanging. Death may occur in prison if Saturn aspects the Sun or the Moon rising. Saturn in a quadruped sign conjunction with the Sun causes death by shipwreck, fall of buildings, falls from elevations, recipices. Saturn in Cancer and the Moon in Capricorn at birth cause death by dropsy. The Moon in a sign of Mars or in Virgo with two malefics on either side brings about death by emaciation of the body. If the Moon is in Capricorn or Aquarius with malefics on either side, death will be due to suicide or fall from a mountain. Two malefics in the 5th and 9th houses with no beneficial aspects bring about death in prison. If Mars and the Sun are in the 4th, and Saturn in the 10th, the person will be crucified. The Sun in the 4th, Mars in the 10th, aspected by the weak Moon, causes death from crucifixion. If Mars, the Sun and Saturn occupy the 4th, the 7th and the 10th respectively, death occurs by fire and weapons. Saturn, the Moon and Mars in the 2nd, the 4th and the 10th respectively cause death by insect bites or wounds generated in the body. The weak Moon, the Sun and Mars in the 10th, the 7th and the 4th respectively make the person die in the midst of night-soil filth and faecal matter. Saturn in the 8th with weak Moon aspected by powerful Mars causes death by surgical operation or piles or fistula. In case the above combinations do not hold good, then the following must be applied.

The 22nd *drekkana* (decanate) declares the cause of death and the lord of that drekkana kills the person by that disease which is attributed to him as given at the beginning of this chapter. The place where death occurs will be similar to the sign occupied by the lord of the Navamsa in which the birth falls. Say the birth falls in the Navamsa of Capricorn. Its lord is Saturn. In the Rasi he is in Taurus. Therefore the nature of the place, death occurs in, will be appropriate to Taurus, *i.e.*, the place indicated by the lord of Taurus, *viz.*, Venus indicating drawing rooms well furnished with exquisite furniture and tapestry. If the lord of the sign occupied by the lord of the Navamsa, the ascendant falls in, is the Sun— the place of death will be a temple, a forest or a religious institution; if the Moon—a fertile place, with green vegetation or a garden: if Mars—hospital, operation room, special wards; if Mercury—playground, sports club, gambling den; if Jupiter—treasurehouse, public office, court, lawyer's house; if Venus—rich flats and apartments, nursing houses, and if Saturn—dirty places and dens of prostitutes.

The period, for which a person will remain unconscious before death, will be the time of oblique ascension of the remaining portion of the rising sign below horizon. This period must be double if the lord of the Ascendant aspects the birth, and trebled if benefics aspect the birth.

12

Example.—Say 25° Gemini is rising (latitude 28° N). The remaining portion of Gemini is 5°. Reference to oblique ascension tables in Appendix B gives the duration of Gemini 5 ghatis on 28° N. latitude. The time taken for 5° in Gemini to rise will be 5/30 × 5/6 ghatis or 50 vighatis or 50/60 × 2/5 = 1/3 hour or 20 minutes. Say Mercury, lord of the birth, aspects Gemini. This time must be doubled — 20 × 2 = 40 minutes. That is, the person will be unconscious for 40 minutes before he expires.

After death takes place, the nature of cremation, burial or otherwise, should be ascertained with reference to the 22nd *drekkana* (decanate). The 22nd drekkana will be the rising drekkana rather the first drekkana in the 8th house. If the 22nd drekkana is fiery, then the body will be cremated and turned to ashes. If it is a watery drekkana, the body will be thrown into rivers or tanks. If it is neither a fiery drekkana nor a watery one, the body will be uncared for and dissolved by atmospherical forces.

The final thing would be to find out the world the person has come from and whither he will go for his future existence. We do not know what exactly is the mystery underlying the phenomenon of death. But it is held by all sages that the soul will go from here to some other world after death, and this can be ascertained thus:—

The past birth can be determined by the ruler of the decanate occupied by the Sun or the Moon (whichever is more powerful) and accordingly the particular *Loka* or world where the soul has come from. Find out which is stronger out of the Sun and the Moon. If the lord of the decanate occupied by the stronger of these two planets is Jupiter—the deceased in his past birth belongs to *Deva Loka* (world of immortals). If the decanate belongs to the Moon or Venus, the person has come from *Pitru Loka* (world of manes). If the decanate belongs to the Sun or Mars, the deceased belongs to *Tiriyag*

Loka (world of lower animals). If Saturn or Mescury ist he owner of such a decanate, the person has come from *Naraka Loka* (infernal regions). In the previous birth the status or rank of the person was high, mediocre or mean and debilitated according as the lord of such a drekkana is exalted, ordinary debilitated.

The chapter on death can be brought to a close when we consider the state of future existence of a person after death.

If there are no planets in the 6th, the 7th and the 8th, find out the decanate rising in the 6th and the 8th and determine the strongest of the two. Then attribute that loka or world which is denoted by that planet ruling the above-mentioned decanate. If a planet is found in the 6th, the 7th or the 8th, then the person goes to the world, indicated by the planet. If there are two or more planets, always give preference to the strongest.

Jupiter	*Deva Loka* (world of Immortals)
Moon and Venus	*Pitru Loka* (world of Manes)
Sun and Mars	*Tiriyag Loka* (world of Lower Animals)
Saturn and Mercury	*Naraka Loka* (world of Infernal Regions)

One is said to secure *moksha* or final emancipation if Jupiter occupies 1st, 4th, 7th, 8th or 10th from the ascendant. According to Sastras, *moksha* or highest spiritual bliss is to be sought in preference to other states of existence.

Today many persons die by heart-attacks, cancer, blood pressure and other fashionable diseases peculiar to modern civilisation. By a careful study we can adapt the principles given in ancient texts to suit modern conditions and attempt forecasts of deaths due to the above diseases.

Loka (world of lower animals). If Saturn or Mescury ist he
owner of such a decanate, the person has come from
Naraka Loka (infernal regions). In the previous birth the
status or rank of the person was high, mediocre or mean
and debilitated according as the lord of such a drekkana is
exalted, ordinary debilitated.

The chapter on death can be brought to a close when we
consider the state of future existence of a person after death.

CHAPTER XXVI

The Ashtakavarga System

This is a peculiar system of ascertaining the various sources
of energy for the different planets. Ashtakavarga helps us to
determine the longevity of a person, the yearly results
produced on account of the incessant movements of the
planets changing their positions from where they were at the
time of birth and to estimate the stability or otherwise of
each Bhava or house. Planets will be found in certain
positions at the time of birth. But at any given time after
birth they will be found in different situations both from the
Ascendant and also from their own radix positions. Ashtakavarga liberally translated means eight sources of energy
for each planet including the Ascendant. Rahu and Ketu
are invariably omitted on account of their shadowy nature.
The subject-matter of Ashtakavarga is vast. I have, therefore,
extensively dealt with it in my book *Ashatakavarga System
of Prediction*. In this chapter I have given briefly important
outlines necessary for its study, without entering into details.

Supposing in a horoscope, the Sun is in Cancer. Six
months hence he will not be in Cancer, but in Sagittarius or
Capricorn and in each succeeding month he transits over a
particular sign and consequently forms different angular
positions to his own position at birth and those of other
planets. Ashtakavarga records the results of such transits.

1. The Sun is declared auspicious in the 1st, the 2nd, the
4th, the 7th, the 8th, the 9th, the 10th and the 11th houses

from himself; the same houses from Mars and Saturn; in the 5th, the 6th, the 9th and the 11th from Jupiter; the 3rd, the 6th, the 10th and the 11th from the Moon; the 3rd, the 5th, the 6th, the 9th, the 10th, the 11th and the 12th from Mercury; the 3rd, the 4th, the 6th, the 10th, the 11th and the 12th from the Ascendant; and the 6th, the 7th and the 12th from Venus. Total 48 points.

2. The benefic places of the Moon are the 3rd, the 6th, the 10th and the 11th houses from the Ascendant. The Moon is auspicious in the 2nd, the 3rd, the 5th, the 6th, the 9th, the 10th and the 11th houses from Mars; the 1st, the 3rd, the 6th, the 7th, the 10th and the 11th houses from the Moon herself; the 3rd, the 6th, the 7th, the 8th, the 10th and the 11th from the Sun; the 3rd, the 5th, the 6th and the 11th from Saturn; the 1st, the 3rd, the 4th, the 5th, the 7th, the 8th, the 10th and the 11th houses from Mercury; the 1st, the 4th, the 7th, the 8th, the 10th, the 11th and the 12th from Jupiter; and the 3rd, the 4th, the 5th, the 7th, the 9th, the 10th and the 11th from Venus. Total 49 points.

3. The benefic places of Mars will be the 3rd, the 5th, the 6th, the 10th and the 11th houses from the Sun; the 1st, the 3rd, the 6th, the 10th and the 11th houses from the Ascendant; the 3rd, the 6th, and the 11th houses from the Moon; the 1st, the 2nd, the 4th, the 7th, the 8th, the 10th and the 11th from himself; in 1, 4, 7, 8, 9, 10 and 11 from Saturn; in 3, 5, 6 and 11 from Mercury; in 6, 8, 11 and 12 from Venus; and in 6, 10, 11 and 12 from Jupiter. Total 39 points.

4. Mercury produces good in 1, 2, 3, 4, 5, 8, 9 and 11 from Venus; in 1, 2, 4, 7, 8, 9, 10 and 11 from Mars and Saturn; in 6, 8, 11 and 12 from Jupiter; in 5, 6, 9, 11 and 12 from the Sun; in 1, 3, 5, 6, 9, 10, 11 and 12 from himself; in 2, 4, 6, 8, 10 and 11 from the Moon; and in 1, 2, 4, 6, 8, 10 and 11 from the Ascendant. Total 54 points.

5. Jupiter will be auspicious in 1, 2, 4, 7, 8 10 and 11 from Mars; in 1, 2. 3, 4, 7, 8, 10 and 11 from himself: in 1, 2, 3, 4, 7, 8, 9, 10 and 11 from the Sun; in 2, 5, 6, 9, 10 and 11 from Venus; in 2, 5, 7, 9 and 11 from the Moon; in 3, 5, 6 and 12 from Saturn; in 1, 2, 4, 5, 6, 9, 10 and 11 from Mercury; and in 1, 2, 4, 5, 6, 7, 9, 10 and 11 from the Ascendant. Total 56 points.

6. Venus produces good in 1, 2, 3, 4, 5, 8, 9 and 11 from Lagna; in 1, 2, 3, 4, 5, 8, 9, 11 and 12 from the Moon; in 1, 2, 3, 4, 5, 8, 9, 10 and 11 from himself; in 3, 4, 5, 8, 9, 10 and 11 from Saturn; in 8, 11 and 12 from the Sun; in 5, 8, 9, 10 and 11 from Jupiter; in 3. 5, 6, 9 and 11 from Mercury; and in 3, 5, 6, 9, 11 and 12 from Mars. Total 52 points.

7. Saturn is beneficial in 3, 5, 6, and 11 from himself; in 3, 5, 6, 10, 11 and 12 from Mars; in 1, 2, 4, 7, 8, 10 and 11 from the Sun; in 1, 3, 4, 6, 10 and 11 from the Ascendant; in 6, 8, 9, 10, 11 and 12 from Mercury; in 3, 6 and 11 from the Moon; in 6, 11 and 12 from Venus; and in 5, 6, 11 and 12 from Jupiter. Total 39 points.

The total individual contribution of benefic points by any planet in any horoscope will be the same respective figures given above. The sum-total of all planets will be 337 points for any horoscope. This is constant.

8. These are the benefic positions. The good or bad results must be ascertained as already stated above. It is usual in preparing the Ashtakavarga Tables to denote the benefic places with a zero (0) and malefic places with a dot lines (—). Planets in *Upachaya* (3, 6, 10, 11) places, in friendly and own houses or exaltation signs produce benefic effects if such houses contain more benefic dots for the planets than malefic ones. And planets when they pass through *Apachaya* houses or unfriendly or depression signs produce malefic effects fully. The *Upachaya* and *Apachaya*

houses must be reckoned with respect to the Ascendant or the Moon and not from the positions of planets (*Apachayas* are 1, 2, 4, 5, 7, 8, 9 and 12 houses from Lagna; the rest are all *Upachayas*).

We shall make ourselves clear by applying the rules to a practical horoscope. We shall prepare the Ashtakavarga Table for the Sun in the horoscope given below.

		Moon Saturn	
Rahu ♓	♈	♉	♊
Ascdt. ♒			Sun ♋
♑	Rasi Diagram		Mars Merc. Venus ♌
♐	Jupiter ♏	♎	Ketu ♍

The first from Cancer, where the Sun is found, is Cancer itself; the 2nd is Leo; the 4th Libra; the 7th Capricorn; the 8th Aquarius; the 9th Pisces; the 10th Aries; and the 11th Taurus. So when the Sun passes through these signs, he will produce beneficial results and accordingly in the Sun's Ashtakavarga Table mark a small zero (0) in each of these places and a line (—) in the rest of the houses.

Similarly, prepare diagrams for the Sun with reference to the remaining planets and the Ascendant, and get eight tables for each planet likewise. Now add together all the zeros in the sign of Aries, in each diagram and we shall obtain a figure representing the total number of bindus in Aries due to the position of the Sun with reference to all

houses must be reckoned with respect to the Ascendant or
the Moon and not from the positions of planets (Apachayas)
are 1, 2, 4, 5, 7, 8, and 12 houses from Lagna & the rest are
all Upachayas.)

We shall make ourselves clear by applying the rules to a
practical horoscope. We shall prepare Ashtakavarga
Table for the Sun in the horoscope given below.

	No. 1 Sun's Ashtakavarga with reference to the Sun	Sun 0			No. 2 The Ashtakavarga for the Sun with reference to Mars	Mars 0
0	0			—	Aries ♈	—
—	Sun ♍ 0	Moon Saturn ♏ 0	—	—	Rahu ♓	—
—	—		—	Ascdt 0	—	0

planets and similarly the total zeros and lines in Taurus,
Gemini, etc., can be found out. In other words, this gives
us the total Ashtakavarga of the Sun.

The Sun's Ashtakavarga as a whole stands as per
Diagram No. 3.

This diagram indicates that while the Sun passes through
Aries, for instance, the auspicious effects will be 5/8 and the
malefic effects 3/8. In other words, he produces benefic
effects to the extent of $5/8 - 3/8 = 2/8$ or 1/4. Similarly,
when he passes through Taurus he produces $5/8 - 3/8 = 2/8$ or
1/4 beneficial results without any malefic effects. The same
thing holds good with reference to other places.

The Upachaya houses for this horoscope are Aries, Cancer,
Scorpio and Sagittarius.

In the Ashtakavarga of the Sun given in the next page,
when the Sun transits over these Upachaya houses, viz., Aries,
Cancer, etc., he produces beneficial results fully and not to
the extent of 2/8; while transiting over Taurus (Apachaya
house) he produces malefic influences to the full extent.

Aries due to the position of the Sun with reference to all

00000 : - - - 3 ♓	00000 5 - - - 3 ♈	00000 5 - - - 3 ♉	000 3 - - - 5 ♊
00000 5 - - - 3 ♒	No. 3 Sun's Ashtakavarga		0000006 - - - 3 ♋
00000 5 - - - 3 ♑			000 3 - - - 5 ♌
000 3 - - - 5 ♐	000 3 - - - 5 ♏	000 3 - - - 5 ♎	00 2 - - - 6 ♍

We know the maximum number of benefic dots is 8 and
the circles represent beneficial units while lines represent
malefic units. We can omit inserting malefic units in the
tables and instead mark benefic units alone, so that the
malefic units can be ascertained by deducting the benefics
from 8. The Sun's Ashtakavarga as given in Diagram No. 3
can also be put as in No. 4.

:	5	5	3
5	No. 4 These numbers as stated above indicate benefic units in Sun's Ashtakavarga		6 Sun
5			3
3	3	3	2

9.   The table prepared for each planet containing benefic dots must be subjected to two reductions, *viz.*, *Trikona* reduction and *Ekadhipathya* reduction.

Trikona Reductions

The triangular or Trikona signs are Aries and the signs forming an equilateral triangle with it, *viz.*, Leo and Sagittarius ; Taurus, Virgo, Capricorn ; Gemini and signs forming an equilateral triangle with it ; and Cancer, Scorpio and Pisces.

*10.   When similar figures, rather the same number of beneficial dots, are not found in the triangular signs, then subtract the least of the three figures from the other two and retain the remainders.

11.   No such elimination is necessary provided, no figure is found in one of the three signs.

12.   In the absence of figures in two of the three triangular signs, the figures in the third must also be eliminated.

13.   If there are similar or equal figures in each of three signs, all the figures must be removed.

We shall apply this reduction to the Ashtakavarga table of the Sun obtained above.

The number in Aries, Leo and Sagittarius—the triangular signs of Aries—are 5, 3 and 3 respectively.   According to rule (10), subtract 3 (the least of the 3 figures) from each

---

* In the matter of *Trikona Sodahana* (Triangular Reduction) there are two distinct views. According to one interpretation, when figures in the three triangular signs are not alike, then the least of the three figures is to be subtracted from the figure in each of the other two of the triangular group. According to another interpretation, the figures in the triangular group are to be altered so as to be equal to the least number; we have adopted the former, for reasons we have dealt with in our book on Ashtakavarga.

and the resultant numbers will be 2, 0, 0. The numbers in the triangular signs of Taurus, Virgo and Capricorn are 5, 2, 5. Applying the same rule, we get after reduction 3, 0, 3. In Gemini, Libra and Aquarius we get 0, 0, 2. In Cancer, Scorpio and Pisces we get 3, 0, 2. The Ashtakavarga of the Sun after this Trikona reduction stands thus :—

2	2	3	0
2	No. 5 Ashtakavarga of the Sun after first reduction		3
3			0
0	0	0	0

Ekadhipatya Reduction

After the Trikona reduction, the *Ekadhipatya* reduction must be applied. *Ekadhipatya* means ownership of two houses. *Ekadhipatya* signs are Aries, Taurus, Gemini, Virgo, Libra, Scorpio, Sagittarius, Capricorn, Aquarius and Pisces.

14.   No reduction is necessary if there are planets in both the houses owned by a planet.

15.   Out of the two houses of a planet, one of which is occupied and the other not, (*a*) if the number in the former is smaller than that in the latter, then make the latter equal to the former; (*b*) if the number in the former be greater than that in the latter, eliminate the latter; and (*c*) if the figures in the two are equal, remove the figures in the latter.

16.   If both the signs of a planet are not occupied, and if the figures in the two houses are equal, eliminate both ; if the numbers are not equal, reduce the larger to be equal to the smaller figure.

17.   Do not effect any reduction if there is no figure in one of the two houses.

18.   Cancer and Leo are not subject to this reduction as they are not *Ekadhipatya* Rasis.

We shall now apply this *Ekadhipatya* reduction to the Sun's Ashtakavarga obtained after Trikona reduction.

Out of Aries and Scorpio which are ruled by Mars, Aries is unoccupied and Scorpio occupied. The numbers in them (Fig. 5) are 2 and 0 respectively. According to Rule 17, no reduction is to be applied. We shall take Taurus and Libra, the houses of Venus: Taurus is occupied and Libra vacant, the figures in them are 3 and 0. According to Rule 17, these do not require any reduction. Coming to Gemini and Virgo, the houses of Mercury, we find both are unoccupied (let alone Ketu in Virgo, a shadowy planet) and in them the figures are 0 and 0. As such, no reduction can be applied to these. Coming to Jupiter's houses—Pisces and Sagittarius—both are unoccupied (leaving Rahu) and the figures, there, are 2 and 0. Rule 17 applies to this and accordingly no reduction is necessary. Out of Aquarius and Capricorn, both are unoccupied and the figures are 2 and 3 respectively. Rule 16 applies to this and accordingly reduce 3 the larger figure equal to the smaller figure 2 and we get 2 and 2 respectively. The numbers in Cancer and Leo, *viz.*, 3 and 0, require no reduction as they are not *Ekadhipatya* Rasis.

After the second or *Ekadhipatya* reduction, the Sun's Ashtakavarga Table stands as given in next page.

Similarly for each planet, the Ashtakavarga Table must be prepared. These seven separate Ashtakavargas are known as *Bhinnashtakavargas* meaning broken ones, *i.e.*, relating to each individual planet.

2	2	3	0
2	No. 6 Sun's Ashtakavarga after I & II reduction		3 Sun
2			0
0	0	0	0

In the illustrated horoscope, the following would be the Ashtakavarga Tables for each planet before and after reduction. The use of the tables "before reduction" will be dealt with later on, while now we shall confine ourselves to the explanation of the uses of the Ashtakavarga Tables "after reduction." The tables given in next page.

Use of Ashtakavarga Tables "After Reduction"
Sun's Ashtakavarga

19. No auspicious work must be undertaken or commenced when the Sun transits over signs where there are no bindus or figures in his own Ashtakavarga.

20. During such times as the Sun transits over signs containing no *bindus* (marks), the person suffers from unexpected diseases, misunderstandings and quarrels.

21. Multiply the total of the figures of the Sun's Ashtakavarga arrived at after all the reductions by the figure in the 9th sign from the Sun in his own Ashtakavarga and

Ashtakavarga Tables Before and After Reduction

SIGN	Sun		Moon		Mars		Mer.		Jup.		Venus		Sat.		Total	
	B.R.	A.R.	B.R.	A.R.	B.R.	A.R.	B.R.	A.R.	B.R.	A.R.	B.R.	A.R.	B.R.	A.R.	B.R.	A.R.
Aries ...	5	2	4	0	3	0	4	0	4	0	5	1	4	3	29	6
Taurus ...	5	3	0	4	3	0	5	3	6	1	4	0	4	2	33	13
Gemini ...	3	0	4	0	3	0	7	2	6	2	7	1	3	1	33	6
Cancer ...	6	3	3	0	3	0	2	0	3	0	4	3	7	6	28	12
Leo ...	3	0	2	0	3	0	5	1	5	1	4	0	1	0	23	2
Virgo ...	2	0	4	2	3	0	4	2	7	2	5	1	2	0	27	7
Libra ...	3	0	6	0	3	0	4	0	3	0	4	1	5	2	28	3
Scorpio ...	3	0	5	2	4	1	5	3	5	2	1	0	1	0	24	8
Sagittarius ...	3	0	5	3	4	0	6	2	4	0	6	2	2	1	30	8
Capricorn ...	5	2	2	0	3	0	2	0	5	0	4	0	4	2	25	4
Aquarius ...	5	2	5	1	3	0	4	0	4	1	3	0	2	0	26	4
Pisces ...	5	2	3	0	4	0	6	2	4	1	5	2	4	1	31	8
Total ...	48/14		49/12		39/1		54/15		56/10		52/11		39/18		337	81

Notes—B. R. means marks Before Reduction.
A. R. means marks After Reduction.

divide the product by 27. Note the constellation that is arrived at by counting the remainder from Aswini. When Saturn passes through this constellation or its triangular ones, the death of the person's father or paternal uncle must be predicted in such a constellation if the particular Dasa is inclined to effect *maraka* (death) to the respective parties.

Taking the illustration : The total of the Sun's Ashtakavarga will be 14. This multiplied by the figure in the 9th from the Sun. *i.e.,* 2 in Pisces, we get $14 \times 2 = 28$. This product, divided by 27, yields 1 as remainder. So in this case, first constellation from Aswini must be counted. This will be Aswini itself. When Saturn transits over Aswini, Makha or Moola, the death of the father or the paternal uncle occurs, provided such a period indicates death to him.

22. Multiply the total figure by the figure in the 8th house from the Sun in his Ashtakavarga. The remainder obtained by dividing this product by 12, when counted from Aries, gives the sign through which or through one of its triangular signs, when the Sun passes, the native dies if that is his *maraka* period.

The total of the Sun's Ashtakavarga after all reductions made is 14. This multiplied by 2, the figure in the 8th from the Sun in his Ashtakavarga, gives 28. This divided by 12 gives 4 as the remainder. So we have to take, that when the Sun passes through Cancer, Scorpio or Pisces he will die, in case the Dasa period also indicates the same.

23. Add together the figures in Arirs, Leo and Sagittarius; in Taurus, Virgo and Capricorn; in Gemini, Libra and Aquarius; and in Cancer, Scorpio and Pisces. See which of these totals is the largest and ascertain the *dik* or direction indicated by that set of triangular signs. The person will have success in such a direction.

In the above-given horoscope, the figures in Aries, Leo and Sagittarius = 2; Taurus and its set of triangles = 5; Gemini and its set = 2; Concer and its set = 5. The greatest figure is 5 represented by both Taurus and Cancer. Taurus represents south and Cancer represents north. Therefore, the person shines well in southern or northern countries to his place of birth or the God or Deity he instals to worship in his house will have been placed in one of these directions.

The Moon

24. Multiply the total of the figures by the bindus in the 4th house from the Moon in the Ashtakavarga of the Moon. Divide the product by 27. Find out the constellation obtained by counting the remainder from Aswini. When Saturn passes through this or its triangular ones, the person loses his mother if the period is unfavourable to her.

Total of the (A.R. 2) figures in the Moon's Ashtakavarga = 12. The A·R. figure in the 4th house from the Moon in her Ashtakavarga is 0; 12 × 0 is 0. So take Aswini; when Saturn passes through Aswini, Makha or Moola, the mother dies if the Dasa period also supports this period.

25. When the Moon passes through signs in which there are no figures (bindus), no auspicious work should be undertaken·

26. Direction or *dik*, found out according to Rule 23, in the Moon's Ashtakavarga, gives the quarter where the person's bath-room will be situated in his house.

In the illustration, Aries and its set gets 3; Taurus and its set 6; Gemini and its set 1; Cancer and its set 2. The greatest figure is 6 represented by Taurus which indicates south so that the bath-room in the person's house will be in the southern quarter.

Mars

27. The quarter where the kitchen or the parlour is situated in the native's house can be ascertained by finding the *dik* according to Rule 23 in the Ashtakavarga of Mars.

In the illustration, the 4 trines from Aries respectively get 0, 0, 0 and 1. Cancer gets 1 and the kitchen will be towards the north indicated by Cancer.

28. When Saturn transits over signs in the Ashtakavarga of Mars, containing no bindus, the native suffers from blood diseases, and if Mars is powerful he may also die.

Mercury

29. Saturn's transiting over signs without figures in Mercury's Ashtakavarga kills the native's son.

30. The strong *dik* or direction locates the playground in the person's house.

Jupiter

31. The bindus in the 5th house from Jupiter in his Ashtakavarga when doubled give the number of sons of the person.

32. The treasure box in the house of a person can be located with reference to the strongest direction obtained as per Rule 23.

33. The number of children meeting early death will be the number of planets occupying signs like debilitation and inimical places.

34. Coitus done in the signs containing the greatest number of bindus or figures in the Ashtakavarga of Jupiter results in the birth of a child.

Venus

35. Venus passing through signs containing the largest figure in his own Ashtakavarga gives happiness, marriage, lands and wealth.

36. The *dik* or the point of compass found as before gives the direction of the bed-room.

In the illustrated horoscope given above, Cancer and its set get 5 bindus and as such the bed-room of the native lies in the northern direction (indicated by Cancer) of his house.

Saturn

37. When Saturn transits over a sign devoid of any bindus in his own Ashtakavarga, the native suffers death or losses.

38. When the Sun and the Moon pass through signs in the Ashtakavarga of Saturn, containing the least number of marks, the death of the person occurs if that year is fatal to the native.

39. The *dik* or the compass, obtained as before, points out the direction where the sweepings are gathered.

40. Add together the B.R. bindus in the Ashtakavarga of Saturn from the Ascendant to the sign where Saturn is and from the sign where Saturn is to the Ascendant. These two totals will indicate the years in which the native suffers illness or diseases or miseries. These two totals added together give the year in which the person dies.

Sarvashtakavarga

Sarvashtakavarga means the Ashtakavarga of all the planets considered together. So far we have considered the *Bhinnashtakavarga, i.e.*, the Ashtakavarga of each individual planet and that too after each has been subjected to two kinds of reductions.

We shall now dispense with the Ashtakavarga Table obtained *after* reductions and pitch our attention upon the Ashtakavarga Table obtained *before* reduction. To obtain the Sarvashtakavarga, add together all the B.R. bindus in each sign separately. For example, the figure in the sign Aries of the Sarvashtakavarga will be the aggregate of the bindus or the figures in the sign Aries in the several *Bhinnashtaka-vargas* (individual Ashtakavarga Tables). Similarly, the total bindus in Taurus, Gemini, etc., must be obtained.

As already stated above, the student must bear in mind that this addition of bindus must be carried out before the two reductions are applied.

We shall take the illustrated horoscope given at the beginning of this chapter as an example.

Adding together all the bindus found in Aries in each table given above ("before reduction" figures), we get the Sun's Ashtakavarga 5, *plus* the Moon's Ashtakavarga 4, *plus* Mars' Ashtakavarga 3, plus Mercury's 4, *plus* Jupiter's 4, *plus* Venus' 5, *plus* Saturn's 4 = 29 total, which is of course the figure in Aries in the Sarvashtakavarga Table. After continuing the same process for each sign, we get the Sarvashtakavarga Table thus :

Sign	Fig.	Sign	Fig.	Sign	Fig.	Sign	Fig.
Aries	29	Cancer	28	Libra	28	Capricorn	25
Taurus	33	Leo	23	Scorpio	24	Aquarius	26
Gemini	33	Virgo	27	Sagittarius	30	Pisces	31

The above-mentioned table can also be represented as below which will be easier to understand.

This table will be useful in predicting some of the most outstanding events concerned with the life of the native and in the determination of Ayurdaya or longevity. This is called the *Bindusodhana Ashtakavargayurdaya* (longevity obtained after searching the strength of the eight sources of energy in a horoscope). I shall briefly outline this method for the benefit of my readers.

31 Pisces	29 Aries	33	33
26	Sarvashtakavarga Table		28
25			23
30 Sag.	24	28	27 Virgo

If the calculations are correctly done, it will be seen that he sum of all the figures in the *Sarvashtakavarga* will be always 337, this being the total of bindus of the seven Bhinnashtakavargas. In the particular horoscope, we are illustrating, the total comes to 337; so our calculations are correct.

41. If there are more than 30 bindus in a sign, then planets transiting over it produce happiness, wealth and mental peace and prosperity, if the figure is between 25 and 30, no good will happen, nor will the result be evil effects; if the bindus are less than 25, the results will be very bad.

42. Business enterprises, marriage ceremonies and other auspicious festivities must be commenced when the rising sign is one which contains the largest number of bindus in the Sarvashtakavarga Table

43. The general disposition of such houses or bhavas as contain a great number of bindus will be favourable or prosperous. The rule does not hold good with reference to the 6th, the 8th and the 12th houses.

44. The person will have general happiness and prosperity if the number of bindus in the 11th house (representing gain from the Ascendant) is greater than that in the 10th (representing labour and karma) and if the number of bindus in the 12th (representing loss) is smaller than that in the 11th and if the number of bindus in the Ascendant be greater than that in the 12th.

In our illustrated horoscope, the 11th house is Sagittarius. The number of bindus here is 30; that is greater than 24, the number of bindus in the 10th, and 25 the number of bindus in the 12th (Capricorn) is not smaller than 24, the number of bindus in the 10th; but is equal to it. Nevertheless, the native will be generally happy and will have more gains than losses.

45. Whether a person will be happy in his childhood, youth or old age can be determined as follows. Add together the bindus of the four signs from Cancer; and add together the

bindus of the four signs from Scorpio and also add together the bindus of the four signs from Pisces. Pisces to Gemini, Cancer to Libra and Scorpio to Aquarius denote childhood, youth and old age respectively. Of the three sections of the life, whichever total is greatest, it indicates happiness and prosperity during that period of life. If there are three or more malefic planets in any of these sections, the person will suffer miseries in the part of life indicated by the particular division.

In the illustrated horoscope, the childhood, youth and old age sections get 126, 106 and 105 marks (bindus) respectively and accordingly the happy life of the person would be during his childhood; youth and old age will also be fairly good and not bad.

46. The sum of bindus, obtained by adding those contained in the houses occupied by Saturn, Aecendant and Mars, gives the year in which the native suffers miseries and diseases.

47. Add together the bindus in signs occupied by Rahu, Mars and Saturn. The total will give the year in which the native receives serious injuries from weapons, enters battlefields or gets poisoned or wounded.

48. When the native would get a son, much wealth, etc., can be predicted by adding together the bindus of signs occupied by benefic planets.

In all the above three instances, wherever the age obtained exceeds that obtained by considering *maraka* (death-inflicting) planets or, wherever necessary, such figures must be reduced by the subtraction of multiples of 12 and 27.

These rules, applied to the horoscope we have considered, will give the following results :—

The total of the figures of the sign occupied by Saturn, Ascendant and Mars is 33, 26 and 23 = 82. This figure indicates the age when the native suffers miseries or illness. Since the length of life of the person may not exceed 75 or 76, this figure must be subjected to a reduction. By subtracting 5 times 12 we get 22. The native suffers illness in his 22nd year. In fact he suffered seriously from malaria for 15 days continuously. Miseries and diseases may also be predicted for this person in his 28th, 34th, 47th and 58th years.

The total bindus of the houses occupied by benefics is 47. Subtracting twice 12 from this, we get 23 as the person's age to get a son or a start in life.

49. Multiply the total number of bindus of the Ashtaka-varga of the planet who is the lord of the Ascendant, bindus of the lord of the 9th and bindus of the lord of the 4th by bindus of the 8th house, 9th house and 4th house respectively, and in each case divide the product by 12. The remainder gives the month from Aries in which the native, his father and his mother respectively may die.

In the illustrated horoscope, the lord of the 4th is Venus and his marks or bindus are 52. This multiplied by 33, the number of bindus in the 4th house in the Sarvashtakavarga gives $52 \times 33 = 1716$. This divided by 12 gives $\dfrac{1716}{12} = 143$.

When the remainder is 0 take Aries and the Sun will be in this sign when the native's mother dies.

50. The strongest *dik* or direction obtained must be chosen for building houses, for travelling, etc., and the other directions avoided. The four directions get 82, 85, 88 and 82 respectively and generally the native must choose West (represented by Gemini) as beneficial to him.

Determination of Ayurdaya

The Ayurdaya (longevity) is thus determined with the aid of Ashtakavarga bindus. There are several methods to find out Ayurdaya on the basis of Ashtakavarga, but I shall explain the most common one.

Now again we must divert our attention to *Bhinnashtakavarga* Tables of all the seven planets, "after reduction" and forget for the present the same tables "before reduction".

51. The essentials to be considered in the determination of Ayurdaya are (1) *Rasi Gunakara* and (2) *Graha Gunakara*.

Rasi Gunakara

These are the zodiacal factors or multipliers of the A.R. bindus in the signs. The figures or bindus left, after the two reductions are applied, in the several signs from Aries in the Ashtakavarga of each planet, must be multiplied by their respective zodiacal factors. All the 12 products must be added together.

The *Rasi Gunakara* (zodiacal factors) are as follows :— Aries 7, Taurus 10, Gemini 8, Cancer 4, Leo 10, Virgo 5, Libra 7, Scorpio 8, Sagittarius 9, Capricorn 5, Aquarius 11, and Pisces 12. This is constant for all horoscopes. We shall reproduce the Ashtakavarga of the Sun for ready reference :

2	2	3	0
2	Sun's Ashtakavarga after I & II reductions		3
2			0
0	0	0	0

Apply the above rules to the Sun.

Aries	2 (No. of bindus in it)	×	7 (Zodiacal factor)	=	14
Taurus	3	do.	× 10	do.	= 30
Gemini	0	do.	× 8	do.	= 0
Cancer	3	do.	× 4	do.	= 12
Leo	0	do.	× 10	do.	= 0
Virgo	0	do.	× 5	do.	= 0
Libra	0	do.	× 7	do.	= 0
Scorpio	0	do.	× 8	do.	= 0
Sagit.	0	do.	× 9	do.	= 0
Capri.	2	do.	× 5	do.	= 10
Aquarius	2	do.	× 11	do.	= 22
Pisces	2	do.	× 12	do.	= 24

The sum of the figures 112

Sum = 112.

Applying the same rules to each of the seven planets we get :—

Moon 104 ; Mars 8 ; Mercury 132 : Jupiter 85 ; Venus 81 and Saturn 118.

Keep these figures on one side and consider the other aspect.

Graha Gunakara

These are planetary factors or multipliers of the figures of the planets. Multiply the several A.R. figures in the signs occupied by the various planets by the figures of the planetary factors and add the seven products together.

The *Graha Gunakara* (planetary factors) are :

Sun 5, Moon 5, Mars 8, Mercury 5, Jupiter 10, Venus 7 and Saturn 5.

In the example horoscope, the Sun is in Cancer ; Moon and Saturn in Taurus ; Mercury, Venus and Mars in Leo ; and Jupiter in Scorpio. Considering the Ashtakavarga

Table of the Sun (page 199) there are 3 bindus in Cancer (the place of the Sun). Multiply this by the Sun's planetary factor 5. We get $5 \times 3 = 15$; take the Moon ; she is in Taurus; there are 3 bindus in Taurus in the Sun's Ashtakavarga ; multiply this 3 by the planetary factor of the Moon, *viz.*, 5. We get $5 \times 3 = 15$. When we apply the same rule to the rest of the signs containing bindus we get :

Sun–Cancer	3 (No. of bindus)	×	5 (Planetary factor)	= 15
Moon–Taurus	3	do.	×	5	do.	= 15
Mars–Leo	0	do.	×	8	do.	= 0
Mercury	0	do.	×	5	do.	= 0
Jup.–Scorpio	0	do.	×	10	do.	= 0
Venus–Leo	0	do.	×	7	do.	= 0
Saturn–Taurus	3	do.	×	5	do.	= 15

Total   45

The total of these will be 45 and this number is derived from the Sun's Ashtakavarga ; similarly, ascertained for the Ashtakavarga of other planets, we get :

Sun 45; Moon 60; Mars 10; Mercury 80; Jupiter 50; Venus 15 and Saturn 50.

Add together the Rasi figures and Graha figures so obtained for each planet ; multiply the result by 7 and divide the product by 27. The quotient gives the years of Ayurdaya the particular planet denotes. The remainder must be reduced to months and days.

We shall take the Sun in our example horoscope. The sign total is 112 and the planet total is 45, *i.e.*, 112 *plus* $45 = 157$. This multiplied by 7 and divided by 27 gives $\dfrac{157 \times 7}{27} = 40.70$ years. Since this number exceeds 27, deduct 27 or a multiple of 27. Deducting 27 we get 13.70 years as the term of life granted by the Sun.

We get the following terms with reference to other planets :—

		Years
Sun	—	13.70
Moon	—	15.52
Mars	—	4.66
Mercury	—	0.96
Jupiter	—	8.00
Venus	—	24.88
Saturn	—	16.55

(Fractions are omitted for the sake of convenience.)

These years are subject to reduction or *haranas* on account of their conjunctions with or aspects of other planets.

52. If there is more than one planet in a sign, reduce its term of life by one-half.

53. If a planet is debilitated, deduct one-half.

54. For a planet in Astangata (combustion), deduct one-half. Combustion occurs when the Moon, Mars, Mercury, Jupiter, Venus and Saturn are 12 deg , 17 deg., 14 deg., 11 deg., 10 deg. and 16 deg. respectively from the Sun backwards or forwards ; when retrograde, combustion occurs when Mars, Mercury and Venus are 8 deg., 12 deg., and 8 deg. respectively.

55. If a planet is in its *Tatkalika satru's* Rasi (temporary enemy's house), its term of life must be reduced by one-third. (See page 21 for Tatkalika satrus.)

56. Planets above the horizon (12th, 11th, 10th, 9th, 8th and 7th bhavas) lose one-half of their Ayurdaya.

57. If a planet suffers defeat in *Grahayuddha* (planetary fight), one-third Ayurdaya must be deducted.

58. If the Sun or Moon is of unusual appearance (as in eclipse), deduct one-third Ayurdaya. When one and the same planet is subjected to several reductions, only the highest reduction should be made.

According to the above rules, the Ayurdaya of all the planets require to be halved excepting that of the Sun as he is below the horizon and accordingly we get the following figures :

		Years
Sun	—	13.70
Moon	—	7.76
Mars	—	2.33
Mercury	—	0.48
Jupiter	—	4.00
Venus	—	12.44
Saturn	—	8.27
	Total	48.98

Multiply this sum of years by 334 and divide the product by 365, to convert *Chandramana* (lunar) years into *Sowramanc* (solar) years :

We get $\frac{48.98}{365} \times 334 = 44.87$ years as the longevity of the native.

In actual practice the Ashtakavarga system of predicting longevity has not been found to yield satisfactory results.

But there are other systems, which must also be considered and above all, the maraka planets and their Dasas are of vital importance.

CHAPTER XXVII

Prasna Sastra or Horary Astrology

Horary Astrology deals exclusively with the answering of questions in the light of planetary influences, relating to important events in the daily transactions of human life. This branch indeed forms a most useful and prominent aspect of astrological science inasmuch as it helps us to foretell the occurrence of many important future events beforehand, how and when such events will take place, what their exact nature is whether or not they terminate favourably, who is instrumental for them and how far such events are beneficial or detrimental to the interests of the party concerned, without reference to the birth chart.

Supposing a person wants to know whether his stolen property can be regained or not, whether an individual suffering seriously recovers from his illness or not, whether it would be profitable to invest money in any business transaction, whether a man would be successful in any speculations, whether the lands he is planning to purchase would bring him luck and whether, in fact, so many everyday human events would be beneficial or not, then all these can successfully be answered with the aid of Horary Astrology. The predictions based on its principles seldom go wrong unless the very foundation is shaky.

If any obstacles are thrown on the way of success in any undertaking or enterprise, by ascertaining these beforehand by means of Horary Astrology, we can resort to remedies to minimise or completely overcome such evils, and augment the good, so that the future way for one's progress and prosperity may be smoothened.

In the case of Prasna or Horary Astrology, first ascertain the exact time at which a question or query is put and for that time mark the positions of planets and the Ascendant and determine the balance of the Dasa and Bhukti. Mark also the Navamsa diagram. In fact construct a map of the heavens for the question time just as you would do for birth time. A number of typical questions are also given in my *Astrology for Beginners*.

This Ascendant is called the Prasna Lagna or the rising sign at the time of the question.

1. The success and failure in any undertaking, such as starting of business, examination results, etc., should be predicted with reference to the Prasna Lagna. The object of the querist will succeed if a beneficial sign rises and joins a favourable navamsa, or if the rising sign be in a *Sirshodaya* Rasi. If the beneficial rising sign is aspected by malefics and its lord has also a similar position the querist will succeed after some effort.

Whether a particular query refers to minerals, vegetables or animals must be first ascertained as per rules given below and then, its success or failure prognosticated.

2. If, at the time of a query, the rising sign be 1st, 4th and 7th; 2nd, 5th and 8th; and 3rd, 6th and 9th navamsas, the question refers to minerals, vegetables and animals respectively in an odd sign, and in an even sign, the reverse holds good.

3. If, at the time of query, Saturn is found in an odd sign from the Prasna Lagna, the woman will have a male child, and if Saturn occupies an even sign, a female child will be born. If male planets occupy masculine *Shadvargas*

a male child will be born; if male planets are in female *Shadvargas* a female child will be born.

4. If Saturn is in the 7th house, the querist will be married within 3 months from the date of question. If the Moon in 3, 5, 6, 7 or 11 is aspected by Jupiter, the Sun and Mercury, and if benefics occupy quadrants or trines, the querist will have marriage very early.

5. If at the time of query it is found that the Sun, Venus or Mars joins the 7th house, it means the querist has committed adultery with another man's wife. Jupiter in the 7th indicates his own wife, Mercury, a prostitute, and Saturn a very low-caste woman.

6. Predict the safe return of the person gone to foreign lands, if the query refers to this point, if there is any planet retrograde between the 8th house and the Ascendant.

7. If a query refers to the advent of enemies in a war or otherwise, such enemies would retreat, even if they have come some distance, should be predicted when the 4th, 5th and 6th houses from the Prasna Lagna are occupied by evil planets. The enemy even if he has come for an attack would return back within that period (in months) obtained by reckoning from the Prasna Lagna to the planet fully possessed of strength. If such a powerful planet falls in a fixed sign, double the number of months, if he occupies a common sign, treble the number of months.

Say at the time of a query Cancer rises and Jupiter possessed of full strength is in the 8th, *viz.*, Aquarius. Count from Cancer to Aquarius. This is 8. Since Aquarius is a fixed sign, double 8, you will get 16. That is, if this query relates to any war, the enemy would return within 16 months or peace efforts would be successful within 16 months from date of the commencement of regular hostilities.

8. Success in speculation, etc., should be predicted when benefics are in 3, 5, 7 and 11 and losses when malefics are

in these signs. If the Ascendant is Gemini, Virgo, Libra or
Aquarius with benefics in it, success would invariably follow.

9. Recovery from any illness should be predicted if
benefics are in Prasna Lagna, 5th, 8th and 7th houses and
have auspicious aspects and the Moon is in the 3rd, 6th,
10th or 11th.

10. Predict the safe return of a person from his travels
if there are planets in the 6th or 7th, Jupiter in a quadrant
and Mercury or Venus in a trine at the time of question.

Find out the nearest planet to Prasna Lagna and multiply
the number by 12. The product will indicate the number of
days within which the traveller returns to his native land.
If the nearest planet is in retrograde motion, he will start
to return after that number of days.

11. If a powerful benefic occupies the 11th house from
the Prasna Lagna or if the Full Moon occupies it aspected
by Jupiter or Venus, predict speedy recovery of the lost
property, when a question relates to this subject. If such a
Prasna Lagna falls in a fixed sign, or in a fixed navamsa,
the article will have been stolen by a near relative of the
querist.

The 1st, 2nd and 3rd drekkanas of the Prasna Lagna
indicate the verandah, the central hall or the backyard of the
house of the thief where the stolen thing was deposited.

The particular direction, towards which a stolen article
is removed, can be ascertained either by the Prasna Lagna
itself or by the most powerful of the planets found in
quadrants at the time of query ; when there are no planets
in the quadrants, then have recourse to the Ascendant itself.

In the case of planets, the directions will be as follows : —
Sun—East ; Venus—S.-E. ; Mars—South ; Rahu—S.-W. ;
Saturn—West ; the Moon—N.-W. ; Mercury—North ; Jupiter
—N.-E.

In the case of signs, the directions will be : —Aries—East ;

Leo and Sagittarius—S.-E. ; Taurus—South ; Virgo and
Capricorn—S.-W. ; Gemini—West ; Libra and Aquarius—
N.-W, ; Cancer—North ; Scorpio and Pisces—N.-E.

12. Find out the Navamsa of the Prasna Lagna ; if it is
after the 5th in that sign, then find out its number from the
5th and ascribe 9 times as many miles to it as that number
denotes. If the navamsa falls within 5, then the stolen article
will be some where near the precincts of the querist's place.

Say the Prasna Lagna is in the 7th navamsa, *i.e.*, it is the
3rd from the 5th so that 3 navamsas are passed from the
5th. At 9 miles per navamsa, it will be 27 for 3 and as such,
the stolen article will have been removed to about 27 miles
away from the place of the questioner.

13. Predict the nature of the article stolen by considering
the navamsa of the rising sign, the nature of the thief by the
drekkana and age and caste of the thief by the lord of the
Ascendant.

Say for instance the Prasna Lagna falls in Aries, the
navamsa in Cancer and drekkana in Leo. It is a sign of short
ascension and the article will be a short one ; the lord of
the navamsa is the Moon and say he is very powerfully
situated. Then the article will be a valuable one. As the
drekkana is Leo, the 2nd in Aries, the person involved in the
theft will be a man, dark in complexion, fearful in look, red
eyes and armed. (The characteristics of other drekkanas are
given in the last chapter.)

14. In the rainy season predict early rain when Saturn
and Venus occupy the 7th house from the Sun and the Moon
respectively and if Saturn and Venus are in the 4th and the
8th from the Prasna Lagna.

An Example of Marriage Question

Illustration.—Mr.......... puts the query : "Will I marry
or not ?" The following are the combinations of planets for the
question time :—

The Prasna Lagna is Virgo; its lord is Mercury and he is in Taurus. The query is about marriage and the lord of marriage is the lord of the 7th from the Ascendant and he is Jupiter—Jupiter is in 20° Cancer. Thus the lords of the Ascendant and the 7th house are Mercury and Jupiter respectively and Venus is in conjunction with Mercury. The lord of the Lagna is in conjunction with Venus who is in

Saturn	Mars Sun	Merc. Venus	
			Jupiter
	RASI		
Moon			
			Lagna

his own sign and thus Venus is well placed, and Jupiter also well placed. The prediction must be given that the querist will get married early, the bride will be fair and her introduction would be through a pious and religious man as Jupiter is the lord of the 7th. The subject of Prasna has been dealt with exhaustively with examples in my English translation of *Prasna Tantra.*

CHAPTER XXVIII

Unknown Birth Times

The birth data of many people will not have been recorded properly. In many a case, even the date of birth will be unknown. In such cases it is possible to find out, rather create, a horoscope on the basis of certain fundamental assumptions.

One should not run away with the idea that the principles enunciated herein are conclusive. An attempt is made in the following pages to give the reader an idea of the methods recommended by ancient Hindu astrological writers for erecting horoscopes of persons whose birth dates are not known. And these methods merit further research and investigation by serious students of astrology. It is hoped that workers in this field will continue investigations and carry views herein outlined to a more extended issue since this work is intended to merely lay down general principles.

The rules involved are laborious and take away the patience of the reader. I have given only one important process and have illustrated the same with an example so that the reader may not find it difficult to understand these principles clearly.

The astrologer, as soon as a person, who will not have recollection of his birth date or time, comes to him for consultation, must record the exact time, the direction and other details of his coming and find out the exact positions of planets and the bhavas for that time; or the time at which a person begins to write a letter to the astrologer for knowing his future, must be considered, in case of long distance and a map cast for that time. It must be remembered that this time indicates the birth of the mind in the person as he is prompted to approach an astrologer. Sometimes this would be more genuine than the birth time itself. Birth means the birth of the mind and not merely the body ; similarly the very inclination to know the future, raised in the mind of a man, is given expression to, not at any chosen moment but at random—rather in a sudden manner.

1. When the time of impregnation or birth is not known, cast a horoscope for the time of query of the person and make out the birth chart from the rising sign at the time of query. If the Prasna Lagna (Ascendant at question time) be the first half of the Ascendant, the birth of the querist will have occurred in Uttarayana (Sun's northerly course) ; if it be the other half, the birth will have occurred in Dakshinayana (Sun's southernly course).

2. If the rising Dwadasamsa at the question time is the 1st, 2nd, etc., the sign occupied by Jupiter at the time of birth will be the 1st, 2nd, etc., respectively from the Prasna Lagna.

By knowing the position of Jupiter, fix the age of the person. Jupiter takes roughly 12 years to go round the heavens. If we know the number of circuits passed by Jupiter from the time of birth, the age of the person can be determined. In many an instance the cycle of Jupiter cannot be easily determined and in such cases, find out the number of cycle from the part of the body touched by the querist. Here the maximum life is taken to be 120 years and this is divided by 12 (the number of years Jupiter takes for one cycle) so that we get 10 years corresponding to the following divisions of the human body :

1. Feet and ankles.
2. Knees, buttocks and shanks.
3. Thighs and sexual organ.
4. The loins and the navel.
5. Belly.
6. The chest and breast.
7. Shoulders.
8. Neck and lips.
9. Eyes and brows.
10. Forehead and the head.

Say the Prasna Lagna is in Cancer and the 4th Dwadas-amsa rises. Then Jupiter will be in Libra at the birth of the querist. The number of Jupiter cycles must be determined. Suppose the things are touched by the querist, then it means that Jupiter is in the third round. So the age of the person should be taken to be $12 \times 2 = 24$ *plus* the number of years taken by Jupiter to move from the sign occupied by him at the question time, *viz.*, 3 in this particular instance. That is, the age of the querist is 24 *plus* $3 = 27$ years.

3. The *Ruthu* (season), the querist was born in, should be determined with reference to the ruler of the drekkana rising on the Prasna Lagna or by the planet occupying the first house, preference being given always to the strongest of the two. If the drekkana of the Sun rises or if the Sun occupies the Prasna Lagna, the *Ruthu* (see page 42) will be Greeshma; if Venus drekkana rises or Venus is in Prasna Lagna—Vasantha; if Mars—Greeshma; if the Moon—Varsha; if Mercury—Sarat; if Jupiter—Hemantha; and if Saturn—Sisira, if the *Ruthu* (season) so obtained does not agree with the Ayana (cycle), then change the Moon, Mercury and Jupiter for Venus, Mars and Saturn respectively. Divide the rising drekkana into two equal parts and if the first division is rising, ascribe the first month of the *Ruthu*, and

if second, the second month as the month of the birth of the querist.

Each sign contains 1,800 minutes of arc and each drekkana 600 minutes. We have ascribed 2 months to each drekkana and 1 month to one half so that 1 month is represented by 300 minutes (of zodiacal space). Therefor day get 300/30 = 10 minutes of arc and the particular the birth must be determined by the rising minute Prasna Lagna.

4. The lunar day of birth of the querist is repre by the number of degrees passed over by the Sun i particular sign at the time of question.

5. The nocturnal or the diurnal nature of the l..asua Lagna reveals the birth of the querist during the day or during the night respectively.

6. The degress rising on the Prasna Ascendant indicate the ghatikas of birth after sunrise or sunset as the case may be.

7. The lunar months of birth can also be determined from the navamsa occupied by the Moon at the time of query; or the birth time of the querist will be the Prasna Lagna, or the 5th or the 9th from it, whichever is most powerful.

8. The safest thing in such doubtful cases would be to ask the querist to touch some part of his body and the Moon will occupy the sign typifying the part of the body so touched by the querist of his own accord. If the querist touches his head, face, chest, heart, belly, sexual organ, thighs, knees buttocks and feet, the Moon's position will be in Aries, Taurus, etc., respectively, Pisces corresponding to the feet.

9. If the Moon is in Pisces at the time of query, she will be in the same sign at the birth time of the querist. Some say that if the Moon is not in Pisces at the question

time, then she will . be in that sign which is equal to the number of signs gained by her from the Prasna Lagna.

Let us suppose that a person, who does not know his birth data, puts a query on 12–4–1937 at about 16-44 ghatis after sunrise at Bangalore. The positions of planets at the time of question are shown in the chart given below.

29° 50' Sun Saturn	Moon Merc. Venus	Ketu	
	Query on 12-4-1937 at 16-44 ghatis		9° 54' Ascdt.
Jupiter			
	Mars Rahu		

Then we find according to the above rules that (a) the query is put in the first half of the Ascendant and hence the birth of the querist will have occurred in Uttarayana. (b) The Prasna Lagna falls in the 4th dwadasamsa, the sign occupied by Jupiter at birth will be the 4th from the Prasna Lagna, i.e., Libra. (c) The querist touched his thighs and, therefore, Jupiter will be in the third cycle at the time of query. He has completed 2 cycles or 24 years and has passed 3 years in the 3rd cycle—from Libra (where Jupiter is at birth) upto Capricorn (where Jupiter is at the time time of query)—i.e., the age of the person at the time of query will be 24 plus 3 = 27 years passed. (d) The ruler of the drekkana of the Prasna Lagna is the Moon (1st drekkana) and hence the birth should have occurred in *Varsharuthu* (Sravana–Bhadrapada). Since this *Ruthu* does not agree with the *Ayana*, the *Ruthu* of the alternative planet, that is the *Ruthu* of Venus (Vasantha), should be deemed as the *Ruthu* of the birth. (e) The rising drekkana is first (9° 54' having passed in it) and if it is divided into two equal divisions, each gets 5°. The Prasna Lagna is within the second 5° of this drekkana so that the birth has occurred in the second month of the *Ruthu*, *viz.*, Vaisakha (April–May). (f) The number of minutes passed in the latter half of rising drekkana is 2\ '(4° 54'); each day gets 10 minutes and as such 294'

get $\frac{.94}{10} = 29\frac{4}{10}$, *i.e.*, 29 days have passed and a portion of

the 30th. Therefore, birthday must be the 30th day of lunar month Vaisakha. (g) The Sun is in 29˙ 50' Pisces and therefore lunar day at birth must be the 30th day (New Moon day) of the month of Vaisakha. (h) Cancer, the Prasna Lagna, is a nocturnal sign. Therefore, the birth should have occurred during the day. (i) The duration of day on the birth date is 30–40 ghatis. Converting this into vighatis (1 ghati = 60 vighatis), we get gh. 30×60 *plus* $40 = 1840$ vighatis. The length of day or night of birth being known, it is represented by the rising sign and the longitude of the Ascendant, the exact proportion of the sign that has arisen above the horizon. Here the length of day is 1840 vighatis and the number of degrees that has already arisen above the

horizon is 9° 54' or 9° 9'. Therefore, we get $\frac{9.9}{30} \times 1840 = 607.2$

vighatis or ghatis 10.12 after sunrise. That is, the birth of the querist took place at 10.12 ghatis after sunrise on the 30th day of lunar month Vaisakha 27 years traced back from the year of the question.

Considerable research must be carried on in this branch of astrology and then alone we shall be able to appreciate how far these principles hold good in actual practice. These rules were propounded by the ancient Maharishis, who were master minds. Knowledge to them did not resolve itself to mere observation and statistical study. They discovered many a grand truth by intuition, a process which modern science sadly lacks.

CHAPTER XXIX

Medical Astrology

Medical Astrology is a part of the grand celestial science dealing with the several zodiacal, planetary and stellar influences which affect the health, constitution, functions and habits of life. In fact, Medicine is a branch of astrology. This conclusion is clear on its very face. Configurations of planets in the heavens in certain angular positions emanate certain forces or energies, which, when they are not in harmony with the energies of an individual, bring about certain disturbances in his physical and mental dispositions. To avert the evil influences of planets, the ancients contemplated upon discovering remedies, and the science of Medicine was gradually founded and developed in this manner.

Each sign of the zodiac represents a certain part of the human body and the diseases peculiar to it and each planet also indicates certain types of diseases. Disease and death are due to the disturbances in the laws of proportion and conjunction of natural forces emanating from the planets and the times which these disturbances occur, can be previously ascertained and adequate provision made to arrest or minimise such evil influences.

The planetary positions at birth clearly indicate the nature of the diseases one would suffer from, when and how they would affect us and how best to alleviate them.

1. The twelve signs of the zodiac commencing from Aries in general and from the Ascendant in particular govern

the twelve important organs of the human body and in addition to this, planets in one sign will affect organs governed by the sign of the same element or constitution.

Aries	governs	Head
Taurus	"	Face
Gemini	"	Chest
Cancer	"	Heart
Leo	"	Belly
Virgo	"	Waist
Libra	"	Lower belly
Scorpio	"	Sexual organ
Sagittarius	"	The two thighs
Capricorn	"	The two knees
Aquarius	"	Buttock
Pisces	"	Feet

In general, such signs as are occupied by evil planets indicate want of development or deformity in the organs they represent and those signs which are occupied by beneficial planets indicate beauty and health to the organs represented by them.

Each planet is given control over some humour (do ha) causing disease and the type and seat of disease depend u℣on the nature of the planet and the particular sign occupied by it and the period of suffering is denoted by the Dasas and Bhuktis of such a planet as shown below.

2.	Aries	governs	the face.
	Taurus	"	the neck and throat.
	Gemini	"	upper arm and throat.
	Cancer	"	breast, epigastric region and elbow.
	Leo	"	back and forearm.
	Virgo	"	hands and abdominal region.
	Libra	"	lumbar region and loins.

Scorpio	governs	external generative and urinary organs and anus.
Sagittarius	,,	hips.
Capricorn	,,	epidermis.
Aquarius	,,	legs and ankles.
Pisces	,,	toes.

Virgo, the 6th from Aries, is a mental sign and this must always be considered dealing with the question of diseases. Virgo means Virgin. Virgin is the male or female who has had no sexual connection and who is chaste, pure and unadulterated. The health is perfectly maintained when all the chemical constituents of the blood are present in normal quantities. When they are adulterated, diseases set in. Disease is the result of the virgin health being adulterated. Therefore, when the sign Virgo is badly afflicted by the vibrations of the malefic planets, the whole world must suffer from ill-health, and diseases of some sort or the other make their appearance and take away large tolls of life. In the astrological nomenclature, Virgo is referred to as the sign representing sickness. Mind has a tremendous influence on health and when it is free from agonies and distractions, the health also remains unimpaired. When the mind is affected, the physical body also suffers. Virgo represents that part of the *Kalapurusha* (zodiacal man) in which the liver and the intestines are situated. The Sun, when he enters Virgo every year, renders the public health suffer for want of digestion and from intestinal troubles. The solar plexus is the seat of feeling and sensation. It consists of a group of twelve different ganglia and lies directly back of the stomach. The twelve divisions of the solar plexus correspond with the twelve zodiacal divisions. The solar plexus play an important part in man. In finding out the disease, etc., Virgo alone must be first considered. Similarly the 6th house in any horoscope from the Ascendant rules the

intestinal and digestive organs and since all troubles, more
or less, arise when these organs become inactive, the sixth
sign in a horoscope operates as the sign of disease. This is in
general and in particular horoscopes, the Ascendant represents Aries and so on.

3. Aries, Leo and Sagittarius are fiery signs and control
the vitality of persons; Taurus, Virgo and Capricorn are
earthly signs and control bones and flesh; Gemini, Libra
and Aquarius are windy signs and they govern the breath;
and Cancer and its trines are watery signs and govern the
human blood.

4. The following internal organs are governed by the
12 signs of the zodiac :

Aries or the Ascendant	—	Brain, nerve centres
Taurus or the second	—	Gullet, cerebellum
Gemini or the third	—	Lungs, breath, nerve fibres
Cancer or the fourth	—	Stomach
Leo or the fifth	—	Heart, blood and liver
Virgo or the sixth	—	Bowels, and solar plexus
Libra or the seventh	—	Kidneys.
Scorpio or the eighth	—	Excretory system and bladder
Sagittarius or the ninth	—	Arterial system
Capricorn or the tenth	—	Bones and joints
Aquarius or the eleventh	—	Blood circulation, eyes and breath
Pisces or the twelfth	—	Lymphatic system

5. Head, face, heart, back, hips and thighs are fiery in
nature. Throat, bowels and neck are earthly. Lungs, kidneys
and blood are airy and stomach and digestive, excretory and
lymphatic systems are watery. The zodiacal signs named
above having these qualities also possess dominion on all these
organs.

6. The following anatomical structures are represented
by the different signs of the zodiac :—

Aries.—Cranium, cerebrum, cerebellum, facial bones, upper jaw, pituitary glands. *Taurus.*—Cervical vertebrae, ears, lower jaw, larynx, thyroid gland, oesophagus. *Gemini.*—Humorous, clavicles,shoulders, capillaries, lungs and tracheae scapula, upper ribs. *Cancer.*—Diaphragm, sternum, elbow joint, epigastric region, thoracic duct, ribs in general. *Leo.*—Radius, ulna, spinal column, heart, spinal cord, vertebrae. *Virgo.*—Carpus, alimentary canal, metacarpus, duodenum, phalanges, abdomen. *Libra.*—Ovaries and seminal vesicles, uriters and epidermis, lumbar vertebrae. *Scorpio.*—Pelvic bones, testicles, rectum, sacrum and colon and bladder. *Sagittarius.*—Femur, hips, sacral region. *Capricorn.*—Knee-joint, hairs, nails and skeleton in general, patela. *Aquarius.*—Fibula, bones and muscles of the feet and teeth, tibia, ankles, astragalus. *Pisces.*—Taurus blood circulation, meta-tarsus.

7. Diseases and signs :—

Aries.—Brain derangement, headache, fevers like ague, malaria, sleeping sickness, apoplexy, insomnia, eye troubles, pyorrhea. *Taurus.*—Obesity, absecesses, swellings in the neck, goitre. *Gemini.*—Consumption, pneumonia, rheumatism, asthma. *Cancer.*—Dropsy, smallpox, flatulency, cancer. *Leo.*—Digestive troubles, dyspepsia, diabetes, locomotor ataxia, swoons, fainting. *Virgo.*—Constipation, masturbation, arthritis, anus troubles, venereal complaints. *Libra.*—Bright's disease, lumbago, nephritis, renal, calculi. *Scorpio.*—Fistula, ulcers, nervous troubles, haemorrhoids, rectal affection. *Sagittarius.*—Gout, paralysis, sudden fits, troubles in the hip. *Capricorn.*—Cutaneous troubles, leprosy, leucoderma, tooth ache, elephantiasis. *Aquarius.*—Nervous diseases, spasmodic eruptions. *Pisces.*—consumption, tuberculosis, mucous troubles and tumours.

It may be asked whether the ancient Hindus had any knowledge of these diseases; if not, how could their ruler-ship by the different signs and planets be ascribed? In the

Ayurvedic text-books a number of these diseases are elaborately dealt with. In many of the astrological works, in giving combinations for the occurrence of different types of diseases, the authors have hinted here and there the zodiacal signs which have governance over them. Besides on the basis of the examination of horoscope the information is collected.

8. Apart from the zodiacal influences, the seven planets also possess dominion over the different organs of the human body, their peculiarities, constitution, etc.

The Sun.—Bile, heart, brain, head, eye and bone. *The Moon.*—Breast, saliva, womb, water, blood and lymphatic and glandular systems. *Mars.*—Bile, ears, nose, forehead, sinews, fibre and muscular tissues. *Mercury.*—Abdomen, tongue, lungs, bowels, nerve centres, bile and muscular tissues. *Jupiter.*—Phlegm, blood, thighs, kidneys, flesh and fat and arterial system. *Venus.*—Ovaries, eyes, generative system, water, semen and phlegm. *Saturn.*—Feet, wind, acids, knees, marrow and secretive system.

9. Each planet rules over certain anatomical structures in the human body and certain diseases also. This rulership must be carefully considered.

The Sun.—Cerebellum, brain, blood, lungs, heart, stomach, breasts, ovaries, seminal vesicles, diseases of the heart, appendicitis, fistula, inflammatory complaints. *The Moon.*—Pericardium, veins, lymphatic vessels, intestinal functions, eye, alimentary canal, membrane—genito and urinary derangements, testicle, wind and colic, bronchial catarrah, dropsy, tumours, insanity, defective eyesight. *Mars.*—Muscular tissue, muscles, carebral hemispheres—inflammation of the lungs, heoemoptsis, haemorrhage from the lungs, spitting of blood, consumption, hypertrophy, typhoid and enteric fever, infectious and contagious diseases. *Mercury.*—Nerves, breath, air cells, sense perception, hair, tongue, mouth—nasal disorders, impediments of speech, brain and nervous disorders, asthma, bronchitis, delirium, neurasthania, headaches, neuralgia, palpitation, worms, genito-urinary troubles. *Jupiter*.—Arteries, veins, auricle and ventricle, the pleura, ear, blood apoplexy, pleurisy, degeneration, piles, tumours, diabetes. *Venus*.—Kidneys, aorta, flesh, marrow, skin, cheeks, complexion—suppression of urine, discharge from eyes, cutaneous eruptions, throat diseases, digestive troubles, venereal complaints. *Saturn*.—Spleen, upper stomach, endocardium, ribs, bones, hair, nails, cold, catarrah, diseases incidental to exposure, rheumatism, consumption, bronchitis, asthma, gout, constipation, Bright's disease.

Precautions in Predictions

10.   The house of diseases is the sixth from the Ascendant. The planets therein, the lord of the 6th, the aspects on the 6th and the navamsa the lord of the 6th occupies, should all be considered for predicting diseases. The planets in the 6th house affect the particular part of the body governed by the sign, and the diseases will be those that are indicated by its rulers.

11.   Due attention must be paid to the Ascendant, and the relationship between its lord and that of the 6th. The details given in the earlier chapters of this book about the planetary and zodiacal peculiarities will be of immense use in Medical Astrology.

12.   The general build-up and strength of the physical constitution must be ascertained with reference to the position of the Sun and the mental peculiarities with reference to the Moon. The Sun in the 6th aspected by Saturn is sure to bring about loss of vitality by means of unnatural methods like masturbation and sodomy.

13.   Malefics in the 6th with no beneficial aspects cause continuous illness. (Miss E. A. of New York has Mercury

in the 6th with Saturn and Mars powerfully aspected by Rahu—she suffered from continuous arthritis for more than 25 years.)

I shall give below the combinations for some of the most terrible diseases from which humanity has not claimed immunity as yet—as it will not be possible to include in a small chapter like this, information which relates to the causation of each and every disease on earth.

14. Abdominal diseases, appendicitis, etc., are caused by the movements of the Sun and the Moon in Virgo.

15. The Sun and the Moon in opposition and in conjunction with or aspected by Mars produce sudden accidents.

16. Enteric disorders and bowel disorders are brought about by the Sun in the 6th, aspected by Saturn. Diarrhoea is caused by Jupiter in Virgo being afflicted.

17. Mars in Libra, afflicted by Venus and aspected by Saturn, causes Bright's disease.

18. If Mars and Venus aspect the Ascendant and if there are evil planets in the 6th aspected by other evil planets, the person suffers from chronic constipation.

19. If the Moon is afflicted by Saturn in Aries which governs the pituitary body), and Mars also has influence over the Moon, the person suffers from leprosy.

20. If Mars and Venus are in the 7th and are aspected by malefics, the person suffers from inflammation in the testicles.

21. If the Moon is in Cancer or Scorpio in Rasi or in Navamsa and is powerfully aspected by malefics, the person suffers from diseases in the anus.

22. Saturn and Mars in the 12th and the 2nd ; the Moon in the Ascendant, the Sun in the 7th, respectively, make the native suffer from white leprosy.

23. If the Moon is in the 10th, Mars in the 7th and Saturn in the 2nd from the Sun, the native becomes crippled.

24. If the Moon is between Saturn and Mars and the Sun is in Capricorn, the person suffers from asthma and pneumonia.

25. If the Sun and the Moon mutually exchange their houses either in Rasi or in the Navamsa, the person suffers from consumption.

26. If the Moon is in the 5th navamsa of Sagittarius, or in the navamsas of Aries, Pisces, Capricorn and Cancer or in any other signs and aspected by Saturn or Mars, the person undoubtedly suffers from consumption.

27. If the Sun, the Moon, Mars and Saturn are in the 6th, the 8th, the 2nd or the 12th respectively, the person becomes blind owing to the excessive accumulation of the humour represented by the strongest of these planets.

28. The malefic planets in the 3rd, 5th, 9th and 11th, having no beneficial aspects, produce deafness and this will be given rise to by the humour indicated by the strongest of the planets placed in any of the above signs.

29. If the Moon, the Sun and Mars are in the 7th and have no good aspects, the person suffers from toothache.

30. Weak Moon in the 12th with Saturn will bring about insanity to the native.

31. If Aries, Leo, Scorpio, Capricorn or Aquarius becomes Lagna and malefics aspect it powerfully, the native's head becomes bald.

32. If Saturn is in the 9th or in the 5th and is aspected by malefics, the native suffers from innumerable diseases.

The reader must apply these principles to a number of horoscopes and make a comparative study of the theoretical rules and practical Medical Astrology.

Disease comes under sixth house and this has been exhaustively dealt with in my book *How to Judge a Horoscope*.

CHAPTER XXX

Female Horoscopy*

The combinations hitherto treated of in the previous chapters are applicable to both the sexes but the information given in this chapter is peculiar to the members of the female sex.

For instance, there is puberty in girls which indicates that they are fit for entering the state of motherhood. This is a peculiar characteristic belonging to the feminine sex. The importance of first menses has so much of physical, mental and spiritual significance that it will be impossible to bring them home unless we devote special attention to its study. So many other things such as conception, delivery, etc., are peculiar to the women.

Some of the ancient writers held that even though the horoscopes of the women indicate any Raja Yogas—like bestowing political power, etc., such yogas must be applied to their husbands. Today the order has been rapidly changing. Advocates of sex equality have been springing up like mushrooms. They want to see that no barriers exist between the males and the females, God knows for what purpose. Women have been competing with men in all walks of life. The type of equality, which we have been aiming at seems to be similar to that which the West has realised already and for the results

---

* For further details refer to *Stri Jataka* or *Female Horoscopy* by Prof. B. Suryanarain Rao.

of which it has begun to repent. In ancient India, the equality was of a different nature. History and tradition afford us any number of instances which go to establish that the women never occupied an inferior place in Hindu families or in Hindu society and that a sentiment of reverence and respect had always been associated with their names. With the advent of divorce, companionate marriage and other injurious reforms, the entire fabric of home-life and domestic harmony are threatened with complete destruction. Pure love is being replaced by commercial love. And divorce courts are being resorted to on flimsy grounds or pretexts for getting rid of the husband or wife. A study of the Female Horoscopy will be of immense interest in view of the rapid advancement women have been making in all walks of life.

Important Combinations

1. From the rising sign at birth must be ascertained the complexion, beauty of general appearance. Marital happiness must be consulted from the 8th. From the 7th house should be predicted passions, husband's character, and her own fortunes; pregnancy, issues, conception and abortion should be determined from the 5th house.

2. If the Ascendant or the Moon falls in the Trimsamsa of Aries or Scorpio and if Mars is not well situated, the girl becomes a prostitute before puberty. If the Ascendant falls in the Trimsamsa of Venus, she becomes adulterous; if in Jupiter—virtuous, modest and dignified; if in Mercury—cunning; if in Saturn—dependent and depraved.

3. If Venus and Saturn exchange their navamsas, the girl becomes extremely passionate and gratifies her instincts by unnatural methods.

4. If the 7th bhava falls in the navamsa of Mars, and has the aspect of Saturn, the girl possesses a diseased sexual

organ. If the 7th house rises in a beneficial navamsa, she will
have well-proportioned sexual organ and loves her husband.

5. The woman becomes a widow soon after marriage if
Mars is in the 7th house with absolutely no beneficial aspects,
but having malefic aspects. The Sun in the 7th in a similar
position makes her to be neglected by her husband.

Beneficial Combinations (Raja Yogas)

6. If Jupiter is in the Ascendant, the Moon in the 7th and
Venus in the 10th, the woman becomes the wife of a very rich
man, even if she is born in humble surroundings.

7. If Jupiter is well posited in the *Shadvargas* and is
powerfully aspected by the Moon, the woman's husband will
get a responsible and lucrative position as minister or as an
equal to a king.

8. A woman will have great political power if the
quadrants are occupied by benefics and the 7th falls in a
masculine sign.

9. Mars in 3 or 6 and Saturn in auspicious Shadvargas
cause a very powerful Raja Yoga.

10. A powerful Raja Yoga is caused if Gemini becomes
the Ascendant with waxing Moon there, the Sun in the 11th
and Mercury in the 10th.

11. If the Sun possessing beneficial Shadvargas occupies
the 3rd and Saturn be in the 6th, a powerful Raja Yoga is
caused.

Widowhood

12. Conjunction of the lords of the 7th and the 8th in
the 8th with malefic aspects.

13. Lord of the 7th with Saturn and aspected by Mars.

14. Rahu and the Moon in the 8th with evil aspects.

15. The Moon and Rahu in the 8th and the lord of the
7th with Saturn aspected by Mars.

16. The conjunction of the lords of the 1st and the 8th in the 12th and malefic aspects over the 8th.

17. The 7th house and its lord between two or more evil planets without beneficial aspects.

First Menses and its Influence

This physical change in the constitution of a girl has a tremendous influence over her entire future and a thorough investigation into the results of planetary influences at the time of the first menses is more essential.

As soon as puberty appears in a girl, cast a horoscope for that time just like you would do if a birth time is given and then study the various influences carefully.

The ancient Maharishis appear to have made such wonderful researches in this branch of knowledge that they have been able to trace the influence of weekdays, lunar days, constellations, etc., on the girl during the first menses.

18. If the first menses appear on a Sunday—the girl suffers from diseases ; Monday—good, noble and virtuous ; Tuesday—miserable ;   Wednesday—domestic   harmony ; Thursday—virtuous and chaste; Friday—obedient to husband ; and Saturday—vicious and bad tempered.

19. The following constellations are auspicious for first menses : —Hasta, Chitta, Swati, Visakha, Anuradha, Uttara, Uttarashadha, Uttarabhadra, Sravana, Moola, Revati, Dhanishta, Satabhisha, Aswini, Pushyami, Rohini, and Mrigasira. First menses is condemned in Pubba, Poorvashadha, Poorvabhadra, Bharani and Aslesha.

20. The following times are unfavourable for the appearance of first menses in a girl :—Sunrise, sunset and twilights ; the days of solar entries into the first degree of the sign ; Full and New Moon days ; times of eclipses ; the 8th and 14th days of the dark half of a lunar month ; the time

when the Moon stands in the 8th house from the radix Moon
or that of her husband; in constellations occupied by evil
planets; when halos are seen round the Sun and the Moon;
during the death times of nearest relatives; when abnormal
phenomena like the appearance of comets, etc., occur; when
the Sun moves in the constellations of Bharani, Krittika,
Aridra and Aslesha.

21. The signs of Aries, Cancer, Scorpio, Sagittarius and
Capricorn forebode evil if first menses occur in them; the
rest are auspicious ones.

Proper remedies must be undertaken to avert the evil
influences of planets.

22. If the number of drops of menstrual fluid be one or
two, wealth and good enjoyment in life are indicated; otherwise the consequences will be baneful.

For fuller information on these points, I should refer my
readers to the excellent book *Female Horoscopy* by Prof.
B. Suryanarain Rao.

CHAPTER XXXI

Mundane Astrology

Strictly speaking Mundane means anything that relates to this material world but somehow, at least so far as astrology is concerned, it is interpreted as meaning "state" or "national" and Mundane Astrology means astrology of the State or national astrology which helps us to predict the general events in the different countries like wars, plagues, pestilences, revolutions and incidents that directly affect a State or the head of a State and consequently tell upon the people.

So many calamities in this world could have been prevented had only the different statesmen at the helms of the various governments heeded to the warnings repeatedly given by competent astrologers, regarding the occurrence of unhappy terrestrial events.

If a statesman knew when his country would be attacked, he could either make such preparations as would enable him to present a strong and united front to the enemy, or if he loved peace could devise such plans and negotiations as would bring about the desired honourable peace. In all these important affairs, prevention is much better than cure. Why should a relief propaganda be organised after a certain catastrophe like plague, earthquake or floods has occurred and then repent for the colossal loss of precious human lives and properties. The loss could have been overcome if it had been previously ascertained when such dangerous phenomena would visit us.

My publications *World Prospects in 1939 and 1940* and *World Predictions for 1941 to 1945* and my innumerable editorials in THE ASTROLOGICAL MAGAZINE deal with the practical aspect of Mundane Astrology. Therein I have made successful predictions about events and happenings that were most improbable at the time the predictions were ventured but which were realised subsequently. I have also discussed several national horoscopes and a student of Mundane Astrology will find, in the above books, a lot of data for carrying on research work.

The effects of the planets over the affairs of nations are found to be just as powerful as they are over the life of the individual. Prof. B. Suryanarain Rao was noted for his predictions of national events. Zadkiels I and II have made remarkable predictions. I predicted the second world war nearly one year in advance. Hitler's aggressive designs; Mussolini's collaboration, France's collapse in 1940; return of the Negus to Abyssinia; Japan's Far-Eastern Policy; Fates of Holland, Belgium, etc., German invasion of Russia; Mussolini's fall; Italy's capitulation; the invasion of Europe by the Allies; and the fall of Hitler; end of the war, Indian political developments, Gandhi's assassination, Khruschev's fall, exit of Nkrumah, Chinese invasion of India, Nixon's fall, recent developments in India, etc.,—have all been correctly foretold by me in my books and in the columns of THE ASTROLOGICAL MAGAZINE. There is enough scientific basis to warrant the study of Mundane Astrology by those in control of a national government or to justify the introduction into national affairs of a competent Astrological Bureau to advise on future foreign entanglements. I admit that it is too much to expect, in the present state of Mundane Astrology, for this Bureau to be always right, but if it could

give the Government enough insight into future complications
with foreign powers, that would be worth untold millions
even if this supposed Bureau made only 60 per cent of correct
predictions.

By repeated observation and the development of *yoga
vidya*, the Maharishis were able to foresee all these clearly
and assign certain signs of the zodiac as representing or as
directly ruling certain parts of this world. Varaha Mihira
has given a list of countries governed by the signs and planets
in his *Brihat Samhita* and we have interpreted them in this
light of modern geographical distribution of countries.

Zodiacal Signs and Countries

Aries.—France, Switzerland, England, Denmark, Germany,
Lesser Poland, Syria, Burgandy—Naples, Verono, Capua,
Marseilles, Birmingham, Florence.

Taurus.—Greater Poland, Persia, Ireland, Asia Minor,
Georgia, part of Russia, Holland, Greek Archipelago—
Muntua, Leipzig, Dublin, St. Louis, Rhodes.

Gemini.—South-west of England, U.S.A., Flanders, Lower
Egypt, Belgium, Sordinia, Wales, Tripoli—London, Versailles,
Melbourne, Plymouth, Brabant, San Francisco.

Cancer.—Holland, Scotland, New Zealand, Paraguay—
New York, Constantinople, Tripoli, Algiers, Tunis, Venice,
Manchester, Genoa and Amsterdam.

Leo.—Italy, Sicily, part of France, Chaldea, Bohemia—
Damascus, Bristol, Bath, Conton and Philadelphia, Chicago
and Bombay.

Virgo.—India, Mesopotamia, Asiatic and European
Turkey, Brazil, Crete, Assyria, West Indies, Greece—Paris,
Lyons, Jerusalem and Los Angeles.

Libra.—Some part of India, Portugal, Livonia, Austria,
Alaska, Japan, Tibet—Sheffield, Lisbon, Frankfort, Antwerp,
Charleston, Vienna, Johannesberg.

Scorpio—Bavaria, Judea, Catalonia, Norway, Morocco—Washington, Dover, Liverpool, Baltimore.

Sagittarius.—Spain, Arabia, Hungary, Madagascar—Cologne, Rottenburg, Toledo, Sheffield.

Capricorn.—A part of India, Macedonia, Afghanistan, Mexico, Greece, Saxony, Thrace—Brandenberg, Oxford, Brussels.

Aquarius.—Sweden, some parts of Arabia, Russia, Denmark, Lower Sudan, Abyssinia—Brighton, Hamburg and Bremen.

Pisces.—Normany, Portugal, Galicia, Egypt, Nubia, Sahara—Alexandria, Lancaster, Ratisbon.

We have also an enumeration of the constellations that govern the different countries and the planets and signs that govern the different parts of a country in Varaha Mihira's *Brihat Samhita.*

Houses in Mundane Astrology

The Lagna or the Ascendant of a country will be the particular sign that rules over it. For instance, the Lagna of England is Aries ; that of India is Virgo and so on. The exact rising degree is not definitely known.

The twelve houses from the Ascendant in a national horoscope represent the following important significations :

First house.—General affairs in the State, public health, the conditions of the Cabinet.

Second house.—State revenue, aristocracies in the State, wealth of the people, State imports and commercial transactions, allies and revenue.

Third house.—Telephones, telegrams, railways, aeroplanes, journals and newspapers and the disposition of the neighbouring nations.

Fourth house.—Schools, colleges and other educational institutions, pupils, landed estates, general happiness, trade and agriculture.

Fifth house.—Mentality of the rulers, children in the State new births, crime and places of amusements.

Sixth house.—State loans and debts, diseases of the people and the rulers, territorial attacks, naval and other forces.

Seventh house.— Health of the women, immorality in the country, rate of infant mortality, war, foreign relations, etc.

Eighth house.—Death-rate, State Treasury.

Ninth house.—Temples, mosques and churches, irreligiousness, judicial courts, law and righteousness.

Tenth house.—The ruler, parliament, foreign trade, exports, exploitation, revolutions and lawlessness.

Eleventh house.—Gains from other nations, gains in trade, international relationships.

Twelfth house.—Secret crime, plots, hospitals and such institutions, war and losses.

In giving the national predictions, the following factors must be carefully considered :—

1. A horoscope cast for the commencement of the Lunar year enables one to predict world events during that year with a fair degree of accuracy.

2. Mark the horoscope for the time of the entry of the Sun into Aries, Cancer, Libra and Capricorn and analyse the disposition of planets and the consequent results. These will give the general results for the world during the particular year.

3. Consider the lunations every month and the planetary positions and how they stand with reference to the particular nation or nations.

Say, for instance, the lunation takes place in Aries and Saturn and Mars are there with other malefic influences ; the country represented by Aries suffers greatly from public ill-health, there will be chaos in the debates of the Cabinet and the general affairs during that month will not be satisfactory.

During the same month, the lunation will have taken place in the 10th house from another sign governing another country. The results will be that the death of the monarch is indicated, foreign trade will be at its lowest ebb, lawlessness will prevail and signs of revolution will be apparent. If the same combination occurs in the 2nd house of another country, then financial depression in the State will set in, retrenchment follows, imports affected, etc. Thus it is seen that evil combinations in any sign will affect all the countries in some way or the other.

The most important aspect in Mundane Astrology is the Planetary Cabinet which will be changing portfolios every year and thus the results will also be changing. Planetary Cabinet means simply this—All the seven planets will become king, prime minister, commander-in-chief, lord of vegetation, lord of minerals, lord of juices, lord of grains, cattle, etc., and these offices will be changing every year. The planet which becomes king in one year becomes prime minister in the next year and so on. These details can be ascertained by looking into any standard almanac.

4. The Sun and the Moon are generally royal planets ; if in any year either of these does not become king, then during that year, the royalty will greatly suffer. Similarly, Mars is the permanent commander-in-chief. If, however, in any particular year he does not become the commander-in-chief, the army and navy during that year must suffer. All these details must be considered.

5. The appearance of eclipses plays a great part in national astrology. The influences will be exercised for a period of 6 months before and 6 months after the appearance. The effects of the eclipse will find manifestation in the countries through which the eclipse passes. If two eclipses— of course one solar and one lunar—occur within 14 days, there

generally will be national troubles, assassinations and war activities (*vide* the leading article in the October 1941 issue of THE ASTROLOGICAL MAGAZINE).

There were two eclipses in March 1914 within 14 days, and Prof. B. Suryanarain Rao, in the March 1914 issue of THE ASTROLOGICAL MAGAZINE, predicted the outbreak of the Great War in the August of that year and said that its origin would be in Europe and that it would arise from the assassination of a prince.

That Roosevelt would be elected as the President of America was predicted by the author in the September 1932 issue of THE ASTROLOGICAL MAGAZINE, while the election took place in November, on the basis of a solar eclipse in that year.

It was also pointed out that there would be chaos and confusion in the Parliamentary debates in London, that a new Cabinet would be formed, that U.S.A. would suffer from great financial troubles and that a number of children would die in England on account of some disease. All these came to pass. Mr. Roosevelt's election for the Presidential Chair of America, for the third time, was clearly predicted in the September 1940 issue of THE ASTROLOGICAL MAGAZINE.

Thus eclipses have great significance in Mundane Astrology.

6. The appearance of comets and the directions in which they appear should also be considered. The country represented by the signs, in which comets appear, suffers, and the health of the people will be affected.

7. Lastly, the nativities of individuals themselves who rule either as kings or as Presidents will have great significance and they should be well studied.

8. Earthquakes must also be considered. Thus Mundane Astrology is a very difficult and useful branch and the student

must be careful in venturing predictions. For greater details
regarding the influences of eclipses, appearance of ometcs,
lunations and the planetary cabinet, I should refer the reader
to the *Brihat Samhita* of Varaha Mihira and in a small book
like this, it will not be possible to incorporate more than what
has already been done.

CHAPTER XXXII

Muhurtha or Election

Muhurtha means auspicious. In astrology, Muhurtha comprehends the selection of auspicious times for every new event and hence, we could interpret *muhurtha* as being equivalent in the English word election.

It is an established fact that success in any work entirely depends upon the auspicious moment at which it is commenced. Even though a man may possess the best advantages, he will not be successful in the end if he commences the work in an inauspicious time. This means that he has not considered the value of moving in harmony with natural forces— that is - the invisible influences imbedded in the womb of Time, throw obstacles on his way and deprive him of his success.

Muhurtha, as a matter of fact, helps us to determine, when exactly the influences contained in Time are well disposed, when they are ill-disposed, what combinations of planets produce beneficial influences and how the invisible currents could be made to flow easily, after a business is started in an auspicious moment.

If we start an event in a favourable time, the ethereal currents, liberated from the planets at that particular moment, will work in the minds of others and make them help the person to attain success.

Even in marriages, if in the girl's horoscope widowhood is threatened, it can be averted by selecting a very auspicious moment for celebrating the marriage.

We call such an auspicious moment, when all the beneficial ethereal currents are called into operation, *Shubha Lagna* and the inauspicious moment *Ashubha Lagna*.

1. *Favourable Periods for Administering Medicines.*— Sunday, Monday, Wednesday, Thursday and Friday. Saturday and Tuesday are not favourable.

At the time of administering medicine, benefics should be in quadrant, the 6th, the 8th and the 12th houses from the Ascendant. The constellations Anuradha, Mrigasira, Revati, Rohini, Chitta, Uttara, Uttarashadha, Sravana, Dhanishta, Satabhisha, Punarvasu, Swati, Aswini and Hasta are good.

Find out the time for the Lagna (rising sign) when Saturn, the Sun and Mars are in quadrants on Saturday, Sunday and Tuesday and at this moment perform surgical operations.

2. *Selling and Buying.*—Constellations Visakha, Hasta, Mrigasira, Punarvasu, Dhanishta, Aswini, Aridra, Pubba, Jyeshta, Poorvashadha and Poorvabhadra are good for buying and selling domestic animals. When Leo is rising at the time of this transaction, it is unfavourable. Sunday, Monday, Tuesday, Wednesday, New Moon day, the 4th, the 9th and the 14th days of the lunar month are unfavourable.

3. *Agricultural Operations.*—Commence ploughing operations in the constellations Revati, Hasta, Makha, Uttara, Uttarashadha, Rohini, Uttarabhadra, Mrigasira, Sravana, Dhanishta, Satabhisha, Pushyami and Chitta. Tuesday, Wednesday and Saturday are not good. When the signs Pisces, Taurus, Gemini and Virgo are rising, commence such operations. Avoid New Moon days, Full Moon days, and the lunar days of the 8th, the 9th and the 14th of the dark half.

4. *Digging Wells.*—This must be done when certain signs are rising if water were to fall in the well so dug. In

Aquarius and Taurus, water can be secured in the wells. Scorpio, Libra and Gemini give very little of water and the rest of the signs give absolutely no water. Similarly, no water will be secured if quadrants are occupied by evil planets. Venus and the Moon in quadrants produce much water in the well. When wells are dug in the sign occupied by the Sun, there will be rock found in the well. The rising signs must be watery signs for obtaining a plentiful supply of water and the planets influencing must also be watery ones.

5. *Entering New Houses.*—The lunar months Magha, Phalguna, Vaisakha and Jyeshta are good. Monday, Wednesday, Thursday, Friday and Saturday are good. Uttarashadha, Uttarabhadra and Rohini are good. New houses should not be entered into when the Sun is in Aquarius, Cancer or Gemini. Constellations occupied by evil planets must be avoided. Hasta, Swati, Pushyami, Aswini, Sravana and Punarvasu are generally considered unfavourable.

6. *Shaving.*—Cutting of hair means much loss of vitality and to minimise this, favourable days must be selected. The 4th, 14th and 16th days of the lunar month and New Moon and Full Moon days are unfavourable. The constellations Pushyami, Punarvasu, Revati, Hasta, Sravana, Dhanishta, Mrigasira, Aswini, Chitta, Swati, Satabhisha and Jyeshta are good.

7. *Constructing New Houses.*—The Sun must be in Taurus, Cancer, Leo, Aquarius, Aries, Libra, Scorpio and Capricorn. The period when Jupiter and Venus are in combustion must be avoided. The lunar month of Ashadha, Sravana, Bhadrapada, Aswija and Pushya are not good. The constellations Anuradha, Moola, Aswini, Hasta, Mrigasira, Jyeshta, Swati, Chitta, Rohini, Uttarashadha, Uttara and Uttarabhadra are favourable.

Benefics must be in quadrants (not in the Ascendant) and the 10th house must be occupied by Jupiter, Venus or Mercury and evil planets must be in the 3rd, the 6th and the 11th.

8. *Strength of Constellation.*—By this we will be able to ascertain whether a particular day is favourable to a particular person or not.

The procedure is this. Count from the birth constellation to the constellation of the particular day on which any new work is to be done or any journey undertaken, etc., and divide the product by 9, if divisible. Otherwise keep it as it is. If the remainder is one (*janma*), it indicates danger to body; if 2 (*sampat*) wealth and prosperity; if 3 (*vipat*) dangers, losses and accidents; if 4 (*kshema*) prosperity; if 5 (*pratyak*) obstacles; if 6 (*sadhana*) good results and gains; if 7 (*nidhana*) danger and death; if 8 (*mitra*) good; and if 9 (*parama mitra*) very favourable.

Illustration.—Birth star Mrigasira wants to interview a superior officer for representing his grievances on 6-9-1933, 1 p.m. The constellation of that day is Uttarabhadra and lasts upto 2 p.m. (in Bangalore). Counting from Mrigasira to Uttarabhadra we get 22; dividing this by 9 we get 22/9 = 2 4/9. The balance is 4 and accordingly it represents kshema or prosperity and the business will be successful.

9. *Five Sources of Energy.*—In this, five sources of planetary, stellar and zodiacal energies are concerned. Supposing a man has fixed a particular time on a particular day in a particular month for commencing some important work. Whether or not the five sources of energy operate favourably at that time can be thus ascertained. In all these cases, lunar dates must be considered and the constellations can be found out by the Moon's position. The method of counting the lunar days is given in the earlier chapters.

Take the number of lunar days from the first of each lunar month, the number of weekdays from Sunday, the

number of constellations from Aswini and the number of
zodiacal signs from Aries.   Add all and divide the total by 9.
If the remainder is 1 it indicates (*mrityu*) danger or death ; if
2 (*vahni*) danger from fire ; if 4 (*raja panchaka*) very bad ;
if 6 (*chora panchaka*) bad ; if 8 (*roga panchaka*) disease bringing;
if the remainder is 3, 5, 7 or no remainder at all, then it is
good.

Illustration.—Mr. X wants to start a new business on
17-9-1933 Sunday at sunrise. The constellation is Aslesha
(rules upto 9 a.m.) and the lunar date is 13th of dark half of
the lunar month Bhadrapada.   The rising sign is Virgo.
Calculating the Panchaka for this, we get :—

No. of lunar days	— 13
No. of constellations	— 9
No. of zodiacal signs	— 6
No. of the day from Sunday	— 1
	29

Dividing this by 9 we get 29/9 = 3 2/9 ; 2 remainder. It
indicates *vahni*. So the time selected is not favourable.

10.   *Marriage.*—The 7th house from the marriage Ascendant must be free and without any planet. Mars should not
occupy the 8th and Venus must never be in the 6th. Jupiter,
Venus or Mercury should be in quadrants (excepting the 7th
house or 2nd quadrant),

New Moon day, Full Moon day, the 8th and 6th lunar
days must be avoided. The lunar months of Magha, Phalguna,
Vaisakha and Jyeshta are good. Constellations Uttara,
Uttarashadha, Uttarabhadra, Revati, Swati, Makha, Hasta,
Rohini, Anuradha, Mrigasira and Moola are favourable.

11.   *Nuptials or Consummation Ceremony.*—There should
be no planets in the 8th. Sunday, Saturday and Tuesday are
bad. Taurus, Gemini, Cancer, Leo, Virgo, Libra, Aquarius,
Sagittarius and Pisces are good. New Moon day, Full

Moon day, the 14th, 6th, 8th and 4th days of the lunar month must be avoided. The constellations Satabhisha, Hasta, Rohini, Sravana, Anuradha, Swati, Uttara, Uttarashadha, Moola and Uttabhadra are good.

12. *Name-Giving (Namakarana) of a New-born Child.*— The 8th house must be free. Friday, Wednesday, Thursday and Monday are good. The constellations Anuradha, Sravana, Uttara, Uttarabhadra, Pushyami, Revati, Hasta, Aswini, Rohini, Mrigasira, Dhanishta and Uttarashadha are favourable.

13. *First Feeding of a Child (Anna Prasana).*—The 10th house must be without any planet. The lunar days 8, 12, 4, 6, 14 and 9 and New Moon and Full Moon days are not good. Constellations Sravana, Swati, Anuradha, Aswini, Hasta, Dhanishta, Pushyami, Punarvasu and Mrigasira are preferable.

14. *Rahukala.*—Every day certain evil influences are supposed to be exercised on our planet at the following hours and they must be avoided for any good work. If the sunrise is at 6 a.m., then Rahukala will operate on :—

Monday	from	7-30 a.m.	to	9- 0 a.m.
Tuesday	,,	3- 0 p.m.	,,	4-30 p.m.
Wednesday	,,	12- 0 noon	,,	1-30 p.m.
Thursday	,,	1-30 p.m.	,,	3- 0 p.m.
Friday	,,	10-30 a.m.	,,	12- 0 noon
Saturday	,,	9- 0 a.m.	,,	10-30 a.m.
Sunday	,,	4-30 p.m.	,,	6- 0 p.m.

15. *Upanayana.*—Upanayana means the investiture of sacred thread or, to be more explicit, initiation into the mysteries of *Parabrahma* or the Supreme Intelligence. This ceremony is performed amongst all high caste Hindus, when special religious instructions are given.

The 8th house must be free from planets. Aries, Taurus, Gemini, Cancer, Virgo, Libra and Pisces are beneficial. The constellations Bharani, Krittika, Aridra, Aslesha, Makha, Pubba, Visakha, Jyeshta, Moola, Poorvashadha, Satabhisha and Poorvabhadra are evil constellations and this ceremony must be performed in any one of the remaining 15 constellations, which are beneficial ones. Wednesday, Thursday, Friday and Monday are good weekdays.

16. *Travelling*.—Travelling towards east on Saturday and Monday, west on Sunday and Friday, north on Tuesday and Wednesday and south on Thursday does not produce good results. The astrological writers recommend the following weekdays for travelling towards the different directions :— East—Tuesday ; South—Monday and Saturday; West— Wednesday and Thursday ; and North—Friday and Sunday.

Sagittarius, Taurus, Cancer, Leo and Libra are favourable signs for travelling; the rest are unfavourable.

The constellations Mrigasira, Aswini, Pushyami, Anuradha, Hasta, Punarvasu, Revati, Moola, Sravana and Dhanishta are good.

The best time would be 12 noon when the Sun will be most powerful and this is called *Abhijin Muhurtha*. This moment counteracts all the evil influences; or malefics must occupy 3, 6 and 11.

17. *Commencing Education*.—By education is meant both religious and secular. The Sanskritists call this *Akshara-sweekara* or bestowing of *Akshara* (indestructible forms of sound vibrations) corresponding to the vague term of alphabets, for the first time on the child.

The 8th house must be without any planet. Lunar days 2, 3, 5, 7, 10, 11, 12 and 13 are favourable. Monday, Wednesday, Thursday and Friday are good. The constellations Punarvasu, Aswini, Chitta, Hasta, Swati, Anuradha, Jyeshta, Revati and Sravana are auspicious.

I have dealt with this subject exhaustively in my book entitled *Muhurtha or Electional Astrology*.

CHAPTER XXXIII

Annual Horoscopes

We have discussed in the previous pages how Hindu astrologers predict future events by means of Vimshottari Dasa, which entirely depends upon the birth positions of planets. In the next chapter, the popular Gochara system has been expounded at considerable length. In this chapter we shall deal with a simple method of ascertaining annual results. Owing to the limited space at our disposal we have to be necessarily brief in our exposition. Full details with copious explanations and a number of illustrations will be found in my book *Varshaphal* or the *Hindu Progressed Horoscope*, which presents a unique method of deciphering annual results. The method adumbrated in this chapter can be advantageously used if a snapshot assessment of a year's outlook is desired.

Before predicting events according to rules it propounds, one should devote some thought for properly comprehending the principles. In this method which are going to set forth below, all technicalities have been omitted and one can easily understand and apply the rules without much effort. It must, however, be hinted that our book *Varshaphal* enables one to make more correct and more detailed predictions as the procedure employed therein is certainly more comprehensive and altogether different, though the principle is more or less the same. The horoscope for any particular year depends upon the time of the Sun's return to the same point that he occupied at the time of birth. Take the case of a person born on Thursday 8-8-1912 A.D. at 33-30 ghatis after sunrise. Predictions for the 29th year are required. From the table given below, find the figures corresponding to age. If there are two digits in age, take the sum of the figures corresponding. Add the same to the number of weekday of birth

*Table for the Yearly Horoscope

Age	Days	Ghatis	Vighatis	Paras
1	1	15	31	30
2	2	31	3	0
3	3	46	34	30
4	5	2	6	0
5	6	17	37	30
6	0	33	9	0
7	1	48	40	30
8	3	4	12	0
9	4	19	43	30
10	5	35	15	0
20	4	10	30	0
30	2	45	45	0
40	1	21	0	0
50	6	56	15	0
60	5	31	30	0
70	4	6	45	0
80	2	42	0	0
90	1	17	15	0

* This table has been based on the duration of the year as given in *Surya Siddhanta*. Researches carried out by me have revealed that the duration of the Siddhanta year is not quite correct and that we have to take the duration of the sidereal year as measured by modern astronomy. A revised table is given in my book *Varshaphal* with fuller explanations and the reader is well advised to follow the method given in *Varshaphal* for casting the annual chart.

(Sunday! Monday 2, etc.), and the birth ghatis. The result will be the time and day of the week at which the required year commences. This will correspond with the time in that year when the Sun occupies the exact position he did at birth.

In the horoscope selected above, the native has completed 28 years and entered on his 29th year.

Age past 28

		For 28 we have		
	Days	Gh.	Vig.	Paras
For 20	— 4	10	30	0
For 8	— 3	4	12	0
For 28	— 0	14	42	0
Add to the above the number of weekday and time of birth	— 5	33	30	0
We get	— 5	48	12	0

The 29th year commences on the nearest Thursday to 8th August. That will be 8th August 1940 and the time for setting the horoscope will be Gh. 48-12. The following are Rasi and Navamsa diagrams for the yearly horoscope.

The *Varsha Dasas* are thus distributed. The Sun's Dasa 110 days, the Moon 60, Mars 32, Mercury 40, Jupiter 48, Venus 56, Saturn 4, Rahu 5, and Lagna 10.

To find the Dasas and their balances, the following procedure should be adopted. Take the birth star of the person (Mrigasira in this case) and count from it to the constellation that rules on the day of the anniversary. Divide the number by 9 and take the balance and ascribe the Dasa in the following order: Sun, Moon, Mercury, Jupiter, Venus, Saturn, Rahu and Lagna. Take the extent of the star and find out what fraction of it remains at the commencement of the year and by the rule of three find the balance of Dasa at the time of solar entry and ascribe the days to the other planets and Lagna as per order given above—On 8th August 1950, the star Hasta rules for 26-20 ghatis. At the time of the commencement of new year Chitta rules. The duration of Chitta is 55-30 ghatis and the arc of constellation (Chitta) that has already passed in Gh. 21-52 while that remaining to be passed being Gh. 33.38. Counting from Mrigasira to Chitta, we get 10 leaving 1 as balance when divided by 9. This represents Ravi Dasa lasting for 110 days. If 55.5 ghatis (duration of Chitta) gives 110 days, what will 33.63 (Chitta remaining) give ?

$$\frac{33.63}{55.5} \times 110 = 66.654 \text{ days.}$$

This is the balance of Ravi Dasa and subsequent Dasas succeed as shown in next page:

Dasa	No. of Days	From	To
Sun ...	67	8- 8-1940	14-10-1940
Moon ...	60	14-10-1940	13-12-1940
Mars ...	32	13-12-1940	14- 1-1941
Mercury ...	40	14- 1-1941	23- 2-1941
Jupiter ...	48	23- 2-1941	12- 4-1941
Venus ...	56	12- 4-1941	7- 6-1941
Saturn ...	4	7- 6-1941	11- 6-1941
Rahu ...	5	11- 6-1941	16- 6-1941
Lagna ...	10	16- 6-1941	26- 6-1941
Sun ...	43	26- 6-1941	8- 3-1941
	365		

General Estimates

Consideration of Birth Horoscope.—In any estimate of results the radical horoscope is of much importance. The Dasa and Bhukti ruling at the present time should be carefully noted as also Gochara positions. In the example illustrated, *Guru Dasa, Budha Bhukti* will be operating throughout the 29th year of the native. As both Jupiter and Mercury are well situated and they have association with the 10th house, the period is likely to prove beneficial. According to Gochara, the subject is having 7½ years' Saturn and both Jupiter and Saturn are in the 12th and Rahu in the 5th— all these being bad. As this is the second time that the native has been undergoing 7½ years Saturn, the evil effects will only be moderate. Combining the above two sets of influences, the resultant is still favourable. Now let us examine the yearly horoscope.

Lord of Lagna, Venus, is in the 2nd or house of wealth and is aspected by Saturn—a yogakaraka. In the navamsa, the Lagnadhipathi is ordinary—being bad by association and

good by ownership and liberation. In general, the results will
be middling in the course of this year, but tending towards
good. Lord of the 10th has neechabhanga. In the navamsa,
Saturn has Shubhakarthari Yoga. Thus, the 10th house indications will be normal, and financial conditions will be
bettered. As Mars occupies the 4th, general happiness will be
lacking. Lord of the 2nd and 5th in the 3rd suggests help to
relatives while the Sun and Mercury in the 11th from the
Moon is indicative of good reputation, name and contact with
high circles. Lord of the 10th (from the Moon) in the 11th
and the parivarthana or exchange of houses between lord of
Lagna (Moon) and the 11th is favourable for business
improvement. The Sun and Mercury in the 3rd in a moveable sign (Cancer) produce travels in connection with business
which will prove profitable to the native. The 7th lord Mars
in the 10th from the 7th assures domestic happiness but his
being aspected by Jupiter, lord of the 8th (in the Navamsa)
gives rise to quarrels and friction. On the whole, financially
and professionally, the year will be good while the conjunction
of the Moon and Rahu does not give mental happiness.

The first Dasa is that of the Sun. This extends from
8-8-1940 to 14-10-1940. The Sun is lord of the 4th and is in
the 3rd with lord of the 5th forming a yoga. Mercury is the
planet for business, trade and speculation. As the Sun is in a
moveable sign and moveable Navamsa in conjunction with
lord of the 2nd and 5th and in the 2nd from the 2nd, he gives
long travelling in connection with business. As everyone
knows Cancer indicates North and the journey will be in the
Northern countries. In *Mars Dasa*, expenses will be great and
income good, domestic quarrels, friction and journeys.
Mercury—The Sun's results may be repeated with slight
modification. *Jupiter*—Misunderstandings, unexpected losses

and mental worry. *Venus*—Financial improvements, domestic happiness and good in general.

We may herewith give the general results of Dasas which should be applied consistent with the strength and weakness of planets obtaining in the yearly horoscope. The results foretold are to be predicted with great caution, prudence and practical knowledge of places, times, conditions and circumstances.

If the *Sun* is powerful, he will give wealth, clothes, jewels, high respect and happiness in general. If the *Sun* is unfavourable, he will cause disappointments, loss of money, mental worries, and bodily complaints. When the *Moon* is powerful, he will give great respect, much money and mental peace ; when unfavourable, increase of enemies, disease, travelling, and hatred among his relations. When *Mars* is favourable, he will cause happiness, official favour, success in endeavours and otherwise good results. When unfavourable, causes hatred, loss of money, injuries and accidents, disputes pertaining to lands, etc. If *Mercury* is well disposed, comforts, success in examinations, business and trade, travelling and mental happiness. When unfavourable, cruel deeds, losses in speculation and business. *Jupiter* :—Favourable, religious interest, progress in education, birth of issues, if Rasi Dasas show such birth—and charitable disposition : when unfavourable, gives travelling, bad company, sinful deeds and much expenditure. *Venus* :—Favourable : female happiness, reputation, good income and a pleasant life; unfavourable : loss of money, fear from enemies, scandals, diseases and exhaustion. When *Saturn* is favourable, houses, happiness, rank, finances and new introductions. When unfavourable, unpleasantness, loss of money, emaciation of body, bad name and diseases. When *Rahu* is favourable he gives good charitable disposition, promotion and success.

When bad, worry, death or unpleasant news, company with base men and increase of enemies. *Lagna* :—Favourable : denotes good results in the commencement and indifferent results later on.

The nature of results of the planetary Dasa depends to a great extent upon their rulerships, aspects and associations. Jupiter, as lord of the 8th in the 5th, will certainly cause sickness to children.

CHAPTER XXXIV

Gocharaphala or Results of Transits

It will be seen that in the preparation of a horoscope, planetary positions will be fixed in their respective longitudes. They are there and they will continue to be fixed. But there is no stoppage of planetary movements. Planets take varying periods for moving from one sign to another. Such movements give rise to the stimulation of radioactive disintegration which, on falling on the individual, can produce psychophysical changes in his character and disposition. Calculations must be made not only in regard to the Dasas and Bhuktis ruling at any particular period but also due consideration should be bestowed on results of transits or Gochara movements of planets. Gochara enables us to predict the effects of the current period.

In predicting Gochara results, the Moon and the birth constellation play a prominent part. Mark the position of the Moon at the time of birth. The sign, in which the birth Moon is placed, is called the Janma Rasi.

The Transiting of the Sun in the 12 Rasis from Radical Moon.—When the *Sun* traverses through the Rasi occupied by the Moon, the person suffers from loss of wealth, loss of prestige, sickness and will have many obstacles and aimless travels. When he transits in the 2nd house, there will be loss of wealth, he will suffer deceit, he will have full of financial worries. In the 3rd house, there will be advent of money, happiness, relief from diseases, recognition from superiors, honours and courage. In the 4th house, there will be diseases, constant attacks from opponents, no peace of mind, pressure from creditors, and sorrow and misery. The Sun transiting the 5th will cause mental agitation, ill-health, embarrassment and accidents. The Sun in the 6th gives rise to release from sorrows, worries and troubles, destruction of enemies and peace of mind. The Sun, transiting the 7th, produces wearisome travelling, colic and anal troubles, humiliation and sickness. In the 8th, Sun's progress gives rise to quarrels with friends, diseases, high blood pressure, royal and official displeasure. The Sun's transit in the 9th house will cause to the native danger, humiliation, dependency, disappointment and separation. One will accomplish his desire and plans, and success will attend on all kinds of undertakings when the Sun is in the 10th. In the 11th, the passage of the Sun will confer on a person honour, health, wealth and success. When the Sun passes through the 12th house, there will be sorrow, creation of a situation which causes loss to everything, quarrels and ill-health.

It must be noted that when passing through the first 10 degrees of a sign, Mars and the Sun produce results. Of the different planets, the Gochara results of the slow moving planets, Jupiter and Saturn, are held to be the most powerful. The triennial results may be ascertained from Saturn, the yearly effects from Jupiter, the monthly results from other planets and the daily influences from the Moon.

We shall first enumerate the likely results that are supposed to accrue on account of transits of the different planets in the different signs from the Moon and then describe the special rules governing Gochara. When the *Moon* transits the sign occupied by her at the time of birth of a person, the native will get excellent food, bed and clothes. When the Moon passes through the 2nd house, loss of respect and of money and obstacles in the way of success are to be predicted. In the 3rd house, the native gets clothes, pleasure from wife and finance; in the 4th, he becomes mentally uneasy; in the 5th, suffers from humility, ill-health, pain of mind and other obstacles; in the 6th, enjoys wealth, health, comfort, redemption from enemies; 7th house, conveyances, good food and financial equilibrium. The Moon transiting the 8th produces misery, ill-health and fear from unexpected sources; in the 9th from herself, pain of mind, chest pain, fatigue of body and the like are caused. When the Moon passes throagh the 10th house, success will attend in every sphere of activity; in the 11th house, the person will enjoy prosperity, will get wealth and new friends; when the Moon transits through the 12th sign, he suffers from accidents and injuries.

It may be remarked in passing that unless *Gochara* is combined with Ashtakavarga, results cannot be predicted with appreciable accuracy. Suppose the Moon is transiting the sign occupied by her at birth. The Moon produces beneficial results provided the benefic dots there are above 4. If they are below 4, then the Moon cannot certainly do as much good as is ascribed to her. Planets produce good, bad or indifferent results during their transits at any particular moment, in accordance with the number of benefic dots which the planets obtain in their respective Ashtakavargas (see my book *Ashtakavarga System of Prediction* for more details regarding Ashtakavarga).

Again, we have to consider what is called Vedha (an obstructing force or point) when delineating results according to Gochara. The Sun, for instance, transiting the 11th, 3rd, 10th and 6th signs from the radical Moon is supposed to yield good results. The smooth flowing of such good results will be obstructed if there are any other planets (simultaneously) transiting the 5th, 9th, 4th and 12th signs from the Moon respectively. To be more explicit with reference to the Sun, if he transits the 11th, the Vedhasthana (obstructing point) will be the 5th; if he transits the 3rd, the Vedasthana will be the 9th; if he transits the 10th; the Vedhasthana will be the 12th. Suppose the Sun is in the 11th; according to Gochara, the results will be honour and health, wealth and success. These good effects are produced only when the 5th (a house of Vedha) is not simultaneously transited by any other planet excepting *Saturn*; conversely, if the Sun is in the 5th, in the course of Gochara, no evil will be produced provided the 11th is being transited at the same time by any other planet, excepting Saturn. Similarly the Vedhasthanas must be considered for all the planets and then the results predicted.

The following are the *Vedhankas* for the different planets. The figures in the nominator indicate the signs counted from the birth Moon when passing through which the respective planets produce good results. Denominator figures indicate *Vedhankas*. Take for instance Mars. The nominator figure 3 indicates that Mars transiting the 3rd gives rise to good effect. The denominator figure 12, just below 3, is the Vedha point. Any planet transiting this Vedha point, when Mars is in the 3rd, deprives Mars from causing good effects. It must be noted that no Vedha occurs between the Sun and Saturn, and the Moon and Mercury. The denominator figure given below each nominator figure is the *Vedhanka* (point of obstruction) for it.

$$\text{Sun}: \quad \frac{11—3—10—\ 6}{5—9—\ 4—12}$$

$$\text{Moon}: \quad \frac{7—1—\ 6—11—10—3}{2—5—12—\ 8—\ 4—9}$$

$$\text{Mars}: \quad \frac{3—11—6}{12—\ 5—9}$$

$$\text{Mercury}: \quad \frac{2—4—6—8—10—11}{5—3—9—1—\ 7—12}$$

Jupiter : $\dfrac{2-11-\ 9-5-7}{12-\ 8-10-4-3}$

Venus : $\dfrac{1-2-3-\ 4-5-8-\ 9-11-12}{8-7-1-10-9-5-11-\ 6-\ 3}$

Saturn : $\dfrac{3-11-6}{12-\ 5-9}$

Let us illustrate the above with the following example :

The Sun is in the 11th with 4 *bindus* which is good. No other planet transits the 5th. Hence he is free from Vedha and gives rise to the full good effect of Gochara ; similarly, the effects are computed for the other planets.

Planets	No. of the sign transiting	Ashtaka-varga Bindus	Vedhas caused, if any
Sun ...	11	4	11th is good ; no Vedha occurs.
Moon ...	11	6	11th is good ; but the position of Mars in the 8th has given rise to a Vedha and hence bad.
Mars ...	8	4	Mars in the 8th is bad.
Mercury ...	11	5	11th is good ; but Saturn in the 12th has caused the Vedha and hence bad.
Jupiter ...	9	4	9th is good ; no Vedha caused ; hence good.
Venus ...	1	4	Position in the 1st is good ; Vedha caused as Mars is in the 8th and hence bad.
Saturn ...	12	3	Saturn in the 12th is bad ; the bindus are 3 and hence exceedingly bad ; but Mercury's position in the 11th has mitigated the evil to some extent : still bad.

From the above, it is seen that only Jupiter and the Sun are good while the others have been inclined to produce evil. Hence the worst evil, *viz.*, death, befell the native, especially because, Saturn is in the 12th and Mars in the 8th.

	Moon Rahu	Ascdt.	Sat.	Sat.	Venus	Ketu
Sun Merc. Jupiter		Birth Horoscope		Sun Merc. Moon	About the end of the second week of March 1937 planetary positions	
Venus		Ketu Mars		Jup.	Mars Rahu	

Gochara results should be judged by reference to Vedhasthanas (obstructing points). The present-day astrologers seldom consider these minute details with the result that most of the predictions made by them are being falsified, thus bringing the fair name of astrology into utter disgrace. In the delineation of *Gochara* (transit) results, there does not appear to be a uniform method in the whole of India. Some rest content with describing results on the strength of the motions of Mars, Saturn and Jupiter, irrespective of the part played by the prevailing Dasa (period) and Bhukti (subperiod). There is no denying the fact that the birth horoscope directly affects Gochara results. Astrological predictions can be accurate when the influences of birth chart are blended with those of Gochara and Ashtakavarga, together with Vedha or obstructing forces.

When *Mars* passes through the sign occupied by the Moon at the time of birth of a person, he will suffer from troubles; in the 2nd house from the Moon displeasure of king, and suffering from quarrels, from enemies and disgrace is indicated. There will be fear from thieves and the body will be afflicted with bilious and windy complaints. Mars transiting the 3rd gives rise to gain of objects, pleasure from children, good health, access to riches and new clothes. In the 4th sign, Mars produces evil results such as fever, digestive troubles, blood discharges and depravity of character. Enemies will increase, fresh diseases will make their appearance and mental peace will be completely absent when Mars passes through the 5th house. In the 6th house, relief from troubles, worries and ill-health should be predicted; he leads an independent life, obtains riches and becomes pretty cheerful. When transiting the 7th, the native quarrels with wife or husband, eye troubles, stomach-ache, indigestion, etc., are also likely to be felt. Mars transiting in the 8th produces quite unfavourable effects, such as discharging of blood, loss of wealth, disgrace and mental worry. The same results are repeated at the time of his passing through the 9th. In addition, the subject becomes extremely weak. His transiting the 10th and the 11th produces quite favourable results. Amounts due will be realised. Success will attend on his ventures. Business will improve. In the 12th house, however, he will suffer from various expenses, troubles, diseases of the eye, pinpricks from an angry wife, from bilious complaints and various other worries.

When *Mercury* passes through the sign occupied by the Moon at the time of birth of a person, such person will suffer loss of wealth caused by the advice of wicked men, by talebearers, by imprisonment and quarrels. He will, besides, receive disagreeable intelligence when in his journey. When

Mercury passes through the 2nd house, the person will suffer disgrace but gains success and wealth. When he passes through the 3rd house, the subject will get friends, will be afraid of troubles from the king and from his enemies, he will quit his place due to his wicked deeds. When Mercury passes through the 4th house, the person's kinsmen and family will increase and there will be much gain ; in the 5th house, the person will quarrel with his wife and sons and will not enjoy the company of an excellent wife ; in the 6th house, the person will be liked by all and will gain renown ; in the 7th house, the person's appearance becomes less bright and there will be quarrels. When Mercury passes through the 8th house, the person will get sons, success, clothes and wealth and will become happy and powerful. When he passes through the 9th house from the Moon, the person will meet with obstacles in his work ; in the 10th house, the person's enemies will meet with ruin and the person will get wealth, will enjoy the company of his wife and will be dressed in the flannel. When Mercury passes through the 11th house from the Moon, the person will get wealth, comfort, sons, women, friends and conveyance and will be happy and will receive good intelligence ; in the 12th, the person will suffer disgrace from his enemies, will suffer from diseases and will not enjoy the company of a good wife.

When *Jupiter* passes through the sign occupied by the Moon at the time of birth of a person, such person will lose his wealth and intelligence, will quit his place and will suffer from many quarrels. When Jupiter passes through the 2nd house from the Moon, the person will have no enemies and will enjoy wealth and women. When Jupiter passes through the 3rd house from the Moon, the person will quit his place and will meet with obstacles in his work. When Jupiter passes through the 4th house from the Moon, the person will suffer from troubles caused by his kinsmen, will become patient and resigned and will delight in nothing. When Jupiter passes through the 5th house from the Moon, the person will get servants, prosperity, sons, elephants, houses, bullocks, gold, women, clothes, gems and good qualities. When Jupiter passes through the 6th house from the Moon, the person will be so much afflicted at heart that he will take no delight in the agreeable faces of beautiful women, in the music of the peacock and the cuckoo and in houses made pleasant by the frolic of children playing like the young of the deer. When Jupiter passes through the 7th house from the Moon, the person will enjoy good bed, the company of an excellent woman, wealth, good meals, flowers, conveyance and the like and he will be of good speech and intelligence. When Jupiter passes through the 8th house from the Moon, the person will suffer from imprisonment, diseases, heavy grief, the fatigue of journey and serious illness. When Jupiter passes through the 9th house from the Moon, the person will become efficient at work and influential and he will get sons, success in work, wealth and gain. When Jupiter passes through the 10th house from the Moon, the person will quit his place and suffer loss of health and wealth. When Jupiter passes through the 11th house, the person will return to his country and will recover his health and wealth. When Jupiter passes through the 12th house, the person will suffer grief in his return journey.

When *Venus* passes through the sign occupied by the Moon at the time of birth of a person, such a person will enjoy excellent perfumes, flowers, clothes, houses, bed, meals and women. When Venus passes through the 2nd house from the Moon, the person will get sons, wealth, grain and presents from the king; will have a prosperous family, will enjoy flowers and gems and will be of bright appearance. When Venus passes through the 3rd house from the Moon, the person will become influential, wealthy and respectable and will get clothes. His enemies will meet with ruin. When Venus passes through the 4th house, the person will get friends and will become greatly powerful. When Venus passes through the 5th house, the person will be happy, will get kinsmen, sons, wealth and friends and will not suffer defeat by the enemy. When Venus passes through the 6th house from the Moon, the person will suffer disgrace, will be afflicted with diseases and will be exposed to danger. When Venus passes through the 7th house, the person will suffer injuries through women. When Venus passes through the 8th house from the Moon, the person will get houses, articles of lacquer and beautiful women. When Venus passes through the 9th house from the Moon, the person will become virtuous, happy and wealthy and he will get plenty of clothes. When Venus passes through the 10th house from the Moon, the person will suffer disgrace and will also suffer quarrels. When Venus passes through the 11th house from the Moon, the person will get wealth of his friends and will also get perfumes and clothes. When Venus passes through the 12th house, the person will get very few clothes.

When *Saturn* passes through the sign occupied by the Moon at the time of his birth, such person will suffer from poison and from fire, will quit his kinsmen, will suffer from imprisonment and torture, will travel to foreign lands and live with his friends there, will suffer miseries, loss of wealth and of sons, will suffer also from the fatigues of foot journey and from humiliation. When Saturn passes through the 2nd house from the Moon, the person will suffer from loss of beauty and comfort, will become weak and will get wealth from other men but will not enjoy this wealth long. When Saturn passes through the 3rd house from the Moon, the person will get wealth, servants, articles of enjoyment, camels, buffaloes, elephants, asses and horses. He will become influential, happy, free from diseases and will become greatly powerful and will defeat his enemies in fight. When Saturn passes through the 4th house from the Moon, the person will be separated from his friends, wealth, and wife and ever suspecting evil in everything, will never feel happy. When Saturn passes through the 5th house from the Moon, the person will be separated from his sons and wealth and will suffer from quarrels. When Saturn passes through the 6th house from the Moon, the person will be freed from his enemies and diseases and will enjoy the company of women. When Saturn passes through the 7th or 8th house from the Moon, the person will be separated from his wife and sons, will travel on foot in a pitiable condition. When he passes through the 9th house, the person will have all that has been stated for Saturn passing through the 8th house and will, besides, suffer from hatred, chest pain, imprisonment and in consequence will not properly observe the daily duties. When Saturn passes through the 10th house, the person will get work and will suffer loss of wealth, learning and fame. When Saturn passes through the 11th house from the Moon, the person will become cruel and will get women and wealth. When Saturn passes through the 12th house from the Moon, the person will suffer from much grief. Rahu transiting the 12th house produces results similar to those of Saturn, and Ketu to those of Mars.

CHAPTER XXXV

Practical Horoscopes

For real progress in any science, theory and practice must keep pace with each other. I have till now treated of all the important theoretical principles involved in the study of astrology and shall now close the book with a few practical horoscopes illustrating such theoretical postulates.

The following horoscopes will greatly help the student if he carefully analyses them in the light of the short remarks which I have given for each horoscope illustrated. In the selection of horoscopes, I have been careful to see that they are taken from different classes of people—kings, presidents, orphans those that lost their mothers and fathers earl those that had more than one marriage, debauchees, philosophers and in fact people of all temperaments and dispositions which will prove quite interesting and helpful in the light of astrology.

The date, place and time of birth given for each horoscope are fairly correct and the reader can find out the exact positions of the planets by himself, if he so desires, as here, I have given the planetary positions only in Rasi (sign). I like to give the following 20 horoscopes for the benefit of my readers :—

1. *Birth Data* :—Male, born on 29th July 1883, 2 p.m., near Doria, Italy.

Planetary Positions :—The Moon, Mars and Saturn in Taurus; the Sun, Venus and Mercury in Cancer; Jupiter in Gemini; Ascendant in Scorpio; Rahu in Libra; Ketu in Aries.

General Remarks :—One of the greatest men of Europe; born in humble circumstances as a blacksmith's son; often starved without food; was a great revolutionary; has a sudden downfall and a violent end.

2. *Birth Data* :—Male, born on 11th July 1872, 7-45 a.m. (77° 25' E. and 13° N.).

Planetary Positions :—Ascendant—Cancer ; the Sun— Gemini; the Moon—Leo ; Mars—Gemini; Mercury—Cancer; Jupiter—Cancer ; Venus—Gemini ; Saturn—Sagittarius ; Rahu—Taurus; Ketu—Scorpio.

General Remarks :—Father died in the 2nd year, great strides in life; mark the position of the Sun in Gemini with a malefic Mars and powerfully aspected by Saturn ; two wives; mark how Venus is afflicted; lost two sisters early.

3. *Birth Data* :—Male, born on 10th August 1874, 1-40 a.m. (93° 30' W. and 41° 50' N.).

Planetary Positions :—Ascendant—Taurus; the Sun, the Moon, Mars and Mercury—Cancer ; Jupiter and Venus— Virgo ; Saturn—Capricorn; Rahu Aries ; Ketu—Libra.

General Remarks :—A great politician and equal to a king in status ; saved Europe from anarchy; humane and tactful.

4. *Birth Data* :—Female, born on 30th October 1920, 8-30 p.m. (12° N. and 76° 38' E.).

Planetary Positions :—Ketu—Aries.; Ascendant and the Moon—Taurus; Jupiter and Saturn—Leo ; Rahu and the Sun—Libra ; Mercury and Venus—Scorpio ; Mars— Sagittarius.

General Remarks :—Mark the aspect of Saturn on the Ascendant and the Moon, and the conjunction of malefics in Libra ; suffered seriously from smallpox in the 8th year and also from dropsy; hot constitution; superior airs, died in her 14th year.

5. *Birth Data*:—Female, born on 12th June 1909, at 4–25 a.m. (77° 25′ E. and 13° N.).

Planetary Positions:—Ascendant, the Sun and Rahu— Taurus; Venus and Mercury— Gemini; Jupiter—Leo; Ketu— Scorpio; Mars—Aquarius; the Moon and Saturn—Pisces.

General Remarks:—Fair looking; modest and chaste; mark the position of Mars in the 12th from the Moon—a strong combination for widowhood which took away her husband in her 14th year.

6. *Birth Data*:—Female, born on 11th January 1928, at 8–30 a.m. (77° 25′ E. and 13° N.).

Planetary Positions:—Ascendant—Aquarius; Jupiter— Pisces; Rahu—Taurus; the Moon—Leo; Venus, Saturn and Ketu—Scorpio; the Sun, Mercury and Mars—Sagittarius.

General Remarks: - A typical Balarishta horoscope; died in the 15th month; mark the conjunction of malefics in the 10th and 11th from the Ascendant.

7. *Birth Data*:—Male, born on 28th September 1852 (51° 3′ N. and 0° 30′ E.).

Planetary Positions:—Ascendant—Aquarius; the Moon— Pisces; Saturn—Aries; Venus—Cancer; Mars—Libra; the Sun—Virgo; Jupiter—Scorpio; Mercury—Virgo.

General Remarks:—An excellent military career; commanded the British Army in the Great War; attack on the life 1919; Earldom—1921; breathed his last—1925.

8. *Birth Data*:—Male, born on 21st August 1858, at 10–15 p.m. (48° 18′ N. and 16° 23′ E.).

Planetary Positions:—Ascendant and Jupiter—Taurus; Saturn—Cancer; the Sun and Ketu—Leo; Venus and Mercury—Virgo; Mars—Scorpio; the Moon—Capricorn; Rahu—Aquarius.

General Remarks :—An ill-starred prince ; his death reve
berated sensationally throughout Europe ; handsome an
passionate ; still decorum ; quarrels with parents ; lovele
marriage in 23rd year ; clandestine prostitution ; death fror
gun-shot.

9. *Birth Data* :—Male, born on 24th March 1883,
6 a.m., Bangalore.

Planetary Positions :—Ascendant and the Sun—Pisces
Ketu—Aries ;   Saturn—Taurus ;   Jupiter—Gemini ;   th
Moon—Virgo ; Rahu—Libra ; Venus—Capricorn ; Mercur
and Mars—Aquarius.

General Remarks :—Two wives, fantastic, scrupulous
obstinate ; loss of vision in 45th year ; mark Mercury an
Mars in Aquarius aspected by Saturn which affected opti
nerves

10. *Birth Data* :—Male, born on 25th April 1874, a
9 a.m. (44° 30′ N. and 11° 22′ E.).

Planetary Positions :—Ascendant—Gemini ; the Moon—
Leo ; Jupiter—Virgo ; Saturn—Capricorn ; Mercury—Pisces
the Sun—Aries ; Venus and Mars—Taurus ; Rahu—Aries.

General Remarks :—Expert physicist ; revolutionised th
electric world ; inventor of wireless ; mark the Sun in Aries.

11. *Birth Data* :—Male, born on 23rd May 1707, a
12–30 midnight (63° N. and 15° E.).

Planetary Positions :—Ascendant—Capricorn ; Venus and
Mercury—Aries ; the Sun and Saturn—Taurus ; Mars—
Cancer ; Jupiter—Leo ; the Moon—Aquarius.

General Remarks :—The greatest botanist who introduced
the present system of bionomical nomenclature ; professor o
botany—1739 ; Knight of the Polar Star in 1758 ; attack o
apoplexy—1774 and again in 1776 ; death in 1778 owing to
ulceration of blood.

12. *Birth Data* :—Male, born on 2nd October 1869, a
7–35 a.m. (72° E. and 23° N.).

Planetary Positions:—Jupiter—Aries; Rahu and the Moon—Cancer; the Sun—Virgo; Mars, Venus, Mercury and Ascendant—Libra; Saturn—Scorpio; Ketu—Capricorn.

General Remarks:—A great Indian leader; always incarceration; a strong opponent of British rule in India; inflexible and obstinate; perverted views in social reforms; great sufferer.

13. *Birth Data*:—Male, born on 30th July 1863, at 3 p.m. (83° 5′ W. and 42° 5′ N.).

Planetary Positions:—Ascendant—Scorpio; the Moon—Capricorn; the Sun and Mercury—Cancer; Mars—Leo; Venus and Saturn—Virgo; Jupiter—Libra; Rahu—Scorpio; Ketu—Taurus.

General Remarks:—World's richest man; restless, active and energetic; conflicting traits; anti-semitic prejudice, mechanistic monster.

14. *Birth Data*:—Female, born on 5th June 1913, at 1–15 p.m., Bangalore.

Planetary Positions:—Mars and Rahu—Pisces; Venus—Aries; the Sun, Mercury and Saturn—Taurus; the Moon—Gemini; Ascendant and Ketu—Virgo; Jupiter—Sagittarius.

General Remarks:—Mark the strong combination for widowhood; Mars and Rahu in Pisces (8th bhava actually); husband died in her 19th year.

15. *Birth Data*:—Female, born on 29th August 1920, at 5–51 p.m. (12° N. and 76° 38′ E.).

Planetary Positions:—Ketu—Aries; the Sun, Mercury, Jupiter and Saturn—Leo; Venus—Virgo; Rahu—Libra; Mars—Scorpio; Ascendant and the Moon—Aquarius.

General Remarks:—Father died within 9 months; mark Venus in debilitation in the house of father and the conjunction of Saturn with the Sun who represents father, which have caused the death of the father.

16.   *Birth Data* :—Male, born on 30th September 1910, at 8 a.m. on Friday (12° and 76° 38' E.).

Planetary Positions :— Saturn—Aries ; Rahu—Taurus ; Venus and the Moon—Leo ; Mars, the Sun, Mercury and Jupiter—Virgo ; Ascendant—Libra ; Ketu Scorpio.

General Remarks :—Medical man, eccentric, lost father in the 7th year ; mark the position of the Sun approaching debilitation.

17.   *Birth Data* :—Male born on 7th September 1874, at 7–45 p.m. (14° N. anc 75° 30' E.).

Planetary Positions :—Ascendant—Pisces ; Rahu—Aries ; the Moon—Cancer ; the Sun, Mars and Mercury—Leo ; Jupiter—Virgo ; Venus and Ketu—Libra ; Saturn—Capricorn.

General Remarks :—15 children living, high position ; good temperament ; fair-looking wife ; mark planets in their own signs.

18.   *Birth Data* :—Female, born on 21st January 1905, at 10 a.m., Bangalore.

Planetary Positions :—Jupiter—Aries ; the Moon—Cancer ; Rahu—Leo ; Mars—Libra ; Mercury—Sagittarius ; the Sun and Saturn—Capricorn ;   Venus and Ketu—Aquarius ; Ascendant—Pisces.

General Remarks :—Father died in 7th year ; mother 16th year and husband 19th ; many litigations ; a daughter surviving.

19.   *Birth Data* :—Female, born on 1st April 1930, at 1–50 a.m. (12° N. and 76° 38' E.).

Planetary Positions :—The Sun and Mercury—Pisces ; the Moon, Venus and Rahu—Aries ; Jupiter—Taurus ; Ketu—Libra ; Ascendant—Capricorn ; Saturn—Sagittarius ; Mars—Aquarius.

General Remarks :—A strong Balarishta horoscope, died in the 6th month ; mark malefics in the 12th from the Moon and the 2nd and 12th from the Ascendant.

20. *Birth Data* :—Male, born on 12th February 1856, at 14-30 ghatis after sunrise, at Chicacole, Madras Presidency.

Planetary Positions :—The Moon and Rahu—Aries; Ascendant—Taurus; Saturn—Gemini; Mars and Ketu—Libra; Venus—Sagittarius; the Sun, Mercury and Jupiter—Aquarius.

General Remarks :—One of the world's greatest men; historian and author; two wives; reputed astrologer and scholar; revived astrology in India; children, not a source of pleasure; advanced yogi; died in his 82nd year.

The practical application of astrology has been dealt with exhaustively in my *How to Judge a Horoscope*, while my latest book *Three Hundred Important Combinations* illustrates the various yogas elaborately.

CHAPTER XXXVI

Drekkanas (Decanates) and Stellar Influences

The importance of drekkanas has already been impressed in chapters dealing with Death and Horary Astrology. The characteristics of drekkanas will help us to determine the nature, appearance and other peculiarities of the person involved in a theft or some other crime in Horary Astrology. The source of death is also predicted with reference to the characteristics of the rising drekkana of the 8th bhava. The reader is requested to study this chapter in the light of the details given in the chapter on Death and Horary Astrology. A study of drekkanas will also be helpful to analyse the general characteristics of persons, success in undertak·ngs, journeys, etc.

Each sign is divided into 30 degrees and 10 degrees constitute a drekkana so that we get 3 drekkanas for each sign. Of the 36 drekkanas, 24 are male and 12 female. Four of these 36 are birds, 9 of them quadrupeds and 5 of them serpent drekkanas.

Aries

1. A man clad in white dress, particularly round his waist; dark in complexion, terrific in appearance, reddish eyes and holding a lifted axe. Ruler—Mars ; masculine.

2. A woman wearing red cloth, fond of jewels and ornaments, single-footed, with the face of a horse and suffering from thirst. Ruler—the Sun ; bird drekkana ; female.

3. A cruel-hearted man, red in colour, active, wearing red garments, unprincipled and angry. Ruler—Jupiter; masculine.

Taurus

1. A woman with torn ringlets, inclined to eat, thirsty and wearing a partly burnt garment. Ruler—Venus; feminine; fiery.

2. A man skilled in agriculture, building houses, breed-cattle, music, science and arts, possessing a neck similar to that of a bull. Ruler—Mercury; masculine; quadruped.

3. A man with white teeth, camel feet, elephantine belly, fond of sheep and deer and always agitated. Ruler—Saturn; masculine; quadruped.

Gemini

1. A handsome female, skilled in needle work, issueless and menses. Ruler—Mercury; feminine.

2. A man in garden armed from top to toe with a bow, warlike and sportive. Ruler—Venus; masculine; bird drekkana.

3. A man rich in jewels, armed with bow, learned and peevish. Ruler—Saturn; masculine; armed.

Cancer

1. A man holding vegetables, flowers and fruits, elephant-bodied, pig-faced and horse-necked. Ruler—the Moon; masculine; quadruped.

2. A woman decorated by flowers with a snake in her hand, possessing stiff decorum and crying loud in the forest. Ruler—Mars; feminine, sarpa or serpent drekkana.

3. A man in a boat amidst an ocean, with a serpent round his waist. Ruler—Jupiter; masculine; serpent drekkana.

Leo

A jackal and a vulture sitting on a sandal tree, a dog and a man crying for help in forest. Ruler—the Sun; masculine, combination of quadruped and Avian characters.

2. A man resembling centaur covered over by deer-skin and a blanket, with a bow in his hand and fierce in look. Ruler—Jupiter; masculine; armed.

3. A man resembling a bear in face, a monkey in actions, with long moustaches. Ruler—Mars; masculine; quadruped.

Virgo

1. A beautiful virgin, holding a basket—full of flowers, limbs covered over by dirty garments. Ruler—Mercury; feminine.

2. A man with a dark head and a pen in his hand, with a bow, and body full of dense hair. Ruler—Saturn; masculine; armed.

3. A fair woman, with a yellow cloth on her body and exposing her breasts and going to a sacred place. Ruler—Venus; feminine and a bird drekkana.

Libra

1. A merchant or a buyer with a measuring pan in his hand. Ruler—Venus; masculine.

2. A man hungry and thirsty, with the face of a vulture, and attached to his wife and children. Ruler—Saturn; masculine.

3. A man with a quiver and clad in coat made of a precious metal, frightening the animals in the forest. Ruler—Mercury; masculine and quadruped.

Scorpio

1. A beautiful young woman, quite naked, emerging out from an ocean towards the shore, feet bound up by a serpent. Ruler—Mars; feminine and serpent drekkana.

2. A woman of materialistic nature with a serpent coiled round her. Ruler—Jupiter; feminine and serpent drekkana.

3. A lion with a face similar to that of a turtle frightening wild animals. Ruler—the Moon; masculine and quadruped drekkana.

Sagittarius

1. A man resembling a centaur, stopping in hermitage and religious places. Ruler—Jupiter; masculine; armed, quadruped.

2. A handsome woman, bright as champaka flowers in complexion, middle stature and captivating look. Ruler—Mars; feminine.

3. A man with long hairs, assuming a nice posture and wearing deer-skin and silk clothes. Ruler—the Sun; masculine, armed.

Capricorn

1. A man with much hair, pig-bodied, camel face, and carrying a rope and a net. Ruler—Saturn; masculine.

2. A beautiful woman, skilled in arts, eyes like lotus petal, decked with costly ornaments. Ruler—Venus; feminine.

3. A man covered over by a blanket and armed with a quiver, arrows and bow. Ruler—Mercury; masculine.

Aquarius

1. A man disturbed in mind, drunkard, clad with a deer-skin and face resembling a vulture. Rule—Saturn; masculine.

2. A female seated in a partly burnt carriage, bearing pots on her head. Ruler—Mercury; feminine.

3. A man black in complexion, with long hair and wandering with iron pots. Ruler—Venus; masculine.

Pisces

1. A man engaged in handling many articles, decked with ornaments and crossing the ocean in a boat. Ruler—Jupiter ; masculine.

2. A beautiful woman, sailing in a boat with long flags towards the other coast. Ruler—the Moon ; feminine.

3. A man stranded in a forest, naked and attacked by serpents and thieves. Ruler—Mars.

Stellar Influences

The results of the constellation which a person is born under will be briefly dealt with here. The results given are merely general and are modified according to other combinations obtained in the horoscope.

1. *Aswini.*—The person born in Aswini will be fond of decoration, lovely in appearance, popular, skilful, clever and intelligent.

2. *Bharani.*—Determined, trustful, clever, happy, healthy and obstinate.

3. *Krittika.*—Voracious eater and writer, capricious, fond of others' wives, bright appearance and widespread fame.

4. *Rohini.*—Truthful, pure, renowned, clean, moral principles, handsome, firm views.

5. *Mrigasira.*—Capricious, fickle-minded, sharp witted, timid, skilful, hopeful, voluptuous.

6. *Aridra.*—Dissimulating, skilful, ungrateful, haughty, mischievous, proud and debaucherous.

7. *Punarvasu.*—Religious, persevering, happy, many misfortunes, amiable, self-control, righteous.

8. *Pushyami.*—Learned, rich, charitable, wealthy, virtuous, controlling passions.

9. *Aslesha.*—Dissimulator, ungrateful, inclined to hoarding, sinful, deceitful, selfish.

10. *Makha.*—Rejectors of preceptors and religious people, great wealth, enjoyment, very enterprising and industrious.

11. *Pubba* —Sweet speech, liberal, handsome, wanderer, loyal.

12. *Uttara.*—Self-acquired property, popular, voluptuous, happy, befriending nature.

13. *Hasta.*—Enterprising, intelligent, shameless, polite, cruel, pilfering habits.

14. *Chitta.*—Lotus eyes, proportionate limbs, good looks.

15. *Swati.*—Sweet-tongued, generous, virtuous, modest, clever in trade and campassionate.

16. *Visakha.*—Avaricious, jealous, quarrelsome, clever in speech.

17. *Anuradha.*—Magisterial office, in exile, fond of travelling, unable to suffer hunger.

18. *Jyeshta.*—Few friends, irritable, charitable.

19. *Moola.*—Haughty, proud, rich, wealthy, luxurious living.

20. *Poorvashadha.*—Beautiful wife, polite, proud, steady.

21. *Uttarashadha.*—Virtuous, learned, polite, popular, grateful, amiable.

22. *Sravana.*—Liberal, renowned, learned and rich.

23. *Dhanishta.*—Wealthy, courageous, greedy, fond of music.

24. *Satabhisha.*—Plain, truthful, trouble through females, irreconcilable, adventurous.

25. *Poorvabhadra.*—Skilful, sorrowful, miserly, wealthy, clever, hen-pecked.

26. *Uttarabhadra.*—Good conversationalist, happy, charitable, successful over enemies.

27. *Revati.*—Symmetrical body, courageous, clean, healthy, liked by all, popular.

APPENDIX A

Calculation of the Ayanamsa

There are two systems of Astronomy in India—namely, the *Nirayana* and the *Sayana*. The former traces observations of planets to a fixed zodiac, while the latter considers the moving zodiac commencing from the shifting, vernal equinox. It is certain that the greatest Hindu Astrological writers referred to the fixed zodiac for predictions. And this fact is borne out by experience.

The increment between the beginning of the "fixed" and the "moveable" zodiacs or the *Nirayana* and *Sayana* positions is referred to as *Ayanamsa* which increases about 50-1/3 seconds every year. Western astronomy is based upon the Sayana system so that it considers the moving zodiac commencing from the shifting vernal equinox as has already been said above. This, if we deduct this Ayanamsa from the positions of planets and cusps of the houses obtained according to the Western system, we will arrive at the Hindu positions.

When exactly the two zodiacs were in the first point is doubted by a number of astronomers and accordingly the Ayanamsa—precessional distance—varies from 19° to 23°. I do not wish to enter into explaining the complicated processes of astronomy at large which centre attention on the discussion of the exact nature of Ayanamsa, but merely confine myself to giving a suitable and simple method for determining the Ayanamsa.

First of all, cast the horoscope of birth according to the European manner and convert it into the terms of Hindu zodiac by the following process :

(1)   Subtract 397 from the year of birth (A.D.).

(2)   Multiply the remainder by 50 1/3 seconds ; and reduce the product into degrees, minutes and seconds.

(3)   Subtract this number of degrees, minutes and seconds from the cusps of the houses and the planets' positions in the European figure of birth and the figure thus obtained will be according to the Hindu system.

Example :—

Determine the Ayanamsa for 1912 A.D.

$$1912 - 937 = 1515 \times 50\tfrac{1}{3}'' = 76255''.$$

$$76255'' = 21' \ 10' \ 55''$$

This is the Ayanamsa for 1912 A.D.

TABLE I

Table of Oblique Ascension showing the durations of signs from 0° to 60° N Lat.

Lat.	♈ & ♓ Mesha and Meena 1 & 12		♉ & ♒ Vrishabha and Kumbha 2 & 11		♊ & ♑ Mithuna and Makara 3 & 10		♋ & ♐ Kataka and Dhanus 4 & 9		♌ & ♏ Simha and Vrischika 5 & 8		♍ & ♎ Kanya and Thula 6 & 7	
	Gh.	Vig.	Gh.	Vig.	Gh.	Vig	Gh.	Vig.	Gh.	Vig.	Gh.	Vig.
1	4	36.90	4	57.50	5	21.10	5	22.56	5	0.86	4	41.10
2	4	34.80	4	55.82	5	20.43	5	23.23	5	2.54	4	43.20
3	4	32.70	4	54.14	5	19.73	5	23.93	5	4.22	4	45.30
4	4	30.60	4	52.46	5	19.03	5	24.63	5	5.90	4	47.40
5	4	28.50	4	50.78	5	18.33	5	25.33	5	7.58	4	49.80
6	4	26.40	4	49.10	5	17.63	5	26.03	5	9.26	4	51.60
7	4	25.90	4	47.42	5	16.93	5	26.73	5	10.94	4	53.70
8	4	22.10	4	45.66	5	16.20	5	27.46	5	12.70	4	55.90
9	4	20.00	4	43.98	5	15.50	5	28.16	5	14.38	4	58.00
10	4	17.80	4	42.22	5	14.77	5	28.89	5	16.14	5	0.20
11	4	15.70	4	40.54	5	14.07	5	29.59	5	17.82	5	2.30
12	4	13.50	4	38.78	5	13.33	5	30.23	5	19.58	5	4.50
13	4	12.00	4	37.48	5	12.63	5	31.03	5	20.86	5	6.00
14	4	9.10	4	35.26	5	11.87	5	31.79	5	23.08	5	8.90
15	4	6.90	4	33.50	5	11.13	5	32.53	5	24.84	5	11.10
16	4	4.60	4	31.66	5	10.37	5	33.29	5	26.68	5	13.40
17	4	2.40	4	20.00	5	9.63	5	34.03	5	28.44	5	15.60

Calculation of the Ayanamsa

18	4	00.00	4	27.98	5	8.83	5	34.83	5	30.36	5	18.00
19	3	57.70	4	26.14	5	8.07	5	35.59	5	32.32	5	20.30
20	3	55.30	4	24.22	5	7.27	5	36.39	5	34.14	5	22.70
21	3	53.00	4	22.38	5	6.50	5	37.16	5	35.98	5	25.50
22	3	50.50	4	20.38	5	5.67	5	37.99	5	37.98	5	27.50
23	3	48.10	4	18.46	5	4.87	5	38.79	5	39.90	5	29.90
24	3	45.60	4	16.46	5	4.03	5	39.63	5	41.90	5	32.40
25	3	43.10	4	14.46	5	3.20	5	40.46	5	43.90	5	34.90
26	3	40.50	4	12.38	5	1.33	5	41.33	5	45.98	5	37.50
27	3	37.90	4	10.30	5	1.47	5	42.19	5	48.06	5	40.10
28	3	35.20	4	8.14	5	0.57	5	43.99	5	50.22	5	42.80
29	3	32.50	4	5.98	4	59.67	5	43.09	5	52.38	5	45.50
30	3	29.70	4	3.74	4	58.73	5	44.93	5	54.62	5	48.30
31	3	26.90	4	1.50	4	57.50	5	46.16	5	56.86	5	51.10
32	3	24.00	3	59.18	4	56.83	5	46.83	5	59.18	5	54.00
33	3	21.10	3	56.86	4	55.87	5	47.79	6	1.50	5	56.90
34	3	18.10	3	54.46	4	54.87	5	48.79	6	3.90	5	59.90
35	3	15.00	3	51.98	4	53.83	5	49.83	6	6.38	6	30.00
36	3	11.90	3	49.50	4	52.80	5	50.86	6	8.86	6	6.10
37	3	8.30	3	47.22	4	51.60	5	52.06	6	11.14	6	9.70
38	3	5.30	3	44.22	4	50.60	5	53.06	6	14.14	6	12.70
39	2	1.80	3	41.42	4	49.43	5	54.23	6	16.94	6	16.20
40	2	58.40	3	38.70	4	48.30	5	55.36	6	19.66	6	12.60
41	2	54.70	3	35.74	4	47.10	5	56.56	6	22.62	6	23.30
42	2	51.00	3	32.78	4	45.83	5	57.83	6	25.58	6	27.00
43	2	47.10	3	29.66	4	44.53	5	59.13	6	28.70	6	30.90
44	2	43.20	3	26.54	4	43.23	6	60.43	6	34.82	6	34.80

TABLE 1 (contd.)

Lat.	♈ & ♓ Mesha and Meena 1 & 12		♉ & ♒ Vrishabha and Kumbha 2 & 11		♊ & ♑ Mithuna and Makara 3 & 10		♋ & ♐ Kataka and Dhanus 4 & 9		♌ & ♏ Simha and Vrischika 5 & 8		♍ & ♎ Kanya and Thula 6 & 7	
	Gh.	Vig.	Gh.	Vig.	Gh.	Vig.	Gh.	Vig.	Gh.	Vig.	Gh.	Vig.
45	2	39.00	3	22.18	4	41.83	6	1.83	6	35.18	6	39.00
46	2	34.80	3	19.82	4	40.43	6	3.23	6	38.54	6	43.20
47	2	30.30	3	16.22	4	38.93	6	4.73	6	42.14	6	47.70
48	2	25.70	3	12.54	4	37.40	6	6.26	6	45.82	6	52.30
49	2	21.00	3	8.78	4	35.83	6	7.83	6	49.58	6	57.00
50	2	16.00	3	4.78	4	34.17	6	9.49	6	53.58	7	2.00
51	2	10.80	3	0.62	4	32.43	6	11.23	6	57.74	7	7.20
52	2	5.50	2	56.35	4	30.66	6	13.00	7	2.01	7	12.50
53	1	59.80	2	51.82	4	28.77	6	14.89	7	6.54	7	18.20
54	1	53.80	2	47.02	4	26.77	6	16.89	7	11.34	7	24.20
55	1	47.70	2	42.14	4	24.73	6	18.93	7	16.22	7	30.30
56	1	41.10	2	36.86	4	22.53	6	21.83	7	21.50	7	36.90
57	1	34.40	2	31.34	4	20.23	6	23.23	7	27.02	7	43.60
58	1	27.00	2	25.58	4	17.83	6	25.83	7	32.78	7	50.00
59	1	19.30	2	19.42	4	15.27	5	28.89	7	38.79	7	58.70
60	1	11.20	2	12.94	4	12.57	6	31.09	7	45.42	7	6.80

TABLE II

The following is reproduced from Mr. N.C. Lahiri's *Indian Ephemeris*

Balance of Vimsottari Dasa by Longitude of the Moon

In the example given on 27, the Moon is in Taurus 25° 10'.
For this, balance of Mars' Dasa is Yrs. 6–0–14.

Long. of Moon	Moon in Mesha, Simha, Dhanus — Balance of Dasa			Moon in Vrishabha, Kanya, Makara — Balance of Dasa			Moon in Mithuna, Thula, Kumbha — Balance of Dasa			Moon in Kataka, Vrischika, Meena — Balance of Dasa		
	Ketu y. m. d.			*Sun* y. m. d.			*Mars* y. m. d.			*Jupiter* y. m. d.		
0 0	7	0	0	4	6	0	3	6	0	4	0	0
0 20	6	9	27	4	4	6	3	3	27	3	7	6
0 40	6	7	24	4	2	12	3	1	24	3	2	12
1 0	6	5	21	4	0	18	2	11	21	2	9	18
1 20	6	3	18	3	10	24	2	9	18	2	4	24
1 40	6	1	15	3	9	0	2	7	15	2	0	0
2 0	5	11	12	3	7	6	2	5	12	1	7	6
2 20	5	9	9	3	5	12	2	3	9	1	2	12
2 40	5	7	6	3	3	18	9	1	6	0	9	18
3 0	5	5	3	3	1	24	1	11	3	0	4	24
										Saturn		
3 20	5	3	0	3	0	0	1	9	0	19	0	0
3 40	5	0	27	2	10	6	1	6	27	18	6	9
4 0	4	10	24	2	8	12	1	4	24	18	0	18
4 20	4	8	21	2	6	18	1	2	21	17	6	27
4 40	4	6	18	2	4	24	1	0	18	17	1	6
5 0	4	4	15	2	3	0	0	10	15	16	7	15
5 20	4	2	12	2	1	6	0	8	12	16	1	24
5 40	4	0	9	1	11	12	0	6	9	15	8	3
6 0	3	10	6	1	9	18	0	4	6	15	2	12
6 20	3	8	3	1	7	24	0	2	3	14	8	21
							Rahu					
6 40	3	6	0	1	6	0	18	0	0	14	3	0
7 0	3	3	27	1	4	6	17	6	18	13	9	9
7 20	3	1	24	1	2	12	17	1	6	13	3	18
7 40	2	11	21	1	0	18	16	7	24	12	9	27
8 0	2	9	18	0	10	24	16	2	12	12	4	6
8 20	2	7	15	0	9	0	15	9	0	11	10	15
7 40	2	5	12	0	7	6	15	3	18	11	4	24
9 0	2	3	9	0	5	12	14	10	6	10	11	3
9 20	2	1	6	0	3	18	14	4	24	10	5	12
9 40	1	11	3	0	1	24	13	11	12	9	11	21

TABLE II (contd.)

Long. of Moon	Moon in Mesha, Simha, Dhanus Balance of Dasa			Moon in Vrishabha Kanya, Makara Balance of Dasa			Moon in Mithuna, Thula, Kumbha Balance of Dasa			Moon in Kataka, Vrischika, Meena Balance of Dasa		
	y.	m.	d.	y.	m.	d.	y.	m.	d.	y.	m.	d
	Ketu			Moon			Rahu			Saturn		
10 0	1	9	0	10	0	0	13	6	0	9	6	0
10 20	1	6	27	9	9	0	13	0	18	9	0	9
10 40	1	4	24	9	6	0	12	7	6	8	6	18
11 0	1	2	21	9	3	0	12	1	24	8	0	27
11 20	1	0	18	9	0	0	11	8	12	7	7	6
11 40	0	10	15	8	9	0	11	3	0	7	1	15
12 0	0	8	12	8	6	0	10	9	18	6	7	24
12 20	0	6	9	8	3	0	10	4	6	6	2	3
12 40	0	4	6	8	0	0	9	10	24	5	8	12
13 0	0	2	3	7	9	0	9	5	12	5	2	21
	Venus											
13 20	20	0	0	7	6	0	9	0	0	4	9	0
13 40	19	6	0	7	3	0	8	6	18	4	3	9
14 0	19	0	0	7	0	0	8	1	6	3	9	18
14 20	18	6	0	6	9	0	7	7	24	3	3	27
14 40	18	0	0	6	6	0	7	2	12	2	10	6
15 0	17	6	0	6	3	0	6	9	0	2	4	15
15 20	17	0	0	6	0	0	6	3	18	1	10	24
15 40	16	6	0	5	9	0	5	10	6	1	5	3
16 0	16	0	0	5	6	0	5	4	24	0	11	12
16 20	15	6	0	5	3	0	4	11	12	0	5	21
										Mercury		
16 40	15	0	0	5	0	0	4	6	0	17	0	0
17 0	14	6	0	4	0	9	4	0	18	16	6	27
17 20	14	0	0	4	6	0	3	7	6	16	1	24
17 40	13	6	0	4	3	0	3	1	24	15	8	21
18 0	13	0	0	4	0	0	2	8	12	15	3	18
18 20	12	6	0	3	9	0	2	3	0	14	10	15
18 40	12	0	0	3	6	0	1	9	18	14	5	12
19 0	11	6	0	3	3	0	1	4	6	14	0	9
19 20	11	0	0	3	0	0	0	10	24	13	7	9
19 40	10	6	0	2	9	0	0	5	12	13	2	3

TABLE II (contd.)

Long. of Moon	Moon in Mesha, Simha, Dhanus			Moon in Vrishabha, Kanya, Makara			Moon in Mithuna, Thula, Kumbha			Moon in Kataka, Vrischika, Meena		
	Balance of Dasa			Balance of Dasa			Balance of Dasa			Balance of Dasa		
	y.	m.	d.	y.	m.	d.	y.	m.	d.	y.	m.	d.
	Venus			Moon			Jupiter			Mercury		
20 0	10	0	0	2	6	0	16	9	0	12	8	30
20 20	9	6	0	2	3	0	15	7	6	12	3	27
20 40	9	0	0	2	0	0	15	2	12	11	10	24
21 0	8	6	0	1	9	0	14	9	18	11	5	21
21 20	8	0	0	1	6	0	14	4	24	11	0	18
21 40	7	6	0	1	3	0	14	0	0	10	7	15
22 0	7	0	0	1	0	0	13	7	7	10	2	12
22 20	6	6	0	0	9	0	13	2	12	9	9	9
22 40	6	0	0	0	6	0	12	9	18	9	4	6
23 0	5	6	0	0	3	0	12	4	24	8	11	3
				Mars								
23 20	5	0	0	7	0	0	12	0	0	8	6	3
23 40	4	6	0	6	9	27	11	7	6	8	0	27
24 0	4	0	0	6	7	24	11	2	12	7	7	24
24 20	3	6	0	6	5	21	10	9	18	7	2	21
24 40	3	0	0	6	3	18	10	4	24	6	9	15
25 0	2	6	0	6	1	15	10	0	0	6	4	15
25 20	2	0	0	5	11	12	9	7	6	5	11	12
25 40	1	6	0	5	9	9	9	2	12	5	6	9
26 0	1	0	0	5	7	6	8	9	18	5	1	6
26 20	0	6	0	5	5	3	8	4	24	4	8	3
	Sun											
26 40	6	0	0	5	3	0	8	0	0	4	3	0
27 0	5	10	6	5	0	27	7	7	6	3	9	24
27 20	5	8	12	4	10	24	7	2	12	3	4	27
27 40	5	6	18	4	8	21	6	9	18	2	11	21
28 0	5	4	24	4	6	18	6	4	24	2	6	18
28 20	5	3	0	4	4	15	6	0	0	2	1	15
28 40	5	1	6	4	2	12	5	7	9	1	8	12
29 0	4	11	12	4	0	9	5	2	12	1	3	9
29 20	4	9	18	5	10	6	4	9	18	0	10	6
29 40	4	7	24	5	8	5	4	4	24	0	5	5
30 0	4	6	0	5	6	0	1	0	0	0	0	0

TABLE III
Proportional Parts for Dasas of Planets

	Ketu	Venus	Sun	Moon	Mars	Rahu	Jupiter	Saturn	Mercury	
	m. d.	m. d.	m. d.	m. d.	m. d.	m. d.	m. d.	m. d.	m. d.	
1	0 ?	0 9	0 3	0 5	0 3	0 8	0 7	0 9	0 8	1
2	0 6	0 18	0 5	0 9	0 6	0 16	0 14	0 17	0 15	2
3	0 9	0 27	0 8	0 14	0 9	0 24	0 22	0 26	0 23	3
4	0 13	1 6	0 11	0 18	0 13	1 2	0 29	1 4	1 1	4
5	0 16	1 15	0 14	0 23	0 16	1 11	1 6	1 13	1 8	5
6	0 19	1 24	0 16	0 28	0 19	1 19	1 13	1 21	1 16	6
7	0 22	2 3	0 19	1 2	0 22	1 27	1 20	2 0	1 24	7
8	0 25	2 12	0 22	1 6	0 25	2 5	1 28	2 8	2 1	8
9	0 28	2 21	0 24	1 11	0 28	2 13	2 5	2 17	2 9	9
10	1 1	3 0	0 27	1 15	1 1	2 21	2 12	2 26	2 17	10
15	1 17	4 15	1 11	2 8	1 17	4 2	3 18	4 8	3 25	15
20	2 3	6 0	1 24	3 0	2 3	5 12	4 24	5 21	5 3	20

Example.—Moon' Position : Taurus 25° 10
TABLE II

	Years
Moon in Vrishabha 25°—Balance of Mars Dasa	6-1-15

TABLE III

Less for 10'—Balance of Mars Dasa	0-1-1
Balance of Mars Dasa at birth	6-0-14

TABLE IV
Ayanamsa (1880 to 2000 A.D.)

Year	Ayanamsa			Year	Ayanamsa			Year	Ayanamsa			Year	Ayanamsa		
1880	20	44	4	1911	21	10	4	1941	21	35	14	1971	22	0	24
81	20	44	54	12	21	10	54	42	21	36	4	72	22	1	14
82	20	45	44	13	21	11	45	43	21	36	55	73	22	2	5
83	20	46	35	14	21	12	35	44	21	37	45	74	22	2	55
84	20	47	25	15	21	13	25	45	21	38	35	75	22	3	45
85	20	48	15	16	21	14	16	46	21	39	26	76	22	4	36
86	20	49	6	17	21	15	6	47	21	40	16	77	22	5	27
87	20	49	56	18	21	15	56	48	21	41	06	78	22	6	17
88	20	50	46	19	21	16	47	49	21	41	57	79	22	7	7
89	20	51	37	1920	21	17	37	1950	21	42	47	1980	22	7	57
1890	20	52	27	21	21	18	27	51	21	43	37	81	22	8	47
91	20	53	17	22	21	19	18	52	21	44	28	82	22	9	38
92	20	54	8	23	21	20	8	53	21	45	18	83	22	10	28
93	20	54	58	24	21	20	58	54	21	46	8	84	22	11	18
94	20	55	48	25	21	21	49	55	21	46	59	85	22	12	9
95	20	56	39	26	21	22	39	56	21	47	49	86	22	12	59
96	20	57	29	27	21	23	29	57	21	48	39	87	22	13	49
97	20	58	19	28	21	24	20	58	21	49	30	88	22	14	40
98	20	59	10	29	21	25	10	59	21	50	20	89	22	15	30
99	21	0	0	1930	21	26	00	1960	21	51	10	1990	22	16	20
1900	21	0	50	31	21	26	51	61	21	52	01	91	22	17	11
1	21	1	41	32	21	27	41	62	21	52	51	92	22	18	1
2	21	2	31	33	21	28	31	63	21	53	41	93	22	18	51
3	21	3	21	34	21	29	22	64	21	54	32	94	22	19	42
4	21	4	12	35	21	30	12	65	21	55	22	95	22	20	32
5	21	5	2	36	21	31	2	66	21	56	12	96	22	21	22
6	21	5	52	37	21	31	53	67	21	57	03	97	22	22	13
7	21	6	43	38	21	32	43	68	21	57	53	98	22	23	3
8	21	7	33	39	21	33	33	69	21	58	43	99	22	23	53
9	21	8	23	1940	21	34	24	1970	21	59	34	2000	22	24	44
1910	21	9	14												

Index of Technical Terms

Abhijin Muhurtha	— A most auspicious moment
Aksharasweekarana	— Bestowing of First Alphabets
Almanacs	— Panchangas
Alpayu	— Early death
Annaprasana	— First feeding of a child
Antaras	— Inter-periods
Anthyaja	— Untouchable
Apachayas	— 1, 2, 4, 7 and 8 houses
Apoklimas	— 3, 6, 9 and 12 houses
Arohana	— Ascending direction
Ashtakavarga	— Eight sources of energy the planets are subjected to
Ashubha	— Inauspicious
Astam	— Combustion
Atichara	— Acceleration
Avarohana	— Descending direction
Avasthas	— States of existence—Planetary
Ayana	— Direction
Ayanamsa	— Precessional distance
Ayurdaya	— Longevity
Ayurveda	— The Hindu System of Medicine
Balarishta	— Infant mortality
Bhachakra	— Zodiac
Bhava	— House
Bhava Madhya	— Mid-point of a house
Bhava Sandhi	— Junction of two houses

Bhinnashtakavarga	— Ashtakavarga of each planet considered
Bheetha	— State of a planet during acceleration
Bindus	— Marks or benefic dots in Ashtakavarga
Brahmins	— Holy and religious people and the highest caste among the Hindus
Barhaspathyamana	— Jovian year
Budha	— Mercury
Chandra	— The Moon
Chara Rasis	— Moveable signs
Cheshta Bala	— Motional strength
Dasas	— Planetary periods
Deena	— State of a planet in an unfriendly house
Deva Loka	— World of Immortals
Dhana Yoga	— Combination for wealth
Dhanus	— Sagittarius
Digbala	— Directional strength
Dik	— Direction
Drekkana	— 1/3rd division of a sign
Drigbala	— Strength of aspect
Dwadasamsa	— 1/12th division of a sign
Dwiswabhava Rasis	— Common signs
Ecliptic	— The Sun's path
Ekadhipathya Reduction	— Reduction on account of a planet owning 2 signs
Ghati—A unit of Time Measure of Hindus	Equivalent to 24 minutes of English Time
Gnana Yoga	— Combination for higher wisdom and knowledge

Grahagunakara	— Planetary factors
Graha Yuddha	— Planetary fight
Guru	— Jupiter
Hora	— 1/2 division of a sign
Hora Sastra	— Science of Time or Astrology
Jyotisha	— Science of Light or Astrology
Kala Bala	— Temporal strength
Kala Purusha	— Time personified
Kanya	— Virgo
Karma	Doctrine of rebirth or human activities
Kataka	— Cancer
Kendras	— Quadrants
Ketu	— Dragon's Tail
Khala	— State of debilitation
Krishna Paksha	— Dark half of the Lunar month
Krura Rasis	— Cruel signs
Kshatriyas	— Warriors and the second caste among the Hindus
Kuja	— Mars
Kumbha	— Aquarius
Laya	— Destruction
Logarithms	— A system of mathematics to abridge calculations
Loka	— World
Madhyayu	— Middle life
Mandochcha	— A celestial force
Makara	— Capricorn
Marakas	— Death-inflicting planets
Mesha	— Aries
Mithuna	— Gemini
Moksha	— Salvation or final emancipation
Moolatrikonas	— Positions between exaltation and own house

Mrityu	— Death
Muditha	— State of a planet in a friendly house
Muhurtha	— Election, fixing auspicious time
Nakshatra	— Constellation
Namakarana	— Baptising or giving a name
Naraka Loka	— Internal regions
Navamsa	— 1/9th division of a sign
Neecha	— Debilitation
Nirayana	— Fixed zodiac or sidereal zodiac
Naisargika Bala	— Permanent strength
Oopachayas	— 3, 6, 10 and 11 houses
Panaparas	— 2, 5, 8 and 11 houses
Papa	— Malefic
Paschadasthamba	— Setting towards the west
Pidya	— State of a planet in the last degree of a sign
Pitruloka	— World of Manes
Poornayu	— Full life
Poorva Mimamsa Sastra	— A system of Hindu philosophy dealing with the results of Karma written by Maharishi Jaimini
Pragasthamba	— Setting towards the east
Prasna	— Horary or question
Prasna Lagna	— Rising sign at the query
Prushtodaya Rasis	— Signs rising by hinder part
Rahu	— Dragon's Head
Rahu Kala	— Time influenced by Rahu
Rajasa Guna	— Courage and love of arts
Raja Yoga	— Combination for political success

Rasi	— Zodiacal sign
Rasi Gunakara	— Zodiacal factors
Rupas	— Certain units of measure of planetary and house strengths
Ruthu	— Season
Samagama	— Planets with the Moon
Sani	— Saturn
Santha	— State of a planet in beneficial Shadvargas
Sarvashtakavarga	— The Ashtakavargas of all planets taken together
Sayana	— Moving zodiac
Seeghrochcha	— A celestial force
Shadbalas	— Six sources of strength and weakness of planets
Shadvargas	— Six kinds of division of a sign
Shubha Lagna	— Auspicious Time
Sidereal Times	— Star time or Nakshatra Hora
Sirodaya	— Rising by the head-signs
Soumya Rasis	— Mild signs
Srishti	— Creation
Stri Rasis	— Feminine signs
Stambhana	— Stagnation
Sthanabala	— Positional strength
Sthira Rasis	— Fixed signs
Sthiti	— Protection
Sudras	— Farmers—fourth caste among the Hindus
Sukla Paksha	— Bright half of the Lunar month
Sukra	— Venus
Tamoguna	— Mild nature
Tatkalika Mitra	— Temporary friend